The Major Film Theories

The Major Film Theories

An Introduction

J. Dudley Andrew
The University of Iowa

Oxford University Press

London   Oxford   New York

1976

for my mother and father
from whom. . .

OXFORD UNIVERSITY PRESS
Oxford   London   Glasgow
New York   Toronto   Melbourne   Wellington
Nairobi   Dar es Salaam   Cape Town
Kuala Lumpur   Singapore   Jakarta   Hong Kong   Tokyo
Delhi   Bombay   Calcutta   Madras   Karachi

Copyright © 1976 by Oxford University Press, Inc.
Library of Congress Catalogue Card Number: 75-25465
First published as an Oxford University Press paperback, New York, 1976

printing, last digit: 10 9 8

Printed in the United States of America

Preface

There have been, to my knowledge, two histories of film theory: Guido Aristarco's *Storia delle teoriche del film* and Henri Agel's *Esthétique du cinéma*. While I am indebted to these works, I have no wish to emulate them in their attempts to list every theorist and disentangle each line of theory.

Instead this book hopes to set off the major theorists one against the other, forcing them to speak to common issues, making them reveal the basis of their thought. I have chosen, therefore, those theorists who wrote about film in a broad sense, and who did so with the force of extended argument. The countless thinkers who have on occasion theorized about cinema (including great thinkers like Panofsky, Susanne Langer, Maurice Merleau-Ponty, Gabriel Marcel, and André Malraux) receive hardly any attention here. Primitive theorists like Ricciotto Canudo, Louis Delluc, and Vachel Lindsay are also slighted because, in my estimation, their theories do not bear the weight of comparison with the other figures in this book.

Priority has been given to those theorists whose writings are readily available in English. Unfortunately this eliminates from discussion major theorists in French, in Russian, and especially in Italian. Since this volume is intended as an aid to, not a substitute for, the reading of the theorists themselves, an extended treatment of figures whose books are both difficult to obtain and untranslated as well seems off the point. True, the final chapters of this book do deal with some contemporary French theorists whose work is still in French, but this seems warranted since their ideas are in the current marketplace and, in several instances, in the process of translation.

The scheme of this book does have some historical appearance, but only incidentally. I retain the classic distinction between formative theory and realist or photographic theory, a distinction which is commonplace and which is related to the cliché that all cinema has roots in either Méliès or Lumière. In film theory it so happens that the first great age of thought was nearly homogeneously formative. Until 1935 or so it is difficult to find a realist capable of standing up against Hugo Munsterberg, Rudolf Arnheim, Sergei Eisenstein, Béla Balázs, or V. I. Pudovkin. Then the situation changed, and the seeds of early realist theory grew into the lush tradition of André Bazin, the *Cahiers du cinéma* critics, and in America of Siegfried Kracauer and *cinéma-vérité* artists like Richard Leacock, D. A. Pennebaker, and Michael Roemer.

It is valuable to set these movements in opposition since that is in fact exactly how they developed. The formative theorists wrote in answer to the brute realism which film producers advertised and which the public thought it was receiving. Later, the realists specifically attacked the formalists because they tossed out cinema's special call to realism as they tried to make it stand alongside the prestige arts.

Again it must be emphasized that no attempt has been made here to include every thinker in each camp. Instead, I have chosen those thinkers who best articulate a position which has behind it either extensive thought or an important tradition. By working back to this tradition or to this core, I hope to give the reader some footholds with which he can more easily and more successfully climb back into the original works. It will become apparent that while the formative thinkers, for instance, concur on many, indeed most, issues relating to film, their reasons for holding such positions and their arguments sustaining those positions vary enormously. While most film students may be ready to compare theories as divergent as Eisenstein's and Bazin's, it seems more fruitful to me to compare theorists of the same camp. This book is meant to promote such comparison.

The final section of the book deals with contemporary theory, with the thought which, at the moment of my writing, is still developing, still working toward a final formulation. For the most part contemporary theory has tried to bypass the formative/realist debate either by incorporating both camps in a dialectic, as Jean Mitry has done, or by lifting the discussion to a level of abstraction where that distinction is no longer quite so pertinent (as both the phenomenologists and semiologists have done to some extent). Because of the wealth of current theory and its rather confused state I have restricted myself to works done in France, where, despite the diversity of approaches, there is a sense of debate and of common concerns. This final section will at best provide the reader with a series of signposts by which he can recognize the major issues and consider the various positions in the light of classical film theory.

Here, too, some figures will be missed, figures who may seem or may become important. But what interests me and what should interest all film scholars and students is the project of film theory itself, not the classification of each and every theorist. Even if what follows were an exhaustive treatment of all film theories, it would be foolish for the reader to put down this book with the relieved sense of having ingested a summary of what has been thought about film. I would have him instead begin to theorize on his own, inspired (though never restricted) by the men and arguments which have gone before him.

Every book requires a time and a place to be written. I would like to acknowledge the National Endowment for the Humanities for giving me the time to organize and articulate these essays. The University of Iowa with its tradition of serious theoretical study of film (marked by more than a dozen dissertations in this area) provided an atmosphere of encouragement. Dr. Sam Becker has been the active embodiment of that encouragement and the very image of that tradition of theory.

Most centrally I must acknowledge the five years of extraordinary students who have peopled my courses in film theory and who helped me reach the insights and comparisons these essays may attain. Let me cite especially several former graduate students, most of whom are now teaching film theory themselves, whose papers and discussions brought me to the understanding of one figure or another. Donald Frederickson's clear and rigorous treatment of Hugo Munsterberg made me aware of the power of his little-known theory and of the complex tradition supporting it.

Jeffrey Bacal and James Spellerberg made me face aspects and issues in the thought of Eisenstein which have become central to my vision of the great Russian. Brian Lewis and David Bordwell supported and broadened immeasurably my view of Jean Mitry.

More personally, let me thank Christian Koch, Dennis Nastav, Anthony Pfannkuche, Ellen Evans, and Donald Crafton, not only for their contributions to my comprehension of the subject, but for their critiques of the whole enterprise of theorizing. In part because of them, this book has been an active part of my life rather than a task. Whatever tasks remained were lightened and often borne by Larry Ward at Iowa, and by the meticulous work and personal good humor of John Wright at the Oxford University Press.

Iowa City   ·   J.D.A.
June 1975

Contents

Contents

The Major Film Theories

Introduction

THE SUBJECT

What is film theory? What do we do in film theory? Film theorists make and verify propositions about film or some aspect of film. They do so for both practical and theoretical reasons. In the realm of practicality, film theory answers the questions asked by those engaged in making films. Cameramen might want to understand the gains and losses of the wide screen; a producer might want to think out all the ramifications of the 3-D process. In such cases, film theory brings to light what filmmakers undoubtedly comprehend intuitively.

Film theory is more often studied, as other arts and sciences, for the sheer pleasure of knowing. Most of us simply want to understand a phenomenon we have experienced fruitfully for many years. Certainly, there is no guarantee that film theory deepens the appreciation of film, and in fact many students claim a loss of that original unreflected pleasure which all of us once had in the movie theater. What replaces this loss is knowledge, an understanding of how things work.

This situation in which knowledge of an experience begins to substitute for the experience itself is a peculiarly modern phenomenon. One need only browse through the local bookstore to see

3

how many experiences which are by themselves not experiences of the mind are being looked at rationally. Most current would be the phenomenon of man's sexual life which has been scrutinized by so many manuals and psychotherapeutic handbooks. Religion, as well, has been replaced for many by the philosophy of religion or cultural anthropology, both of which substitute an activity of reason for one of another order. The whole field of psychology has as its goal the conscious understanding of unconscious processes. This list could go on and would include, of course, aesthetics, the rational inquiry into the realm of art, a realm which is not by any means an entirely rational one.

To ask whether reason can aid experience is to ask a question beyond the scope of this small study, but it is to ask a question which we must always bear in mind, lest our inquiries become a replacement for our film viewing. I believe that those who study film are able to experience more kinds of films than those who do not study and that students of the art see the simple films, the films of their youth, in a fuller and more intense way. In any field knowledge can enervate experience, if the knower lets it. Yet it need not, for knowledge should be related to experience rather than be a substitute for it. This brings to mind the Socratic proposition that the unreflected life is not worth living. We must always remember too the schoolboy's reply to Socrates: "The unlived life is not worth reflecting upon."

Film theory is another avenue of science, and as such is concerned with the general rather than the particular. It is not concerned primarily with individual films or techniques, but with what might be called the cinematic capability itself. This capability governs both filmmakers and audience. While each film is a system of meanings which the film critic tries to lay bare, all films together form a system (Cinema) with subsystems (various genres and other kinds of groups) susceptible to the analysis of the theorist.

In America the film theory most well known is the *auteur* theory which, properly speaking, is not a theory at all but a critical method. Like all critical methods it relies on certain theoretical principles, but they are directed not so much at systematic understanding of a general phenomenon as at the evaluation of particular examples of that phenomenon. In this case the object of study is an individual film or an individual director. As Andrew Sarris says, "At the very least the auteur theory can help the student decide which film to pay attention to and which to ignore." He and his fellow *auteurists* have developed a sophisticated way of laying out a film or a body of films to draw attention to significant details and patterns which illuminate the personality and vision of the filmmaker. *Auteur* theory is also a way of ranking directors in a hierarchy of worth. As such, it may be very useful but it is certainly not a theory. Like its blood brother "genre criticism," it organizes our film history for us and makes us sensitive to certain aspects of it, showing us what movies we have valued or ought to begin valuing.

Both these methods avoid the dangers of impressionistic connoisseurship which haunt the unsystematic critic, for they follow an organized approach and some invariable principles which can be applied to a series of films, one after the other. But even this is not theory in its pure sense, for its goal is an appreciation of the value of individual works of cinema, not a comprehension of the cinematic capability. We might call criticism "applied film theory," just as we call engineering "applied physical science." But we must always remember that film criticism can be random and casual or, as in the two cases at issue here (genre and auteur study), it can be systematic, progressive, and formal.

While most criticism begins with some general theoretic principles, most theories begin with questions generated by individual films or techniques; but the answers must always be applicable to more films than the one which generated the question. In the same way, a botanist may be drawn to ask a general question by the appearance of a particular flower, but his finished theory must be applicable to more flowers than the one he first observed; otherwise he would be not a scientist but a connoisseur.

The goal, then, of film theory is to formulate a schematic notion of the capacity of film. It may be argued that film is not a rational activity and that no schematic description will ever be adequate to it. But this brings us back to our problem of knowledge and experience. When asked, "What possible value is there in trying to account scientifically for film?," the film theorist must answer that the schematization of an activity allows us to relate it to other aspects of our life. By putting an activity into rational terms we can discuss it alongside other schematized activities, be they rational or not. The film theorist should be able to discuss his field with the linguist or the philosopher of religion.

No one would ever equate a film theory, which after all is merely an order of words, with the experience of a film. But at the same time who would deny the value of geology just because it reduces the phenomena of earthly substances to chemical and mathematical formulas? It is precisely such formulas which allow us to see the place of the earth in the whole of the universe. Similarly, the generality of film theory gives us a way of understanding an experience in new terms, in terms which let us place it in the universe of our experience as a whole. No longer must our film experience be an isolated aspect of our existence. Some may cry out that by placing cinema in a larger world, by treating it in terms which enable us to cross over between it and other kinds of experiences, we destroy the uniqueness and sanctity of the experience of film. But most of us are happy to be able to think about and talk about that which we have so loved and continue to love. And most of us think of film not as a sacred way of being with the world but as another variant way of being human, different from, but related to, such things as literature, religious ritual, and science. Film theory hopes to articulate this mode of being human, this cinematic capability.

THE METHOD

We may expect that all film theorists will approach their subject logically, though we know that the logic of one theorist will differ from that of another. In his own way each theorist will pose what he feels to be an important question about film and, having answered that (or, in the act of trying to answer that), he will be forced to ask other related questions. Film theories then are reducible to a sinuous dialogue of questions and answers, and we may compare them provisionally just by examining the kinds of questions asked and the priority given each question. Our study, however, would be trivial if we merely enumerated all of the questions addressed by each theorist and the responses given. Such a list would by itself never generate the comparison, contrast, and schematization of ideas on film.

In order to compare theorists we must force them to speak to similar issues by categorizing their questions. Every question about film falls under at least one of the following headings: raw material, methods and techniques, forms and shapes, purpose or value. These categories, adapted from Aristotle,* divide the phenomenon of film into the aspects which make it up and which can be interrogated.

1. "The raw material" includes questions about the medium, such as those which seek its relation to reality, photography, and illusion, or those which follow out its use of time and space, or even those which aim at such processes as color, sound, and the make-up of the movie theater. Anything which is seen to exist as a given state of affairs with which the cinematic process begins belongs to the category of "raw material."

2. "The methods and techniques" of cinema comprises all questions about the creative process which shapes or treats the raw material, from discussions of technological developments (like the zoom shot) to the psychology of the filmmaker or even the economics of film production.

3. "The forms and shapes" of film is the category containing questions about the kinds of film which have been or could be made. Questions about cinema's ability to adapt other artworks lie here, as do questions about genre and audience expectation or effect. Here we are looking at films from the standpoint of a completed process in which the raw material has already been shaped by various creative methods. What determines those shapes and how are they recognized as valuable by an audience?

4. "The purpose and value" of cinema is the category which interfaces with the larger aspects of life, for here fall all questions which seek the goal of cinema in man's universe. Once raw material

* Aristotle's breakdown of the four "causes" of any natural phenomenon (material, efficient, formal, and final) is developed in his *Physics,* II, section 3.

has been shaped by a process into a given significant form, what does this mean for mankind?

Whether or not this is the perfect breakdown of questions about cinema, it seems to be a just and useful breakdown, and every theorist implicitly answers each kind of question. We can tell a great deal about a theorist by seeing which category of question most intrigues him. In any case, in each of the analyses that follow, an attempt is made to see the kinds of answers and issues each category of questions brings up. This way comparisons of theoretical positions are rather easy to make. No doubt this approach does injustice to some theorists, because it imposes a kind of logical schema on their remarks which may fit them clumsily, but it provides the constant perspective which will allow us to attain an overview of film theories, and it gives us the coordinates so we can begin to map those theories.

While there are countless questions which can be catalogued within these categories, we need in fact be concerned with only a few. The reason for this is that film theory forms a system in which the answer to any one question can be seen to lead easily to the next question, and any one question can be rephrased in terms of another. These two propositions about film theory are essential: 1. the transposition of questions and 2. the interdependence of questions. Let's look at each briefly.

1. *Transposition*

Film theorists may begin with a question related to one category and touch the others only by implication. A theorist like Pudovkin was very interested in questions about the creation of a film. He discussed technical questions from the standpoint of the filmmaker. What kind of editing best organizes a scene? What kind of acting is suitable for a historical epic film? What should we do with the new invention, sound?

Other early theorists were interested in film from the spectator's viewpoint: How does a spectator respond to parallel editing or to a *cinéma-vérité* film which tries to gain in immediacy what it loses in visual attractiveness? Some theorists go straight to the projected images themselves for their questions. What is the nature of film?

What is its relation to reality? How are picture and sound related? Is film a spatial or a temporal art? In its essence what is distinctive about film?

A single phenomenon may be studied from any one perspective or may be transposed and be questioned from all perspectives. For instance, Pudovkin's question about the kinds of use to which sound film might be put could be rephrased to read: "Will synchronous sound make the image appear more real to the spectator and thereby increase the illusion of the fiction film?" This transposition can be further redefined to fit into the material perspective: "Is sound more real than picture because it is the reproduction of an aural fact whereas an image is a representation in two dimensions of a visual fact?" So even though two theorists may begin from differing perspectives, we can relate their views by transposing the questions.

2. *The Interdependence of Questions*

Not only can a single question be asked from different perspectives, but a single question can be seen to contain within it a number of dependent questions. The answer a film theorist gives to a question which interests him can sometimes be extrapolated to serve all the questions to which it relates. This is how we can venture to guess, for instance, Munsterberg's opinion of wide-screen ratios from his answers to the questions of color and sound. Color, sound, and screen dimensions are all questions relating the technology of film to the art of the film. We can generalize from even the smallest statement made by a theorist about sound to his opinion of this larger, more generic question of technology. In other words, within each category questions can be organized into a hierarchy from the most general to the very specific. This allows us to move continually toward ever-more-general questions.

Optimally we can take all of the questions a theorist asks and factor out the four basic questions which serve as our categories. 1. What does he consider the basic *material* of film to be? 2. What *process* turns this material into something significant, something which transcends that material? 3. What are the most significant *forms* which that transcendence assumes? 4. What *value* does the whole process have in our lives? In the essays which follow there will be an attempt to organize discussion of each theorist into sections dealing with these four types of questions. Chapter subheadings are variations of the theme of each category. Occasionally two categories must be treated as one in order to preserve the particular character of a given man's thought. But in every case theorists will confront the same kinds of issues about film and about its value and purpose.

To summarize: by transposing questions and by following out their branches of interdependencies, we are able to compare the most diverse theorists, theorists who begin from different perspectives and ask seemingly different questions. If this were not possible, film theory would become a mere collection of unrelated questions randomly answered by various men. But with these two propositions, that is, by seeing film theory as a system, all questions and all perspectives are interconnected.

This does not mean, of course, that all the answers given to the questions will be the same, or that all the theorists will have the same perspective or ask essentially the same questions. What it does mean is that film theory is a logical enterprise and that, while we must note the distinctiveness of the approach of any particular theorist, we must at the same time be able to compare and contrast his views with our own and those of other theorists.

In other words, we must examine not merely the questions the theorist asks (though again this will reveal much about him) but the basis from which those questions spring and the consequences they imply. We must see every theory as broadly as possible, that is, we must see it systematically.

The Formative Tradition

Since ours has proved to be a century of criticism it is not surprising that theories of cinema were being propounded before the cinematographic process was even twenty years old. Never before has an art been dogged so quickly by intellectuals trying to understand it or, more often, trying to set it properly on its way.

The first serious essays about film naturally sought to carve out a place for it in modern culture. Film had grown up like a vine around the great trunks of serious and popular culture. It had even begun to alter the culture's view of its history. Yet it must have been difficult at first to separate cinema from the events it recorded, and more difficult still to see it apart from the established arts and entertainments on which it depended for its form and for its very methods of reaching an audience.

The first "theories" sound more like birth announcements than scientific inquiries. Men who felt an immediate sympathy for film and who wanted to see it blossom on its own realized that they had first to free it from the other phenomena which supported it and with which the public naturally associated it. This meant an immediate attack against the realism of the screen and against those who, like Lumière, were certain that cinema had no lasting import beyond the events it could record.

These theorists struggled to give to cinema the stature of art. Cinema, they claimed, was the equal of the other arts because it changed the chaos and meaninglessness of the world into a self-sustaining structure and rhythm. During this epoch, comparisons were made between cinema and virtually every other art. Poet Vachel Lindsay was the first American to publish a theory of film (*The Art of the Moving Picture,* 1916), and he specifically showed that cinema enjoyed the properties of all the other arts, including architecture. In France a whole coterie of film enthusiasts incessantly compared film to music, concentrating on its ability to shape the flow and look of reality. Following the initial steps of Ricciotto Canudo, and under the banner raised by Louis Delluc, leader of the French avant-garde film movement until his death in 1924, this group not only wanted to see cinema regarded as an art but they insisted that it was an independent art.

Innumerable essays of this period (1912-25) loudly differentiate cinema from theater. Most suggest that because cinema in its infancy was economically obliged to record theatrical performances, it had never looked beyond the theater for its own essence. The avant-garde of the twenties stressed the qualities of music, poetry, and above all dream inherent in the film experience. Delluc tried to sum up his conception of the new art in one mystic word, *photogénie,* that special quality available to cinema alone which can transform both the world and man in a single gesture. Cinema is photography, to be sure, but photography which has been raised to a rhythmic unity and which in turn has the power to raise and uplift our dreams. The articles and books of Germaine Dulac, Jean Epstein, and Abel Gance overflow with lyric statements about the uniqueness of cinema. Aesthetic propositions are advanced but seldom supported in a rigorous way. It was enough in the twenties to conceive and forcefully present new ways of seeing cinema (as "plastic shape," or "frozen time," or "synchronized to the tempo of our daydreams").

While poetic film theory appeared in France alongside the first *ciné*-clubs and the avant-garde *ciné*-artists, the Establishment film industry in Germany was busily creating the movement we call *expressionism.* This movement, which takes seriously the formative dictum to transform daily life, had no real theorist to speak for it, despite the fact that of all the movements in the history of film, it lies closest to the ideas of the intelligentsia it stems from. Certainly we have interesting remarks of expressionist actors, designers, writers, and directors relating to cinematic method and function, but no extended expressionist film theory was ever formulated.

When in 1925 the German movement lost its original power and the French avant-garde disintegrated, the center of advanced thought about film moved to Moscow. Russia had begun its famous State Film School in 1920 and around this school there developed heated and productive discussion. Lev Kuleshov, Dziga Vertov, V. I. Pudovkin, and especially Sergei Eisenstein are the names most often associated with this period. Nearly all questions pertaining to cinema were framed as questions of editing by this group. Eisenstein's ideas went furthest here, but we should never forget that his writings were composed in the context of a vast and vibrant atmosphere of debate.

The end of the silent film triggered a great number of important essays. By 1929 the number of journals devoted to film theory (including in English such magazines as *Close Up* and *Experimental Cinema*) indicate that a significant world community looked at cinema as an artform. Aestheticians rose up everywhere to debate the new direction which cinema should take after sound had disturbed its equilibrium. All this debate took place in a definitely formative atmosphere.

Paradoxically, the coming of sound seems to mark the decline of the great age of formative film theory. Nevertheless, by 1935 it was taken for granted in nearly all educated circles that cinema was an art, independent of all other arts, yet having in common with them the process of transformation whereby dull matter is shaped into scintillating and eloquent statement. If most of us still see cinema in much this way, if most articles on cinema still hold to this general perspective, it is in large part because of the powerful viewpoint propounded between 1915 and 1935.

1

Hugo Munsterberg

When Hugo Munsterberg wrote *The Photoplay: A Psychological Study* in 1916, he wrote without precedent, and perhaps for this reason his is not only the first but also the most direct major film theory. His mind was not distracted by the din of argument; nor was his memory supplying him with obstinate counter-examples, because cinema was hardly sophisticated enough to try anything other than to satisfy those functions it knew it could handle. Since Munsterberg claims that he looked at films only for about ten months prior to writing his book (he had been ashamed to be seen in a movie theater), his visual heritage in cinema was obviously restricted. He tried to make up for this with the energy and thoroughness of the scholar by carefully researching film and by studying its history as much as he could. Nevertheless he was clearly interested in discussing not the earliest cinema, but those wonderful story films of 1915 which evidently he viewed almost daily.

Munsterberg's book is divided into an aesthetics and a psychology of cinema and he was preeminently qualified in both areas. He is often identified as one of the founders of modern psychology and he wrote widely on the subject for the scholar and the layman alike. In philosophy his credentials are even more impressive. He had been imported from Germany to Harvard by William James and he eventually became chairman of the philosophy department, during the era not only of James, but of Royce and Santayana as well. He seems to have had a tenacious intelligence, and when in 1915 he turned that intelligence on the cinema, he wouldn't rest until he had explained its workings to himself and justified its importance to the intellectuals of the time who thought it crude and silly.

MATTER AND MEANS

Munsterberg's book opens with a historical introduction, the fruit of his attempt to learn all he could about the medium. This section labeled as it is, "Introduction," may seem autonomous and tangential to his theory, especially for the reader who realizes that Munsterberg's reputation lies in philosophy and psychology, certainly not in history. Besides, Munsterberg follows a long tradition in scholarship when he examines the genesis of film before performing an analysis of it. The questions "What do I want to examine?" and "How did this get here?" have a natural precedence over such questions as "How does it work?" and "What can I do with it?" But we should not be misled here, for Munsterberg's casual introduction dovetails into the heart of his argument. What at first looks like a simple chronology of important events serves on second glance to summarize the means by which the institution of film, as well as any given example of cinema, can exist.

Munsterberg's history of film is divided cleanly between what he calls film's "outer" and "inner" developments, between the technological history of the medium and the evolution of society's uses of that medium. Munsterberg argues that technology provided the body of this new phenomenon and society has animated that body, forcing it to play many actual roles. Without technology there would be no moving pictures and without psychosociological pressures, these pictures would sit unprojected in attics and museums. It is society's craving for information, education, and entertainment that allows cinema to exist at all.

Munsterberg's introduction culminates in a hymn of praise to the narrative capability of film. It recounts the legend of a young cinema compelled in its first years to the slavish documentation of stage-plays, freeing itself inevitably but heroically to find its own destiny as a medium of narrative. This medium he called, in the language of his day, the "photoplay."

The history of film, then, shows an ineluctable propulsion from (stage one) the toying with visual gadgetry to (stage two) the serving of important societal functions such as education and information, and finally, through its natural affinity for narrative, to its true domain, (stage three) the mind of man. After this introduction, Munsterberg never again mentions any kind of cinema except narrative cinema. For him, cinema is indeed mere gadgetry without narrativity. Only when the gadget worked on the narrative capacity of the mind did the photoplay come into being and, through it, the artistic wonders of film we all recognize.

Munsterberg was always more concerned with the spectator end of the "communications arc" than with the filmmaking side. It is interesting that Munsterberg never discussed the director or scriptwriter as a creative force. Evidently he felt that the impersonal powers of technology and sociology worked through filmmakers to give rise to movies. What they operated on, what filmmakers made cinema out of, was Munsterberg's prime concern and startling inspiration: the mind of man. The first half of his book develops this inspiration. Cynics could quip that only an idealist philosopher like Munsterberg could possibly conceive of the mind as raw material; but Munsterberg would be ready to counter with an impressive array of concrete psycho-physiological evidence.

Like the Gestalt psychologists, whom he preceded by only a few years, he felt that every experience is a relation between a part and whole, between figure and ground. It is the mind which has the ability to resolve this relation and organize its perceptual field. He ascribes the sensation of viewing movement to the displacement of a figure on its ground and mentions that we can, through willed attention, reverse that relation, altering our perception of the movement. The motion of the clouds and the moon makes the best example of this experience. We can, on particular nights, watch clouds pass swiftly across an imperious moon, but the next moment

A classic figure/ground dilemma.

the moon begins to glide for us through a murky forest of clouds. All depends on how our attention structures the percepts.

Munsterberg had a hierarchic notion of the mind; that is, he felt it was comprised of several levels, the higher levels depending on the operation of the lower. Each level resolves the chaos of undistinguished stimuli by a veritable act, virtually creating the world of objects, events, and emotions that each of us lives in. At its primary level, the mind animates the sensory world with motion. It is well known that his description of the so-called *phi-phenomenon* put him decades ahead of later theorists who would account for the illusion of moving pictures by recourse to the theory of "retention of visual stimulus." Munsterberg characteristically went beyond this passive view to an active one in which the mind at its most primitive level confers motion on stimuli.

He recognized that the retina does retain visual impressions momentarily after a stimulus has been removed, as when we close our eyes after looking at the sun, but he shows that this passive phenomenon is not able to account for the way we bring a series of still pictures to life. The phi-phenomenon does account for this by emphasizing the active powers of the mind which literally make sense (motion) out of distinct stimuli. Munsterberg describes this phenomenon by recounting some famous experiments in perception, but he never tries to explain it. The phi-phenomenon is for him a given. It shows that at its most basic level the mind has its own laws and constructs our world in exercising them. It shows as well that the technology of film implicitly recognizes these laws and works its effects on the mind itself. The complex machinery (cameras, projectors, and all the processing gadgetry) producing intermittent still pictures has been developed to work directly on the raw material of the mind. The result is motion pictures.

This single, basic mental capability was enough to let Munsterberg conceive of the entire cinematic process as a mental process. Cinema, for him, is the art of the mind just as music is that of the ear and painting that of the eye. All of its technology and sociology proceed from this belief. All inventions and uses for the cinema have been developed to shape and create films out of the mind of man. It is the mind which is the quarry for the filmmaker and the stuff of movies.

It seemed obvious to Munsterberg to describe all cinematic properties as mental. Besides the basic quality of motion, he notes that closeups and camera angles exist not simply because of the lenses and cameras which make them technically feasible, but because of the mind's very way of working, which he labels "attention." Not only does the mind live in a moving world, it organizes that world by means of this property of attention. In the same way the motion picture is not a mere record of motion, but an organized record of the way the mind creates a meaningful reality. Attention operates on the world of sensation and motion, just as angle, composition, and focal length are properties a step above sheer recording of intermittent photographs.

At an even higher level Munsterberg confronts the mental operations of memory and imagination which go beyond simple attention to give this world a sense, an impact, a personal direction. The filmic properties which respond to these mental operations are the various kinds of editing all of which confer on both motion and significant camera work a dramatic direction and organization. At the highest mental level are emotions, which Munsterberg considers to be complete mental events. While he never distinguishes, in this book at least, between the mind and its emotions, the latter must organize the powers and activities of the former. The cinematic aspect corresponding to emotion is the story itself, the highest unit or ingredient available to this narrative art, and the one which directs all the lower processes of film.

Thus in ascending his psychological hierarchy, Munsterberg has carefully pointed to the material analogues in cinema which relate to each stage of mentality. The primitive illusion of movement given to us by the mind's operation on intermittent photographs is supplemented by select attention attained via angle, composition, image size, and lighting. Corresponding to memory and imagination are the natural resources of editing, which compress or expand time, create rhythms, and render flashbacks or dream scenes. Finally, Munsterberg claims: "To picture emotions must be the central aim of the photoplay."[1] Since the materials of cinema are the resources of the mind, the form of cinema must mirror mental events, that is, emotions. Film is the medium not of the world, but of the mind. Its basis lies not in technology but in mental life.

At last we can see why Munsterberg pays only fleeting attention to documentaries and instructional movies. They may perform valuable social functions, but they can never attain the stature of the photoplay which is a form based on cinema's true raw material, the movements of the events of the mind. We can see as well why he felt color and sound would prove worse than superfluous to the cinematic experience. They are technical developments which don't activate a new level of the mind. For him the technology of 1915 was already ideally suited to shape the greatest masterpieces of which cinema would ever be capable and to enhance our lives by thus fulfilling the goals of art. How different his position is from that of Bazin who, thirty years later, would claim that film must be seen as an evolving phenomenon, perpetually developing an ever-more-perfect technology which will serve unthought-of goals by giving us unimaginable forms of cinema. It never crossed Munsterberg's mind that the purpose of the highest cinema could be other than the traditional purpose of art or that its form might not follow the established precepts of all successful art.

FORM AND FUNCTION

Munsterberg was first and always a philosopher, an idealist in the neo-Kantian school. And it is the Kantian aesthetics which he delivers to us pre-packaged at the outset of Part II of his book. To use our system of categories, it was the value, function, or purpose of cinema which first must have gripped his mind as he found himself returning time and time again to the movies in 1915. For him the experience of being lost in a film story proved that film was an art, having the purpose of art, and it is toward the aesthetics of film that his psychology of film tends.

Following Kant, Munsterberg employs an entirely different kind of analysis when he turns from psychology to aesthetics. Psychology is part of a scientific mode of thought. It tries to explain aspects of what Kant called the *phenomenal realm,* the realm of sense experience where things are linked in time, space, and causality. Munsterberg's historical introduction described the epidermis of film, treating film like an object in nature. Part I moved to psychology because Munsterberg saw film as an object for experience requiring that we relate it to the seat of experience, the mind. History, in short, described the object we usually call film, and psychology showed how that external object creates the internal object which is really the film. Together these analyses account for the "phenomenal" aspects of cinema.

The second half of his book goes outside science to philosophy in order to account for the form and function of film, that is for the *noumenal realm.* While science is able to show how a thing has come into existence and how it works in our lives, it is unable to describe the value of that object. For this we must go to philosophy and specifically to the value-philosophy and the neo-Kantian aesthetics which Munsterberg had practiced and promoted for forty years.

Aesthetics plays an important role in the overall philosophy of Kant and an even more important role in Munsterberg's system. The sciences of the phenomenal world can never get outside that world to the basis of life and consciousness. They are locked within a world of causality. Kant found that for science to be construed as correct or "true" we have to believe in the transcendence of certain logical categories that exist in the noumenal, not the phenomenal sphere. These categories are unprovable, yet without them all our science and everyday common sense falls apart. Logic isn't alone in this noumenal realm. He also placed ethical first principles there which serve to justify our normal moral sense, giving us the ability to judge one action as better than another and, more important, allowing us to go beyond ourselves in so judging. Just as we demand that everyone accept the logical principles by which we make sense of the material world, so we demand that everyone recognize the transcendence of certain moral principles without which we couldn't properly speak of right and wrong actions.

Logic and ethics are joined by aesthetics to round out Kant's inquiry into the noumenal. Here too certain innate and transcendent

principles are shown to underlie our basic sensual life. We find ourselves attracted or repelled by various objects and experiences and
Kant needs to show that this "affective" aspect of our lives is not
completely governed by sheer physical causality, that we aren't
completely and passively at the mercy of our psyches and the random stimuli of the world. He argued that while most of our feelings and judgments are based on the pleasure principle and are
therefore explicable within the normal domain of psychology, our
experience of the truly beautiful places us momentarily outside of
all considerations of personal gain or pleasure. We confront an object or experience for itself and we feel that it is justified in itself.
This is why Kant calls the object of beauty an object having "pur-
posiveness without purpose." It looks perfectly designed, so that
each of its parts work toward a magnificent whole, but we can do
nothing with it except experience it. It is cut off from other objects
and experiences just as we are cut off momentarily from the normal
continuity of self-interest which comprises our daily life and projects. Both the mind and the object are free-floating during this experience. Kant says the mind is "distinterested," that is, not intent
on turning this object to use, while the object is "isolated," held
out against all the other objects in the world. We don't look at it
to see how it can aid us, nor to find out its place in the larger
scheme of things. During the aesthetic experience that object becomes for us the whole context, an end in itself, a *terminal value*.

What pleased both Kant and Munsterberg was that this value
doesn't help us at all, gains us nothing. We have no cause to uphold
it. Therefore, they reasoned, our selfless attraction to this value
proves the existence of transcendence, proves the reality of the entire world of values. Materialists have always argued that logic
and ethics are fabricated by a frantic mind unable to cope with the
arbitrary world of matter and morals. Having to justify our common sense and our common morality, we invent the "noumenal"
realm and claim that it makes *the* world hold together, whereas in
reality it is a simple psychological ploy designed to hold *our* world
together. Such materialists actually use psychology to explain the
universals man senses around him. They try to account for the
noumenal by the phenomenal. Both Kant and Munsterberg were

sensitive to these charges and went to aesthetics to shore up the defenseless world of transcendence. They found that in the pure experience of beauty man encounters a transcendence which doesn't affect him directly and which the psychology of the materialist cannot explain away. Beauty saves both Truth and Goodness.

In the art object the mind suddenly finds in the world an object constructed perfectly for it, assuring the rightness of both the object and the perceiving mind, both of which escape for a moment the hectic minute-to-minute tension which exists between man and the world. For Munsterberg the isolated art object must appeal to the disinterested perceiver in all its uniqueness, first stirring the mind and then putting it to rest. Certain films, he found, fully accomplish this.

Evidently the effect was so strong for him that he refused to believe film was an inferior art form. Those who claim it is a mere carrier of the art of the theater, ignore the fact that when we see a photograph of a Renaissance painting we crave to see the original and so are not really satisfied by the object before us, but when we see a good film we are satisfied and don't consider it displaced theater. Our minds invade this object on the screen and are cut off from all other engagements. The film then flows to its conclusion shaped in such a way that it *sustains itself* away from the real world and *sustains us* in what has been called a state of "rapt attention." Instead of trying to use such a film or even to comprehend it, we are content to perceive it for itself, isolated from everything else, valuable in itself. Such is Munsterberg's answer to film's final goal. He is so sure of this answer that he never bothers to argue for it in this essay. It is for him a fact of experience.[2]

Aesthetic experience first strikes us in our contemplation of nature. When in our daily routine we suddenly stop for no reason "to really see" and enjoy that which before we had scarcely noticed, we are isolating this object or landscape from its background and we are isolating ourselves from our routine. This instance of nature pleases us not because it helps our lives but because it insists that, as Mikel Dufrenne says, "We are made for this world and the world is made for us." Our experience puts us to rest and desires nothing more, even when the object is violent or strange.

We cultivate aesthetic experience in art objects, which are objects constructed in the world for no practical reason. Often they are cut off from the world by a spatial border (a frame or a proscenium arch) or by a temporal border (we listen to a symphony in a hall from 8:00 p.m. to 8:45 p.m. and then we go back out onto the street). Artworks are objects, Munsterberg would say, following Kant, built to the measure of our minds, objects whose *raison d'être* is to be experienced perfectly and out of all context.

Munsterberg must show how film can be such an art object. He proceeds negatively. First he indicates, as we have seen, that film is not a mere transmission channel for theatrical artwork. Then, perhaps too briefly, he tells us that neither is film a transmission channel for the aesthetic experience of the natural world. It is true that the filmmaker may provide a picture of Niagara Falls for those of us who have never seen it; and he may show us for the first time the beauty of a flower we have known but have never really "seen before," simply by putting these natural objects on the screen where they are perforce useless. But Munsterberg would never claim this to be film's total aesthetic capacity. After all, why do we need a duplication of nature, and one which cannot render the smell of the flower or the spray of the falls? Films of natural beauty have a practical purpose of whetting our appetite for the aesthetic experience of nature, but they can never substitute for such experience. They are at best like the photograph of the Renaissance painting which eventually entices us to the Uffizi gallery in Florence.

Finally Munsterberg turns to the positive side of his argument. If a part of nature or a piece of drama is to function aesthetically in a film, it does so, he states, by submitting to the poetics of the screen, forming a new object, a film object of contemplation. For Munsterberg this is a mental object, an object which flows and finds its rest according to the laws of the mind. Here we can recognize the coincidence of his aesthetic theory and his psychology of film. The belief that film's only claim to aesthetic validity lies in its transforming of reality into an object of imagination has its echo in the psychological claim that film in fact exists not on celluloid, nor even on the screen, but only in the mind which actualizes it by conferring movement, attention, memory, imagination, and emotion on a dead series of shadows.

Not all films attain the height of becoming aesthetic objects. What must a film be like to attain this stature? In other words, how must moving pictures be transformed into imagination? Munsterberg shows his Kantian roots most explicitly here when he claims that reality is characterized by the primary orders of time, space, and causality. These three basic ways of relating objects ensures their status in the continuum of reality. Nor can we even conceive of the world without them. Now the filmmaker has the means to displace precisely these three categories of experience, conferring on appearances whatever spatial, temporal, and causal relations he chooses. Although Munsterberg doesn't say so explicitly, this view of the potential of film brings it quite close to the world of dream. Naturally, Munsterberg would appreciate this rapport both on aesthetic and psychological grounds.

The film must follow a purely mental world, replacing the relations of appearances in the world with mental relations. The film differs from the dream mainly in completeness. Whereas the dream may arouse certain fantasies and emotions, leaving us bewildered or trembling on awakening, the aesthetic film will dispel all the energies it calls into play. It will take appearances from nature, reorder them in light of the mind, and, by doing so, stir our emotions. It will then neatly tie up those appearances, giving them a final order which at once asserts the priority of mental laws over chaotic appearances and at the same time completes the spectator's experience in a way which leaves him lacking nothing. The spectator has given himself over to an object of the imagination and is left in the world but wonderfully cut off from its cares and demands. Munsterberg couldn't be more succinct in summing up:

> The photoplay tells us a human story by overcoming the forms of the outer world, namely space, time, and causality, and by adjusting the events to the forms of the inner world, namely attention, memory, imagination and emotion. . . . [These events] reach complete isolation from the practical world through the perfect unity of plot and pictorial appearance.[3]

This practical aesthetic led Munsterberg to an advanced view of censorship. All material is suitable for film, he argued, even the most violent and prurient, so long as it reaches its proper conclusion, releasing the energies it has aroused. "Unity" becomes the catchword here as in so many theories of art. The absolute formal unity of the artwork ensures that nothing in it will directly affect our practical lives. The experience is entirely self-contained. Just as the space and time of the film are imaginary and don't affect the space and time of our everyday existence, so also the causality at work in the film doesn't flow directly into our lives. The sentiments we see on the screen, tender, violent, erotic, virtuous . . . all grow out of an interlocking system which ends when the film ends. These feelings move us during the film, but the film's unity allows us to contemplate them dispassionately as we are ushered back into the sounds of traffic outside the theater. If the film's *form* is unified, then the film's *goal* will be served and we will disinterestedly involve ourselves with an isolated and intrinsically valuable object.

There are a number of serious questions raised by Munsterberg's aesthetics, but they could be addressed to countless aestheticians since Kant. It is most important to note the consistency of Munsterberg's thought. While some of his answers may strike us as short-sighted (his refusal to allow sound, color, documentary, spontaneity, etc.), it should be remembered that he did provide film with a carefully thought out apology taken from a respected tradition of psychology and philosophy, and that cinema desperately needed such support in that era. Perhaps Munsterberg's full impact is still to come. The reprinting of his study has provoked considerable interest in his theory and Jean Mitry, for one, has said, "How could we have not known him all these years? In 1916 this man understood cinema about as well as anyone ever will."[4]

2

Rudolf Arnheim

Hugo Munsterberg's ideas, no matter how advanced or cogent, had little effect on subsequent film theory. Rudolf Arnheim, many of whose notions are substantially the same as Munsterberg's in *The Photoplay: A Psychological Study,* has on the contrary had a vast effect. As Arnheim's reputation in the field of art criticism and psychology of perception has grown, so has interest in *Film as Art,* the small book he published (originally in German) in 1932. Like Munsterberg, Arnheim comes from a respected intellectual school, the Gestalt school of psychology. And perhaps for this reason his argument, like Munsterberg's, is quick and consistent. At the same time his absolute adherence to a set of ideas leads him to reject many kinds of cinema, making him seem today rather parochial.

In the first sentence of his essay Arnheim limits his interest to questions of film as an art form only. For support he uses analogies from the other media: we pay no aesthetic attention to postcards (art), military marches (music), and striptease (dance). All media, he says, have multiple uses, only one of which is aesthetic; but it is this artistic function which generally makes us focus on the medium itself. Thus poetry returns us to words, not to messages, and painting focuses our sensibilities on line, color, composition, and other formal properties rather than on representation. Film art

27

likewise returns us to the basis of the medium, rather than emphasizing the world it pictures. But what is this basis?

MATERIAL

Munsterberg had found this basis to be the psychological processes of the spectator. Arnheim wants to shift the focus to the material of the medium itself, yet he finds no way to reduce this to anything analogous to the simple materials of the other arts. He concludes that film's material must be all the factors which make it a less than perfect illusion of reality.

Most theorists have held that in some sense cinema is the medium of reality, even if it is a displacement of the real. Arnheim, however, claims that if this be so, film cannot be art since there is no true opportunity for an artist to manipulate such a medium. The artist would merely have to *re*present reality, focusing the audience's attention on what is represented, not on the means of such representation. Like instructional prose writing, such filmmaking would have its values but these would never be aesthetic values, since they are directed at the object rather than at the means.

Arnheim then turns to a decisively brilliant approach. Since film can be an art only insofar as the medium differs from a true rendering of reality, he enumerates every aspect of the medium which is in some way unreal. These include: 1. the projection of solids on a two-dimensional surface; 2. the reduction of a sense of depth and the problem of absolute image size; 3. lighting and the absence of color; 4. the framing of the image; 5. the absence of the space-time continuum due to editing; 6. the absence of inputs from the other senses. Every image in film is fraught with at least these six types of unreal aspects. And it is these aspects which must be the raw material of film art.

It should be clear why Arnheim chides technological developments such as color, 3-D photography, sound and wide-screen. Each reduces the impact of film by bringing it more into accord with natural experience. Arnheim's position here is close to Munsterberg's, for the aspects he has enumerated are not deviations

from *reality* so much as from our *experience of the real.* Coming
as he does from Gestalt psychology, which emphasizes wholes over
parts, patterns over individual sensations, Arnheim treats the film
experience as unreal. True, it reproduces many visual facts on celluloid just as they would be seen on the retina, but our feeling for
reality is much deeper than its retinal component.

Let's take some examples. Arnheim points to the fact that we
see a rectangular table as nearly rectangular even when the front
edge is pushed quite close to our eyes. Despite the fact that the
retinal image of the table is trapezoidal (as would be any photograph of it taken from this perspective) our mind compensates for
the distortion. Our vision, in other words, is not a mere result of
retinal stimulation, but involves an entire "field" of perceptions,
associations, and memory. In this case we aren't seeing badly; we
are actually seeing more than our eyes can tell us because vision
is a complete mental operation of which retinal stimulation comprises but a part. Objects diminish in size by the square root of
their distance from us. Our mind compensates for this to a large
extent. But the photograph does not so compensate, giving us an
image of a man's foot, Arnheim says, larger than his head if it is
stretched out in front of him. When examining a photograph, our
mind fails to compensate for this effect, since the photograph is a
two-dimensional object. It is this which makes photographic composition so different from mere arrangement of figures. Composition in film or photography is a function of this visual fact or inadequacy. While being true to the mathematically real, photography
is false to the psychologically real.

Arnheim's notion of the frame as an organizing principle in film,
his concept of the space-time continuum, his insistence that film is
abstract because it fails to provide inputs from our senses of taste,
touch, and smell are other instances where meaning is seen to reside in a *pattern* of stimuli rather than in individual stimuli themselves. Film may mechanically record the sensations which the
retina gathers but it does so mindlessly, consequently non-
representationally. Film art is based on the manipulation of the
technically visible, not the humanly visual.

These are just some of the reasons for the technical limitations

Photograph by Joe Heumann.

of representationalism which allow us to experience the *medium* even as we try to get lost in the illusion of reality. Arnheim holds that the sum of these limitations is the raw material of film art, for it is only these which an artist can control and manipulate for his own expressive purposes. Many people have balked at this notion of film's raw material. The very term "technical limitations of representationalism" sounds unlikely when placed beside terms like "sound," "stone," "gesture," "color," which might be taken as raw materials for some of the other arts. Not only is it a clumsy term; it contains within it the admission that film strives to be representational. This drive toward realism is what André Bazin has called "the myth of total cinema," a psychological force at the heart of all of us pushing film toward perfect illusionism. For Arnheim, this drive is profane and must be checked and dammed up if we are ever to be able to use this medium for higher purposes.

The limitations of illusionism are the means by which we recognize the medium at all and are able to treat a film as a film rather than as reality. These limitations are also the fabric of the medium.

Although Arnheim doesn't say so, film art differs vastly from the other arts on this question of raw material. Music, for instance, is sound which has become conscious of itself and of its own properties, and has been taken out of the world, so to speak, in order to be built into a mental object. Film art, on the other hand, is the self-conscious use not of *something* in the world (sound, stone, gesture, etc.) but of a *process* we use to represent the world. In other words, film art is based on a process, or more accurately, on the retarding of a process.

We might think of the film process as a window through which we are able to see the world. Arnheim would have us turn this window at an angle until the glass begins to refract the light, distorting what is beyond it while revealing its own properties. Suddenly we become aware of the frame of the glass, of its texture, of the kinds of light it allows to pass, and so on. Nonetheless we would never be aware of these qualities if we weren't trying to look through the window. Film art is a product of the tension between representation and distortion. It is based not on the aesthetic use of something in the world but on the aesthetic use of something which gives us the world.

Arnheim never analyzes the implications of this difference of film from traditional art, a difference which will become the cornerstone of Bazin's theory. Arnheim's is necessarily a negative theory based as it is upon a notion of suppression: we must suppress the filmic process of representation in favor of the artistic process of expression. We can do this because the cinematic process has its own peculiarities. It is not so much a window as a prism.

THE CREATIVE USE OF THE MEDIUM

The next step for Arnheim is simple, and it is one for which his studies in art theory have prepared him. Having defined the raw material of film as aspects of its technology, he can elaborate the artistic effects associated with each aspect or limitation. This he does with a store of examples from artistically successful films. Film artists are aware of the unreality of the images they create and they exploit these limitations, forcing the spectator to see not just the object on the screen but the object carefully delimited via the medium. I have already alluded to composition in depth as a function of the two-dimensionality of the picture. Likewise, the frame which restricts the spectator's view can be used by the artist to organize and direct our perception of the object. For each limitation of natural perception there is a gain for potential aesthetic perception, and Arnheim is quick to list such gains. In addition there are specifically filmic possibilities which no one would associate with real perception: fast and slow motion; fades, dissolves, superimpositions; backward motion, the use of still photography, distortions through focus and filter.

Is Arnheim trying to create a dictionary of cinematic art? If such an approach is valid, every manipulative feature of film could be described, together with suggestions of the meaning of such manipulation (e.g., the worm's-eye view suggests weight or forcefulness; the head-on telephoto shot of someone running connotes the futility or arduousness of his effort). Countless handbooks to visual literacy have been written on the basis of Arnheim's work, each hoping to equip viewers with an understanding of what the filmmaker is saying through his special treatment of a subject. Such introductions are often valuable in that they focus the uninitiated viewer's attention on aspects of the medium he had formerly "not seen," but they may also promote an impoverished view of cinema. There are, by Arnheim's reasoning, a finite number of limitations for the artist to manipulate; and while there are numerous ways of manipulating some of them, a list of possible "artistic effects" is really quite manageable. Must we then believe that every image is comprised of a represented object (noun) or action (verb) qualified by artistic effects (adjectives and adverbs)? Must we think of every film as something seen through a prism which had been carefully turned by the filmmaker in order to distort and color whatever he is showing?

The sterility of this view overshadows its convenience. Does any other art merely "comment on" or color the world? Perhaps Arnheim has prompted such a view with his definition of film's raw material. We have noted that film's material seems to differ in kind from the materials of the other arts. His view that film becomes art when the filmic process of representing the world is retarded nevertheless keeps film art dependent on representation. The other arts lift their material out of the world and freely play with it; film would seem to be condemned to commenting on the world because its material is not material in the world at all, but a *process* which was invented to represent the world and is unthinkable apart from that world.

FILM FORM

While Arnheim's prescriptions for the artistic use of film have been widely adopted, his notions of film as an art form are seldom taken seriously. But it is only due to his strict ideas about film form that Arnheim is redeemed and stands above his countless imitators who seem interested only in cataloguing visual techniques and effects. They are unable to show how artistic *effects* are capable of producing *art*. Arnheim's commitment to Gestalt psychology gives him an advantage here.

He discloses his Gestalt heritage in his Preface when he employs the term *impurities* in relation to the form of films. And it is this idea which returns in the last essay of the book, "A New Laocoön." For Arnheim, every medium, when used for artistic purposes, draws attention away from the object which the medium conveys and focuses it on the characteristics of the medium itself. Further, every medium proceeds by means of a central sensory nexus: music is the medium of sound, dance of gesture, poetry of words, and so on.

The nexus becomes a symbolic language to be manipulated by the artist, and the artist must learn to organize this physical material so that his vision or idea shines through. Even if he wants to duplicate aspects of the physical world, he must study his medium diligently so that he can successfully translate his perception of the world into the proper codes of his medium. A painter looks onto a pastoral scene with cows and farm buildings; then he looks at his palette and canvas; finally, after much trial and error, and a heavy reliance on tricks learned from other artists, he splashes the proper blotches of oil onto the canvas and produces relations which everyone will marvel at as being so true to reality. He *transmits* nothing; rather he *translates* one kind of perception into the conventions of his medium. If his goal is the expression of an inner state or emotion he must proceed in the same way. There is no shortcut through the medium.[1]

As artist after artist toys with this material nexus, experiences are quickly accumulated. One learns that some things cannot be well translated into music or sculpture. More important, one learns that the medium is subtlest and most interesting when it adopts certain concentrated or pure shapes. Years of attention paid to the medium should have as an effect the progressive purifying of the medium, so that music in an advanced stage, for example, should be freed from references (lyrics) and theatricalities (performance characteristics) and should render up pure sound. In other words, the aesthetic capacity of its nature seeks a simplification of chaos and at its best finds a realm of purity in the heart of a medium.

While every use of a medium is conventional (i.e., a translation, not a transmission), some conventions are more natural to a given medium than others because a medium has definite physical properties. As time goes by, changing conventions reveal more and more clearly the most powerful peculiarities of the medium until it is purified of all extraneous connections. At this point the medium has found its forms. After centuries of starts and stops, music moved toward the purity of the sonata form in the time of Mozart and Haydn. Other forms coexisted with this one, but it is apparent that music had found a natural posture in the sonata. Even into our own century composers draw on this form because listeners sense its heritage and, more importantly, because it is a pure and therefore powerful use of music.

Arnheim was fearful that film, in constant search for newness, would never develop an audience capable of subtle experience. He was also worried that film artists, moving from form to form, might pass up or give up a pure form of cinematic expression were they ever to find it.

As a matter of fact, Arnheim felt that cinema had found such a form and had given it up. The silent cinema of the twenties was for him the high point in the history of cinema. After twenty years of experimentation, filmmakers had located the peculiarities of the medium and had established a narrative form capable of unifying the most varied effects. With the coming of sound this form was frittered away. Instead of a highly flexible set of physical sign systems, filmmakers provided audiences with a semblance of gross realism. Anyone with an eye for depth and sophistication of expression could see that cinema had bartered its purity. In Arnheim's schema, the peculiarities of the medium were being de-emphasized. Cinematic form, instead of unifying a varied set of sign systems (lighting, gesture, editing, composition), had become in the thirties a kind of laundry bag tying together imitations of reality. A streamlined, exceptionally versatile form was traded off for a form which could not help but emphasize one element, speech, turning film into an impure kind of theater-substitute.

The sound film failed as art in every way. It tried to pass itself off as approaching reality, forgetting that art exists only when attention flows back on the medium. Second, it enshrined one of its parts (dialogue) at the expense not only of other de-emphasized parts, but at the expense of the organic whole. Gestalt psychologists suggest that in the evolution of any organism the loss of a constraint may produce unhealthy growth, growth which doesn't profit the organism as a whole. A cancer results from the loss of natural checks and this cancer may destroy the whole in its expansion. The technological check against sound had kept film energy flowing productively into well-organized, well-balanced films, films in which all aspects worked in harmony. Sound forces every element to serve the plot and dialogue and it tries to insist on the reality of its content. To Arnheim it is indeed a cancer which has destroyed the artistic life of film by distorting its ensemble form.

THE PURPOSE OF FILM

What was it about late silent cinema[2] which so attracted Arnheim? What function was it performing so well? What, for Arnheim, is the purpose of film art? While nothing in *Film as Art* adequately answers these questions, Arnheim's prolific writings in the fields of art history and perceptual psychology contain many references to exactly this problem. The case with Arnheim, then, is quite similar to that with Munsterberg. Both these intellectuals composed rather slight treatises on film (as if cinema were for them a vacation from their true fields), yet these treatises in both cases are backed up by voluminous work in related fields as well as by the prestige of an important intellectual tradition.

That important tradition within which Arnheim wrote, and is still writing, is of course Gestalt psychology. Gaining prominence just after the first world war, Gestalt psychology had its greatest successes in the field of perception. The Gestaltists hold that the mind is active in the experience of reality to such an extent that it gives to reality not only its meaning but its very physical characteristics as well. Basing their beliefs on numerous experiments, the most famous of which involve shifting figure/ground relationships, they have argued that the color, shape, size, density, and brightness of objects in the world are products of the operation of the creative mind on an essentially dumb or neutral nature.

Arnheim has gone so far as to assert that not merely the mind, but all our nervous centers create the world we live in by organizing it. Our eyes, our ears, the tips of our fingers give shape, color, form, and finally higher meanings to the world which stimulates them. This process is called *transformation,* and it occurs constantly in all mentally healthy human beings. The Gestaltists attribute many psychological disorders to sensory misbehavior. For instance, Arnheim speaks of the schizophrenic as one who is locked into a world of a very few visual forms infinitely applied to the world. These few forms are inadequate to cope with the great quantities of stimuli which our own eyes and minds have no difficulty transforming. The schizophrenic is therefore bound to run into conflict with a reality which the rest of us, with our more "healthy" or, at least, more diverse structuring capabilities, force him to live within and acknowledge.

The Gestaltists reserve an important place in their theories for artistic process. It is for them the very model or paradigm of perceptual activity. Well known are their experiments and diagnoses which involve the subject in an act of creating or reading (i.e., transforming) images. But beyond this the Gestaltists have lent their support to the twentieth-century trend to demythologize art, making it seem part of what we all do as human beings, rather than a divine gift which a few geniuses have the right to practice. In the Preface of his *Art and Visual Perception,* Arnheim writes,

> No longer can we consider the artistic process as a self-contained activity, mysteriously inspired from above, unrelated and unrelatable to what people do otherwise. Instead, the exalted kind of seeing that leads to the creation of great art appears as an outgrowth of the humbler and more common activity of the eyes in everyday life.[3]

and later in the same book he goes on:

> Recent [i.e., Gestalt] psychological thinking encourages us to call vision a creative activity of the human mind. Perceiving achieves, at the sensory level, what in the realm of reasoning is known as understanding. Every man's eyesight also anticipates in a modest way the admired capacity of the artist to produce patterns that validly interpret experience by means of organized form (p. 37).

While art may be produced by the same human capability which allows for everyday experience, Arnheim would never suggest that it is of the same order. Art's "admirability" and "exaltedness" come precisely from its generality, that is, from its quality of hovering above the everyday in a world of forms. Art is the organization not of a specific field of sensory data, but of a general pattern applicable beyond itself. Arnheim states that "The artist uses his categories of shape and color to capture something universally significant in the particular" (*Art and Visual Perception,* p. vi). The artist's concern, then, is not so much his subject matter as the pattern he can create through that subject matter. When we admire a painting, we admire not the subject matter reproduced but the organization given it by the painter. In a representational painting we note that the artist has first seen his subject (this is called the *primary transformation,* the transformation each of us constantly performs) and then has imaginatively organized it into a higher pattern which seems to express his particular vision of both the subject matter and all of reality (this is the *secondary transformation*). A cubist painting of a building, for example, is a transformation not of the building but of the artist's particular mode of organizing certain kinds of perceptions.

Now Arnheim has always been very careful not to overstate his case. A work of art is an expression, to be sure, and an expression which brings to light the organizing sentiments of the artist; nevertheless, we mustn't forget that expression begins in the world. Otherwise human beings would be locked, like the schizophrenic, within a closed set of a priori categories of experience. For Arnheim art is a "give and take" with the world. The artist receives raw stimuli from the world which he sees as objects and events; he then projects these objects into an imaginative pattern which he thrusts back into the world. The world responds, forcing him to adapt his pattern until both artist and world are satisfied. In this way, the artwork expresses both the artist and the world.

This position is more moderate than the extreme idealism or mentalism of Munsterberg. Perception and art are both founded on the organizing abilities of the mind, but for Arnheim these are supported by a world which seems to lend itself to certain kinds of organization. It seems important to point out that Gestalt psychology has struggled to base itself on physics, not on philosophy. One of its earliest and greatest members, Wolfgang Köhler, claimed that the "field" concept of human perception introduced by him was directly related to the atomic physics of Max Planck.[4] Modern science, including ecology, has shown that certain general forms or impulses organize natural events and that every individual event takes on meaning only when seen in terms of the whole system. Köhler took this analogy seriously and constructed theories of perception based on the physical properties of electronic and cellular movement which he assumed must occur in the nervous centers. The physical makeup of the brain, in other words, demands that we think in terms of balance, symmetry, contrast, and so on. We perceive the world according to laws which exist in us but which have been given to us by that world of which we are, therefore, integral and homogeneous parts.

Whether or not other Gestalt thinkers would accept these views, Arnheim certainly sees a close rapport between the world and the mind. Certainly man's senses and his brain pattern the world and, in art, pattern it absolutely. This would seem to give the mind authority over nature. But these patterns, Arnheim finds, have the same characteristics as raw nature. He insists on this in closing *Art and Visual Perception:*

> Motifs like rising and falling, dominance and submission, weakness and strength, harmony and discord, struggle and conformance, underlie all existence. We find them within our own mind and in our relations with other people, in the human community and in the events of nature. Perception and expression fulfills its spiritual mission only if we experience in it more than the resonance of our own feelings. It permits us to realize that the forces stirring in ourselves are only individual examples of the same forces acting throughout the universe (p. 434).

From the broadest perspective, then, Arnheim feels that the purpose of art is to perceive and express the general forces of existence. While all human beings resolve the world of raw stimuli into a world of objects and events, the artist goes further by abstracting from those objects and events their general characteristics. Arnheim says that when he finishes a painting the artist has not thrust a self-made pattern on the world, but instead has balanced a play of forces (his own and the world's) until his picture achieves equilibrium. Some artists, he claims, play down their own patterning in the hope of expressing the chaos of nature and of life (the romantics); others are compelled to stamp a timeless form on whatever nature they choose to gather to them (classical artists, the descendants of the Byzantine style). Both methods are self-destructive when carried to their limits, and all artistic styles lie somewhere between them.

Arnheim does not come out in favor of one style of art over another, for he sees in the multiplicity of styles a manifestation of the endless variety in man and in nature. Nonetheless, all styles, in his view, must come to some kind of equilibrium between the mind and nature, for without this the work will be unfinished. The artist may fail at the level of the material he is supposed to pattern, satisfying himself with the mere reproduction of the particulars of nature. The result is brute sensation, sensation available to us without art, sensation never raised to the level wherein it expresses itself. On the other hand, the artist may fail at the level of his abstractions, never achieve a singular appropriate pattern for the material. This failure is called "ambiguity" and it "confuses the artistic statement because it leaves the observer on the edge between two or more assertions which do not add up to a whole" (*Art and Visual Perception,* p. 31). For Arnheim there is one and only one pattern which neatly matches its material bringing both of them into the light of expression. Here, more than anywhere else, he absolutely rejects the realistic theorists to be studied later. Ambiguity for them, especially for Bazin, becomes a value not a liability; nor could the artistic product from their standpoint ever be thought of as a "statement."

No matter how much interplay Arnheim calls for between man and nature in the creation of art, his is finally a mentalist theory of art. He looks for those moments when an equilibrium of forces, yoked by an artist's mind from the stimuli of the world, succeeds in expressing aspects of both the artist and the world which we had never been fully aware of before. Inspiration, in the scientific and artistic spheres, is achieved when the material before one suddenly reorganizes itself into a new and satisfying structure. Both artist and scientist create the "figure in the carpet," the pattern in the Rorschach patch we call reality, a pattern which reality is already predisposed to receive. Thanks to such scientific and artistic restructurings, we can see more deeply, live more fully. As a photographic medium film provides us with more material to pattern. As an artistic medium it can help us pattern that material and show us the ways in which our minds are joined to the physical universe we live in.

Arnheim has written only a few minor articles about the cinema since his book of 1932 but, as recently as 1957, he said "I still believe what I believed then" (*Film as Art,* p. 5) and his most current writings apply the selfsame ideas to still photography.[5] His refusal to budge from his earliest beliefs has exasperated generations of film students, but it gives to his views a presence and solidity which cannot be ignored. Today Arnheim remains silent about the cinema, but his position has plenty of advocates from the visual literacy handbooks directly derived from him to the sophisticated theories of filmic perception which Christian Metz in France is currently developing and for which he openly indebts himself to Arnheim.[6]

3

Sergei Eisenstein

The views of cinema developed by Sergei Eisenstein are infinitely richer and more complex than those of either Arnheim or Munsterberg. Unlike them, Eisenstein was a filmmaker of immeasurable ability whose fame assured his writings on film an immediate and broad readership. Eisenstein was an energetic and eclectic thinker. Unlike Arnheim and Munsterberg, however, he was temperamentally unable to deduce a film theory from a firmly held philosophy, and he cluttered up his theoretical research with massive amounts of arcane data culled from a lifetime of scattered reading in at least four languages.

While he paid public homage to Marx and Lenin and was certainly committed to many of their theories, Eisenstein was not the kind of thinker who embraces a single idea or tradition which he then systematically develops. Eisenstein was interested in countless subjects and numerous theories about those subjects. He would browse creatively in a bookstore or library, ferreting out facts and hypotheses of all sorts which later he would apply to his own special passion, film.

All this gives many of his ideas the look of pop-theory. Just examine his essay "Color and Meaning" (in *The Film Sense*), where he puts together a vast but diffuse list of famous statements on color theory. The list is impressive and altogether fascinating. It will remain an important resource in the theory of color aesthetics, but it is a collection of statements harboring myriad confusions and contradictions which Eisenstein, in his passionate pursuit of the subject, didn't bother to untangle. In his excitement to confirm his intuitive feelings about color and cinema, he hurriedly brought to bear all the sources he could, many hardly relevant to his theory. And this is characteristic. His writing always manifested the drama of discovery which he actually experienced in working out his theory. He would, it seems, suddenly be struck by an intuition and be driven to ransack history, economics, art history, psychology, anthropology, and countless other fields in order to substantiate that intuition. Or at other times it appears that a new idea concerning some aspect of film theory was delivered to him through a nearly random encounter with books, events, people. His seminal essay "The Unexpected" (in *Film Form*) begins, "We have been visited by the Kabuki theater . . ." and goes on to develop a theory of the film image which struck him while he viewed that theater.

While all of us operate in this way to some extent (from intuition to a search for support for that intuition) few writers expose this process as ingenuously as did Eisenstein. The quality of shock which he so stressed in filmmaking is an integral part of his tactics in writing film theory as well. Skim the essay "A Dialectical Approach to Film Form" (in *Film Form*) and you will see graphically how Eisenstein tried to burst ideas upon us rather than weave them into a fabric of linear logic. Even between any two of his essays there is the continual use of abrupt transition rather than any dissolving or match-cutting of ideas. Just as he claimed one must listen for overtones between shots in films, so we must listen for such overtones between his essays.

All this makes reading Eisenstein an interesting but tenuous business; and it makes summarizing him nearly impossible. In what follows I hope merely to try to locate Eisenstein within the categories of questions which we have used in examining other theorists. Optimally such an orientation will give the reader some compass points and several monuments he can rely on as he wanders through the various quarters, avenues, and back alleys which make up this rich theoretic megolopolis which we call the work of Eisenstein.

It is only fair to note at the outset that our concern throughout this chapter will be to try to maintain the same sense of struggle which Eisenstein's ideas seemingly went through on every level. While each statement he made may sound dogmatic and final, they must all be seen to qualify one another. This is the true dialectical mode of thinking, a mode of which Eisenstein was a brilliant practitioner.

We will see first that his conception of the basic material of the medium grew from the belief that the single shot was the film's basic building block (a belief Vsevolod Pudovkin never transcended) to a much more complex conception, that of the "attraction." This latter concept is much less mechanistic than the shot, for it takes into account the activity of the viewer's mind, not simply the action of the filmmaker's will. Nevertheless, Eisenstein never fully abandoned the determinism of his early views and the hope that the filmmaker, through a calculated structuring of attractions, could shape the mental processes of the spectator.

Next, at the level of creative process we will see how his attitude toward montage, generally thought to be unflinching and dogmatic, actually veered from its starting point in a rather dramatic way. The struggle between Eisenstein's fluctuating view of montage is best seen in the changing relation that concept has to certain types of psychology. While Eisenstein seems to have conceived of montage within the psychological model of Pavlov, or at least of the associationists, his later writings on the issue seem much closer to the developmental psychology of Jean Piaget. Once again his initially simple mechanistic notions were questioned and altered by a more complex and less predictable variant, one which brought a respect for the powers of the spectator and for the mysterious workings of perception and understanding.

The tension between the simple, predictable, mechanistic process of filmmaking and the complex developmental experience of film viewing emerged explicitly in Eisenstein's double view, first of film form and then of the purpose of film. He thought of the unified film sometimes as a machine and sometimes as an organism. He spoke of film sometimes as if it were a powerful vehicle for rhetorical persuasion and sometimes as if it were a higher, almost mystical means of knowing the universe, that is, he spoke of it as autonomous art. These two pairs of dialectical opposites (the machine versus the organism and rhetoric versus art) will be looked at separately. In my view it was the very frustration of trying to hold opposed views that allowed Eisenstein to question every view and to remain a productive theorist for over thirty years. His essays are always scintillating because each is infused with an energy derived from the juxtaposition of opposite tendencies. He felt these oppositions in himself, in the world he lived in, and in that subject he spent his life trying to understand, the cinema.

THE RAW MATERIAL OF FILM

Eisenstein studied mechanical engineering in the years before he entered the artistic colony of Moscow, and when he joined that colony he entered a period known as "Constructivism." From the beginning Eisenstein considered the artistic activity to be one of "making" or, more precisely, of "building." For this reason the question of the "raw material" which the artist has at his disposal was constantly paramount in his mind.

What bothered Eisenstein about the films which he saw was their inefficiency. The filmmaker, he felt, was at the mercy of the events which he filmed, even if he staged those events. The audience watched screen events exactly as they watched everyday happenings, making the filmmaker a mere channel through which reality could be reproduced. Eisenstein had faced a similar problem in the theater in the early 1920s when he was involved in the brutal fight between the Moscow Art Theater and the avant-garde theater movements of which he was a part. "The Moscow Art Theater is my deadly enemy," he said, because its concern was with a faithful replication of reality. The Constructivists countered this realism in a series of ways, most of which involved the breaking up of the various aspects of theater into bits which could be recomposed according to the formal wishes of the director. The sets should not provide a backdrop for the dialogue, the Constructivists argued, but should function on equal terms alongside the dialogue, almost in dialogue with the dialogue. The same holds true for lighting, blocking, costuming, and so on, all of which should coexist in a democratic harmony rather than in a feudal hierarchy. Even in the theater, then, Eisenstein was seeking ways in which he could break reality down into useful material for the director to fashion.

The process of thus decomposing reality into usable blocks or units may be termed *neutralization*. He claimed that music and painting are based on the neutralization of sound and tone, respectively. In his essay on color he specifically denied that a given color might have a meaning of its own, that yellow, for instance, might signify jealousy and red, passion. Color meaning, like all meaning for Eisenstein, derives from an interrelation of neutral particles: green takes on a particular meaning when it appears in a relational system involving other colors and other codes.

Eisenstein recognized that the elementary film particle, the individual shot, is different from a tone or a sound. It is already comprehensible and appeals immediately to the mind of the spectator as well as to his senses. In order to give the filmmaker the same power which the composer and painter has, Eisenstein felt, shots must be neutralized so that they might become basic formal elements which could be combined however the director saw fit and according to whatever formal principles he might want. Their native "sense" must be extracted so that their physical properties might be used to create a new and higher signification.

The "unexpected" revelation which the kabuki theater brought about in Eisenstein at last gave him the evidence he needed for his theories of neutralization. Kabuki employs an exaggerated stylization far beyond what we normally allow in Western theater. It doesn't simply heighten the reality of fact or event; nor does it merely give a particular slant or interpretation to facts and events through stylization, as Arnheim thought all art should do; instead it deforms and alters all events and facts until they retain only a physical basis. All aspects of the drama become equal, since all have been stylized into sheer epidermis, sheer physical form. In this way the kabuki rendering of, say, a murder, is quite different from conventional Western *mise en scène*. The stylization of the murder gesture eliminates its primacy and puts it on an equal footing with the other gestures it co-operates with. Moreover, all these stylized gestures function in a larger system containing stylized codes of sounds, costuming, and decor in such a way that one cannot say that these other codes are there to support the gestures. The meaning of a kabuki play, in other words, could never be understood by a recounting of the plot or gestures. It is the form of the ensemble which contains the meaning and this form, in Eisenstein's view, is as abstract and as powerful as a musical or painterly form. Reality no longer holds down the theater. Gesture has become the equal of tone or color.

Following his experience with kabuki theater, Eisenstein hoped to create for film a system in which all the elements would be equal and commensurable: lighting, composition, acting, story, even subtitles must be interrelated, so that film can escape the crude realism of mere storytelling accompanied by supporting elements. Eisenstein claimed that each element functions like a circus attraction, different from the other attractions at the fair but on an equal footing and capable of giving the spectator a precise psychological impression. This is quite different from conventional aesthetics, which sees lighting, blocking, camera work, and so on as supporting the *dominant* action, creating a large impression. For Eisenstein, viewing a film is like being jolted by a continuous string of shocks coming from each of the various elements of the film spectacle, not just from the story.

In his earliest writing Eisenstein believed that the smallest unit of film was the shot and that each shot acted like a circus attraction to deliver a particular psychological stimulus which could then combine with other neighboring shots to build the film. Later Eisenstein became more interested in the possibilities of elements within the shot itself providing several sympathetic or conflicting attractions. In any case Eisenstein felt that film could exist as an art only when it reduced itself to "bundles" of attractions, like musical notes, which could be shaped rhythmically and thematically into the rich textures of full experiences.

In music, all possible pitches in the universe are regulated until they form a keyboard capable of harmonic interplay. Eisenstein wanted a keyboard for film so that the director could utilize every element either alone or in combination with other elements and be

Potemkin, 1925. The Museum of Modern Art/Film Stills Archive

sure of the result. Following Pavlov he believed that film shots, or attractions, could be controlled for specific audience effect.

In sum, Eisenstein never considered the mere recording of life as cinematic. Early in his career he chided filmmakers who used extended takes. What could be gained by continuing to gaze at an event once its significance had made its imprint? For him the raw material of film resided in the elements within the shot capable of provoking a discrete (and potentially measurable) reaction within the spectator.

The main values of such neutralization of elements are transference and synaesthesia. In transference a single effect can be produced by a number of different elements. In a film many elements are present on the screen at once. They may reinforce each other, heightening the effect (this occurs in the conventional cinema Eisenstein deplores); the elements may conflict among themselves and create a new effect; or an unexpected element may convey a needed effect. This last is the height of transference. In *Potemkin* (1925), for instance, when the bourgeois lady says on the Odessa Steps, "Let us appeal to them," she is answered not by a speech or a subtitle, nor even by an action, but by the elongated shadows of the soldiers which move silently, incessantly, and ominously down the steps. Here, where elements of speech and lighting are in dialogue, a transference of effect has occurred.

When several elements combine at the same time, there is the possible of synaesthesia, or multisensory experience. A good example of this is found in Jean Vigo's wonderful film *L'Atalante* (1934). After her wedding night, the bride, Dita Parlo, emerges from the hold of the ship, and the following things occur simultaneously: the camera position shifts instantly from long shot to close up; the sun shines with a blinding light on the face of Dita Parlo which

L'Atalante, 1934.

breaks into an irresistible smile; and the crew gives her an accordion serenade. Here four kinds of elements combine to produce a synaesthetic experience in the viewer. We see, hear, feel, and nearly smell the freshness of that moment. This is possible, Eisnstein feels, because the filmmaker has the ability to build each of these attractions any way he chooses. He at last has a workable material.

In making the filmmaker the equal of the painter, composer, and sculptor, Eisenstein goes much further than Pudovkin with whom he has often been associated. Pudovkin put the filmmaker at the mercy of the shot and insisted that creative filmmaking comes from the proper choice and organization of these bits of reality which already have a definite power. He suggested that the filmmaker see through the confusion of history and psychology and create a smooth train of images which would lead toward an overall narrative event. For Pudovkin the sense of the world already exists in the reality captured by the shots, but it could be heightened and released by fastidious editing. The filmmaker has the means, Pudovkin believed, to force the spectator to experience a film event as if it were a natural event. He can slyly direct and control the attention and emotions of the spectator as he leads him not through the confusion of history but through the clarity of a reality reorganized on film so that its hidden relationships have been brought out. Pudovkin's stress on the individual shot as the basic fragment of film lines him up much closer than Eisenstein to the realist film theorists. Even at his most formative, when he talked of creating events on film by means of editing, Pudovkin stopped far short of Eisenstein. Pudovkin wanted to link shots to lead the spectator surreptitiously to the acceptance of an event, a story, or a theme. Eisenstein noted this and demanded not *linkage* but *collision,* not a passive audience, but an audience of co-creators.

All these differences between the two great contemporaries stem from the crucial concept of raw material. Eisenstein could never accept the notion of the shot as a bit of reality which the filmmaker gathers. He insisted as willfully as he could that the shot was a locus of formal elements such as lighting, line, movement, and volume. The natural sense of the shot need not, should not, dominate our experience. If the filmmaker is truly creative he will construct his own sense out of this raw material; he will build relations which aren't implicit in the "meaning" of the shot. He will create rather than direct meaning.

Most films and film theories today still bear the mark of Pudovkin far more than that of Eisenstein, but it is Eisenstein who has ignited the imagination of those seeking a new cinema. His theory of raw material is infinitely more complex than Pudovkin's, for it contains within it a material side (the aspects of the shot he calls attractions) and a mental, or even spiritual, side (the mind which is attracted). Pudovkin simplified this problem by defining raw material from the position of the filmmaker. A shot is a mere technical step in film production. A shock or an attraction, on the other hand, is a relation between mind and matter; it is a question of audience experience and is thereby a much subtler, much richer concept.

CINEMATIC MEANS: CREATION THROUGH MONTAGE

While the raw material for film is the discrete stimuli within the shots, we must not leap to the conclusion that for Eisenstein such stimuli are equivalent to cinema itself. They are rather like building blocks or, to use his analogy, "cells." Cinema is created only when these independent cells receive an animating principle. What gives life to these stimuli, making a full film experience possible? For this we must move to the famous and central concept of *montage*.

Just as Eisenstein's insight into the material of film had been generated by kabuki theater, so it was his study of haiku poetry which ostensibly led him to an understanding of montage. In the very "alphabet" of the Japanese language Eisenstein saw the basis for cinema dynamics. What is an ideogram, he asks, if not the collision of two ideas, or attractions? The picture of a bird and a mouth means "to sing," while the picture of a child and a mouth means "to scream." Here a change in one attraction (from bird to child) produces not a variant of the same concept but an utterly new signification. In film the senses perceive attractions, but cinematic meaning is generated only when the mind leaps to their comprehension by attending to the collision of these attractions.

Haiku poetry, made up of ideograms, works in a similar manner. It records a short series of sense perceptions, forcing the mind to create their unified sense, and producing a precise psychological impact. Eisenstein gives the following from among several examples:

> A lonely crow
> on leafless bough
>   one autumn eve.

Each phrase of this poem can be seen as an attraction, and the combination of phrases is montage. The collision of attractions from line to line produces the unified psychological effect which is the hallmark of haiku and of montage.

After pointing to the case of haiku, Eisenstein immediately lists the kinds of conflict between attractions available to the filmmaker: conflict of graphic direction, of scales, of volumes, of masses, of depths, of darkness and lightness, of focal lengths, and so on. In a later essay he enumerates the general kinds of effects such collision can yield. He discovers five "methods of montage" from the absolutely mathematical metric montage, where conflict is created strictly in the lengths or duration of shots, to intellectual montage, where meaning is the result of a conscious leap made by the spectator between two terms of a visual metaphor or figure. Most of Eisenstein's writing deals with the methods lying between these two extremes. He says conflict can be organized rhythmically, tonally, and overtonally. Each of these methods depends on a conflict between the graphic elements of the shots. Our senses apprehend the attraction of each shot and our inner minds join these attractions through similarity or contrast, creating a higher unity and a significance. Shots as attractions, then, are mere stimulation. It is the specific interaction of shots (at the level of length, rhythm, tone, overtone, or metaphor) which produces meaning. Montage is for Eisenstein the creative power of film, the means by which the individual "cells" become a living cinematic whole; montage is the life principle which gives meaning to raw shots.

While Eisenstein worked out these central concepts concerning montage quite early in his career, he continued to give attention to problems related to montage all during his life. Specifically, he tried to illustrate how various particular elements could be creatively amalgamated into the film experience. As film's technology expanded, Eisenstein hurriedly indicated the formative potential of each new device. In this he was much more liberal (and, I might say, more palatable to modern readers) than Arnheim, with whom he had some obvious similarities on other matters.

The famous "Statement on Sound," which Eisenstein wrote in conjunction with Pudovkin and Grigori Alexandrov, is a perfect example of the adaptability of his theory of montage. While Eisenstein's ideas about film's raw material and about montage construction had been pronounced before sound had become a viable addition to film, he quickly incorporated this "realistic" invention into his anti-realistic theory.

> There will be commercial exploitation of the most saleable merchandise, TALKING FILMS. Those in which sound-recording will proceed on a naturalistic level, exactly corresponding with the movement on the screen, and providing a certain "illusion." . . .
>
> To use sound in this way may well destroy the culture of montage, for every ADHESION of sound to a visual piece increases its inertia as a montage piece and increases the independence of its meaning—and this will undoubtedly be to the detriment of montage, operating in the first place not on the montage pieces but on their juxtaposition.
>
> Only a CONTRAPUNTAL USE of sound in relation to the visual montage piece will afford a new potentiality of montage development and perfection.[1]

Eisenstein immediately goes on to suggest that experiments with non-synchronous sound "will lead to the creation of an ORCHESTRAL COUNTERPOINT of visual images and aural images." He sees in the sound track a way of integrating dialogue and information, not to mention music, in a manner far superior to the use of sub-titles.

The case of sound is just one of many instances in which Eisenstein proclaimed a "montage" use of realistic technology. In another instance he supported color cinematography because color could form an additional complex code of montage units, or attractions, which could interact with other elements in the film. As a viewing of his *Ivan the Terrible,* Part II, will demonstrate, he must have thought long and hard about the possibilities of such unrealistic use of color. In that film, color was employed alongside black and white footage, and the colors themselves were carefully segregated through filters and costuming to shock the spectator with a new visual element. Similarly he was eager that 3-D be developed, for he saw in it new parameters of relations between volume and space, giving the filmmaker an additional element to control. Finally, he wrote a plea for the use of the perfectly square screen shape, rejecting the encroachments of wider and wider ratios. Since he considered the screen to be a frame rather than a window, he felt that the "dynamic square" offered more varied possibilities for screen shapes.

Always, then, Eisenstein sought to increase the number of variables at the filmmaker's command; but at the same time he was eager that all elements remain at that command and not operate on their own. Montage is the veritable voice of command which builds these elements into a film. Whereas Hollywood welcomed technical developments because of the added realism which they provided for the spectator, Eisenstein sought to subvert the natural realism of sound, color, and 3-D through the breaking up or "neutralization" of these elements, allowing them to function in contrapuntal juxtaposition with the other elements of the film. They provided, as it were, a new range of sounds on the keyboard which could be integrated into the artistic experience by the composer-filmmaker through the energy of montage construction.

Eisenstein's concept of montage has many sources. It was a key notion in Constructivist aesthetics, though never developed so fully as in Eisenstein's film theory. It clearly owes a good deal to the theories of dialectical thinking held by Hegel, Marx, and nearly everyone else in Eisenstein's socio-cultural milieu. It also shares much with many psychological theories of the 1920s, theories Eisenstein surely was acquainted with, given his deep interest in thought processes.

It is fascinating to place montage theory next to some theories of cognition prevalent during the twenties if only because it helps separate Eisenstein from Arnheim, whose Gestalt psychology he could never have accepted. Certainly Eisenstein's interest in Pavlov was enough to estrange him from Arnheim, for Pavlov worked at the level of the significance of individual stimuli, whereas Gestalt psychology emphasizes the "field" or "whole," which absorbs and transforms stimuli and from which stimuli derive whatever significance they have. Eisenstein's concept of montage, however, went far beyond Pavlov. What is often neglected is the probable influence upon Eisenstein of the Associationists, who flourished in the twenties. They stressed the laws of space, time, and causality which relate individual percepts. Like Eisenstein, they broke the cognitive process down into sequences of individual imagistic elements, related not by syntax as is language but by sheer juxtaposition. The noted psychologist E. B. Titchener even suggested that it takes at least two sensations to make a meaning. This provides a clear rationale for Eisenstein's theory of montage.

But it is the famous child psychologist Jean Piaget who provided the most striking psychological parallel to Eisenstein's theory. Eisenstein knew the ideas of the great Swiss thinker through the work of Lev Vygotsky, a Russian psychologist of the period very close to Piaget. No matter how close the actual relation was between Eisenstein and the school of Piaget, the many ideas common to these two men are worth noting:[2]

1. *Ego-centrism.* In Piaget's scheme children aged 2-7 engage in pre-operational thought in which their representations cannot be differentiated from themselves. In many ways Eisenstein looked at the viewing experience as an egocentric activity. The viewer adopts the images on the screen as if they embodied his own pre-cognitive experience.

2. *Primary felt symbol.* In the 2-7-year-old stage Piaget found the predominance of the felt symbol as an organizing operation.

Such symbols are highly iconic in nature; that is, the symbol emulates as closely as possible the physical characteristics of that for which it stands. As an example of this, Piaget cited a child opening her mouth to facilitate learning how to open a box. This example is peculiarly apt in considering Eisenstein's theories, since Eisenstein once spoke of his admiration for a Philippine tribe which would give any member in childbirth spiritual support by opening all the doors of the village (*cf. Film Form,* p. 135).

3. *Montage thinking.* Piaget discovered that young children measure meaning by examining the difference between the two terminal states of a process without paying any attention whatsoever to the intermediate stages linking them. His experiments in this area are well known: a child watches water poured from one container into a taller, thinner container and concludes that there is now more water. The pouring itself was not taken into account. In many respects Eisenstein's editing theories assume just this kind of attention to terminal states. This is one reason that he came out so strongly against the long-take, a film style which necessarily focuses on the unfolding of an event. He preferred to shoot static fragments of an event, energizing them with a dynamic editing principle. For a child in Piaget's scheme and for an audience in Eisenstein's theory, it is more meaningful to show three lions in quick succession, each static, each occupying a different position, but together suggesting fierce arousement, than to show one lion actually rousing itself to fight.

4. *Inner speech.* In his essay "Film Form—New Problems," Eisenstein talked explicitly about the ability of cinema to render the syntax of inner speech, a syntax of image clashes and overlaps which only later was translated and tamed into the logic of uttered speech. Piaget suggested, as might be expected, that children operate in a world of inner speech made up of a collage of images. They slowly learn to modify their personal worlds when this inner speech is repeatedly confronted with an external situation to which it does not conform. Usually inner speech is largely replaced by operative public syntax by age seven. It is characterized by several aspects which relate to Eisenstein's film theory. First, it occurs in "unconscious movement" from image sequence to image sequence.

Second, it is "transductive" in that the child attributes causation to the visually associated elements in juxtaposition. Finally, it exhibits a basic "syncretism" which clusters numerous elements into a single event.

Eisenstein employed none of Piaget's vocabulary, but we can say that he wanted the cinema to resurrect inner speech. He wanted the flow of inner speech to be activated by montage and to build toward an emotionally significant event through visual juxtaposition. In Piaget's terms, he wanted cinema to become or to produce a "global syncretism of individual transductive inferences."

Eisenstein's fascination with primitive societies and with the expressions of children reinforce the conception of cinema art as a return to a pre-logical Eden. He certainly would not be the first aesthetician to see in art a recovery of a supra-logical thinking capacity which unselfconsciously provides an immediate experience or renders an immediate communication.

Montage is the instrument of this heightened consciousness. In language it by-passes public syntax and creates the strongest of poetic effects. In film it takes inarticulate or banal elements and fuses them into ideas too rich for words. At its best, montage shapes these felt ideas into a grand syncretic emotional event, an event capable of reorienting our thought and our action. By itself montage can't perform this feat; we must go outside montage to discover the most powerful and effective shapes and structures film can adopt. Yet montage remains the crucial life principle which energizes every worthwhile film and which provides an entrée to the pre-logical world of imagistic thinking where art has its deepest consequences.

FILM FORM

In the 1920s Eisenstein realized that individual attractions could never account for signification in cinema and so he introduced the unifying and dynamic concept of montage. Toward the end of that decade and all through the 1930s Eisenstein struggled to go beyond simple montage to the level of film form, for it became clear to him that despite the life-giving energy of shot juxtaposition, mere juxtaposition could never of itself determine the impact of a whole film. Montage accounts for signification at the local level but not for the overall significance.

The question of film form actually arose within his consideration of montage itself as a question about what he called *the dominant*. In any given shot there are multiple attractions; which of these should determine the kind of juxtaposition required? If shot A is joined to shot B on the basis of conflicting light values, can the filmmaker then join to them shot C, which interacts with B in regard to screen direction? If so, what happens to the light value of shot C? Do we as spectators simply ignore it? Such questions led Eisenstein to suggest that every shot has a dominant attraction and many subsidiary ones in the context of the unrolling film. In narrative films the story line dictates what should attract us first about a shot. In a police film, for example, we will instantly spot the killer as he hides behind lace curtains. The other attractions of the shot (the motion of the curtains in the breeze; the mottled moonlight and shadows on the room; and so on) play around the central attraction of the figure. In a slightly more abstract film the dominant attraction might be the moonlight and its shadows and the film would follow the progress of changing light values. In such a film the figure behind lace curtains would no longer usurp our attention. Many experimental films in the twenties and thirties attempted organization along lines other than plot.

The notion of the dominant was prevalent in Russia during the twenties and no doubt Eisenstein was familiar with the crucial essay entitled simply "The Dominant," written in 1927 by the noted literary critic, Roman Jakobson. A literary work is made up of a host of interacting codes, Jakobson asserts, but one code becomes the dominant and controls the inflections of the other codes.[3] In certain lyrical poems, for example, sound codes of alliteration and assonance dominate the system and draw to themselves the other codes of narrative, repetition, images, and so on.

This concept seems in conflict with the notion of *neutralization,* wherein all codes become effectively equal. Eisenstein vacillated between these ideas, considering all systems to have a dominant, on the one hand, while, on the other, encouraging artists to break away from its tyranny. In the most obvious case, we can say that every film pursues several lines, the most apparent of which is the narrative or story line. In most films it is the story line which dominates the film bringing all other aspects "into line" with it. Clearly Eisenstein was eager to subvert this convention of giving more independence and importance to those other, "subsidiary" codes.

In treating subsidiary codes, Eisenstein returned to his musical analogy, suggesting that every shot is made up of a series of tones and overtones aside from its dominant. The dominant is that which most fully strikes the viewer's attention, while tones and overtones are "secondary stimuli" playing at the periphery of both the image and the viewer's consciousness. Eisenstein admitted that all his early consideration of montage was concentrated on juxtapositions of the dominants within a film scene. Later he began to emphasize editing which would bring out other lines of development within a film.

It becomes clear that Eisenstein began to think of the film experience as a nexus of complementary lines, rather than as a staccato system of discrete stimuli. If we consider shots to be like the discrete notes of a piano piece being shaped by a composer into several lines, we must recall that the dominant line in traditional music would no doubt be the melody line, but any good piece must be rich in tones and overtones created by attention to the peripheral harmonics of the keyboard in relation to the developing piece.

In his essay "The Filmic Fourth Dimension" (in *Film Form*), Eisenstein meditated specifically on this musical analogy. While he admitted that a dominant does exist, he came out for a neutralization of elements (which he called a "democratic equality of rights for all provocations, or stimuli, regarding them as a . . . complex," *Film Form,* p. 68). He then suggested that filmmakers begin working with the overtones as much as with the dominant in order to create the equivalent of the "impressionism" of Debussy or Scriabin. In passing, we might note that of all composers, they are the two most frequently associated with synesthesia, Scriabin even composing musical evocations of colors.

Stimulated by his sense of musical form, Eisenstein began making references to "total experience," and "the feeling of the whole."

The filmmaker must not merely mechanically join montage pieces along a dominant line, but must sensitively orchestrate a vibrating whole so that the viewer can receive a host of organized stimuli weaving variously throughout his mind but creating a final impression, a feeling of totality. Such interconnected montage thinking is "polyphonic montage" and its result is "unity through synthesis." These notions are of a higher level than montage just as montage was of a higher level than the attractions it juxtaposed. Montage is the energy of cinema which makes the raw material come alive, but the concept of synthetic unity is what directs this energy toward an overall goal, toward a meaningful shape.

Virtually all of Eisenstein's ruminations concerning film form and unity can be reduced to an interplay between the images of "art machine" and "art organism." Again and again he insisted that art must be the intersection of nature and industry. In one of his earliest essays he was already trying to yoke these traditionally antithetical concepts:

> Montage thinking—the height of differentially sensing and re-
> solving the "organic" world—is realized anew in a mathematic
> faultlessly performing instrument machine (*Film Form,* p. 27).

Eisenstein's characteristically clarion style proclaims the successful confrontation of an organic world with an art machine. But this youthful optimism gave way to many doubts and continual re-examination of these images. We can say that as he grew older his conception of film form shifted markedly from an interest in mechanical shape (born during the Constructivist period) to organic form, but at no time did the conflict between the two ever disappear entirely.

In order to grasp, even in outline form, Eisenstein's complicated views concerning film form, let us look at these two images separately and in some depth.

The Art Machine

The image of art as a machine comes first, no doubt, from the many classical rhetoricians who spoke of art as a device for controlling the responses of an audience. In more recent times the nine-teenth-century realists, especially Taine and Zola, contributed to the elaboration of this image. But most of Eisenstein's debts for his image of art as machine are unquestionably owed to the Construc-tivists with whom he worked. They took seriously the dictum of Marx and Lenin that art, first of all, is work like any other work. One need only glance over the paintings and prints of this era or read the descriptions of theatrical sets (many of which Eisenstein worked on) to see how religiously this idea was held. Eisenstein was also a partisan of a new theory of acting called *bio-mechanics*. In the twenties it successfully challenged the Stanislavski method, the heart of the abhorred and utterly naturalistic Moscow Art The-ater. The very name bio-mechanics demonstrates the orientation of the avant-garde in Russia in the twenties.

What are the properties of a machine which make it a viable ana-logue for an artwork? It is, first of all, an intentional construction designed with specific goals in mind. It is invented to accomplish a purpose or to solve a problem which exists prior to its invention. It is fully designed before it is constructed and at all stages it is recti-fied until its engineering conforms to its purpose. Both the con-struction and the functioning of the machine are largely predictable. Wherever possible the engineers employ familiar parts and familiar methods in order that the finished machine correspond closely to the design. The machine itself is then altered and modified until it cleanly and efficiently performs its operation. If it is a good ma-chine its performance will be predictable. If the machine begins to fail, it can be fixed by replacing the troublesome parts. As time goes by it may lose its effectiveness and be superseded by a newer model designed to perform the same function but in an even more efficient fashion, responding to advances in science and technology.

Now many of these aspects of a machine appealed to Eisenstein's sense of the nature and purpose of film. We have seen that for him the raw material of film is the "attraction" and that a film is a series of shocks set off in the spectator, a kind of psychological machine. From this it follows that the form of a film depends on the kind of experience the filmmaker wishes to evoke. The creative process in fact begins with the artist making himself fully aware of the *end* he has in mind, then deciding on the best possible *means* of attaining that end.

The means involves a series of steps, each of which operates at a successively higher level of abstraction within the spectator. First comes the raw material, the bare attractions which may be defined as anything in the film which makes a difference to the spectator. Through simple juxtapositions of these primary stimuli, basic cinematic meanings are created. These innumerable moments of montage-meaning begin to coalesce into lines of development, including a dominant line and several attendant lines. The most common such lines are characterization, plot, overall lighting tone, and so on. The spectator takes these clusters of dramatic meaning and actually re-creates the story of the film by resolving the tensions with which he is confronted.

Conflict in character, plot, tone, and all higher levels of meaning is exactly analogous to the physical conflict Eisenstein felt was at the basis of primary montage. The repeated and nearly countless conflicts between attractions produce the grand conflicts and tensions of the drama. Here, of course, the conflicting elements are quite easily identified: a certain set of characters set off against another set; a past action set against the present; wintery decor and lighting played against a springlike atmosphere, and so on.

This dramatic level begins to dissolve into an even higher level of generality within the spectator's mind. He sees the story as merely a single instance of a general theme which could be stated by other stories and other oppositions. At the highest level, then, the spectator becomes aware of the central problem or problems which the filmmaker had hoped to engender within him. The film has functioned as a machine, utilizing reliable fuel (attractions), energized to create a steady stream of motion (montage), developing a controlled and total dramatic meaning (story, tone, character, etc.), leading toward an inevitable destination (the final idea or theme).

Since Eisenstein believed that the mind works dialectically by making syntheses between opposing elements and that the crowning moment of a film comes when the mind synthesizes the opposing ideas which give a film its energy, he wanted to allow the spectator to be aware of synthesizing the entire film, from the smallest particles to the controlling ideas. Whereas D. W. Griffith and Pudovkin had hoped to lead the spectator forward in a trance toward a conclusion which would suddenly burst upon him from nowhere, Eisenstein always insisted that the spectator aid in forging the meaning of the film. In this, of course, his theory resembles the theories of drama which Bertolt Brecht was building at the time.

In his film *Strike,* for instance, Eisenstein didn't hesitate to juxtapose bizarre images, like the face of a man and the picture of a fox, or the picture of a crowd and one of a bull being slaughtered. These images, each providing a strong stimulus, remain meaningless until the mind creates the links between them through its metaphoric capability. The story itself emerges from numerous such metaphors, the mind creating an interplay between specific workers struggling against a specific managerial system. Before the end of the film the spectator begins synthesizing the controlling ideas of the film, ideas about capital vs. labor. The film achieves its effect when the spectator realizes the conclusion (or synthesis) of the collision of such major ideas. The synthesis in this case is one which demands the overthrow of capitalism and the ascendancy of the working class.

The film machine exists to deliver the theme to the spectator. All the filmmaker's attention is focused on the means needed to lead that spectator to a confrontation with the theme. And the filmmaker must lead him there with his eyes open, exposing to the spectator his means, his mechanism, not merely because this style is preferable to the illusionary realism which is the hallmark of Hollywood but because the film derives its energy from the conscious mental leaps of the spectator. The audience literally brings to life the dead stimuli, forcing lightning to leap from pole to pole until a whole story is aglow and until the theme is illuminated beyond both doubt and ignorance. Without the audience's active participation there would be no artwork. This mechanistic theory of art must always focus on the structure and habits of the human mind more than on the subject of the artwork, for the human mind is the means by which the film exists and the destination of its message. The organic theory, on the contrary, stresses the film object itself as self-sufficient, self-sustaining.

The Organic Analogy

Eisenstein never gave himself totally to the mechanistic theory outlined above. From the first there was the hint in his writing of a conflicting theory, the organic. This hint developed into the dominant theme of his writing in the thirties. The lengthy and crucial essay, variously entitled "Word and Image" (in *The Film Sense*) and "Montage 1938" (in *Notes of a Film Director*), is essentially a meditation on the problems organic theory poses for his earlier ideas on film. The actual sources of Eisenstein's ideas about organic theory are too numerous to recount here. Organic theory has been the most influential model of artistic creation in Western civilization since the beginning of the nineteenth century. Eisenstein's desire to fuse some ideas from this tradition with the more radical Constructivism of his youth is natural.

What aspects does an organism have which makes it comparable to a work of art? Most centrally there is the life principle or soul which lives within every part of the organism, causing it to develop into its proper shape. There is the sense that the organism, when transplanted to a different milieu, will alter itself in adaptation without losing its identity. There is the marvelously intriguing notion of self-reparation by which an organism is able to rectify its own injuries or shortcomings. There is the generative aspect of an organism through which it reaches beyond itself in procreation. Finally, and in sum, there is the sense that an organism exists for itself. While a machine exists to promote a pre-existent end, an organism lives solely for its own continuity.

Of these aspects the one that fascinated Eisenstein the most was that of the all-infusing life-principle. What centuries of Christianity have termed "soul," and what Hegel termed "idea," Eisenstein called "theme." It is theme which makes an organism tend to be the way it is; theme which seems to demand that certain choices rather than others be made in the creative process. Eisenstein wrote:

> Each montage piece exists no longer as something unrelated, but becomes a particular representation of the general theme which in equal measure penetrates all the shot-pieces.[4]

Eisenstein went on to say that in a good film the particular representations, when properly ordered, produce the theme which has itself brought them into being. In trying to come to grips with the difficult problem of circularity such a notion leads to, Eisenstein came back again and again to the situation of an actor. An actor exhibits a chain of gestures the combination of which promotes and finally realizes a complete image (say, that of jealousy). The small gestures which are linked together on the chain are all properly chosen by the exigency of the theme of jealousy even though that jealousy finally exists only when the chain has been completed. The mechanistic side of Eisenstein suggests that the actor from the beginning knows precisely what he wants to convey and need find only the most efficient and powerful means to encourage the audience to leap to that image. The organic side of Eisenstein rebels, claiming that the theme is invisible even to the actor until his chain of gestures has run its course, but that this theme functions all the same in choosing those tiny bits (in this case, the gestures) which make up the whole. These bits are chosen because they, and they alone out of all possible representations, contain within themselves the micro-system of the theme. For the modern reader the notion of montage "cell" takes on a further metaphoric significance in that each montage piece, in addition to functioning in the overall machine of the film, has within it the signature of the genetic code which is the theme. This ensures that the cells will interact in polyphonic montage and create a "monism of ensemble."

Clearly the concept of organic form is attractive; but it has the danger of displacing the responsibility for the outcome of a film from the filmmaker-engineer, giving it over mystically to "nature." An organicist can be tempted to reduce all discussion of film to the statement, "but this film grew into its proper form and it is useless to think about it further." Eisenstein never considered losing himself in such reductionism. To him the theme, as the life principle, begins directing the decisions during the filmmaking process, but that theme could not simply be plucked out of thin air. Conse-. quently the most crucial task of filmmaking for Eisenstein is the discovery of the theme. The work such a discovery implies is tantamount to the construction of the film.

To understand Eisenstein's view of "discovering the theme" we must realize that for him nature does not exist in an easily available manner. This separates him immediately from the major portion of organic theorists, who feel that sheer close observation of nature yields the organic theme which is then capable of infusing an artwork with its natural energy. For Eisenstein both nature and history must be transformed by the mind before they may become true. There is no such thing as bare reality directly apprehensible. The filmmaker's task, the task of the artist, is to apprehend the *true* form of an event or natural phenomenon and then utilize that form in the construction of his artwork.

An obvious example from Eisenstein's own work will help. In 1905 there was an insurrection on the ship *Potemkin* as part of the abortive revolution of that year. For a while the insurrection rallied the people of Odessa and the sailors of other ships nearby. Eisenstein believed that this event could be filmed in countless ways, but only one way would take advantage of the true form of the event. Only one film would be organically tied to the truth of history.

The process by which a filmmaker comes to appropriate the true form of an event is not by merely recording the appearances of the event. Eisenstein had always held that to attain "reality" one must destroy "realism," break up the appearances of a phenomenon and reconstruct them according to a "reality principle." For the Marxist Eisenstein, both nature and history obey a principle of dialectical form. The filmmaker must see behind the surface realism of an event until its dialectical form becomes clear to him; only then is he able to "thematicize" his subject. After this, the choices he makes in both his raw material and in his montage methods will be automatically dictated by this life principle. For his part, the spectator must re-create the theme of the film as his mind energizes the "attractions" before him. The myriad interconections between these cells will ultimately overwhelm the spectator as both film and spectator move toward the final image of the theme. The film is not a *product* but an organically unfolding creative *process* in which the audience participates both emotionally and intellectually. Eisenstein wrote, "The spectator is made to traverse the road of creation the author traversed in creating the image" (*The Film Sense,* p. 32) and he cited Marx for support:

> Not only the event but the road to it is part of the truth. The investigation of truth must itself be true. True investigation is unfolded truth, the disjunctive members of which unite in result (*The Film Sense,* p. 32).

The organic analogy, in sum, displaces to some extent the origin of the form of a film from the filmmaker. Even Eisenstein recognized the inadequacy and immorality of willful montage creation which tries to manipulate the spectator. The apprehension of the organic theme involves an understanding of reality outside of, but only by means of, the creator's consciousness. The creative filmmaker puts himself in the position of understanding reality thematically and of being able to create a film, the intertwining lines of which render that theme. Furthermore the very lines of meaning in this film are made up of fragments or cells, each of which contains within it the stamp of the theme. The entire film is of a piece, even though operating through conflict and collision. This is so because, in Eisenstein's credo, the basic themes of life itself are reducible to conflict. Montage, then, while providing the mechanical energy which allows the film machine to perform its designated task, is formally isomorphic to the organic structure of nature and of history.

Eisenstein seemed satisfied with his "organic-machine." Whenever he investigated the effect of a film on the spectator, he leapt toward the image of the machine. But when he turned to the relation of the artwork to reality he concentrated on the organic interrelation of the cells which make it up. While this confused many of his critics and followers, to him this was nothing other than a change in emphasis. "The error," he said, "lay in emphasizing possibilities of juxtaposition while less attention seemed to be paid to analyzing the material that was juxtaposed" (*The Film Sense,* p. 8).

To sum up, Eisenstein simply wanted a film to get things done like a machine, but he didn't want this machine to be made out of any old parts, some engineered on the spot, others bought at a junk yard, all held together in whatever fashion seemed to work. And so he reached for nature, for the organic in which all parts are inter-related in a self-sustaining system. But this more attractive model (close to the film form dreamed of by Munsterberg and Arnheim) was necessarily "useless." That which is naturally self-sustaining does not promote the revolution, not directly at any rate. Eisenstein vacillated between these two very different notions of film form because he was never completely certain about the function or purpose of film art. We need to examine this uncertainty.

THE FINAL PURPOSE OF FILM

Implicit in all his reflections about the form of film are issues which concern the purpose of film. The most accessible entry into the problems for Eisenstein's theory is through consideration of the relationships between rhetoric and autonomous art. These terms are polar opposites in most theories of art and in our culture there has been a vast normative bias in favor of art over rhetoric. It is only fair to note at the outset that, as far as I know, Eisenstein never considered his theories to be anything other than theories of art. There is not a single instance on record of his referring to film as a rhetorical medium. Nonetheless several critics in the past have accused him of being a theorist of rhetoric and others have tried to support such a claim by analyzing his films as propaganda texts. It is helpful to sketch the issues at stake in any consideration of rhetoric versus art and to try to locate Eisenstein's positions in transit.

Rhetoric

The Greeks constructed elaborate theories of rhetoric even before the science of aesthetics or the idea of art had been developed. In its broadest sense rhetoric is the science of language and communication. More specifically it is the study of the ends, methods, and effects of discourse. For our purposes we can conceive of rhetoric as the examination of discursive situations in which one party wants to convey something to someone else for the purpose of influencing him or at the very least of enlightening him.

It should be obvious that any rigorously held belief in art as machine entails the classical rhetorical situation. The artwork or film becomes a true medium, capable of being adjusted and modified, across which a rhetor (or filmmaker) conveys his ideas with as much clarity and power as he is able. The goal of such a situation is precisely in the audience effect, be it an intellectual or an emotional effect.

The film situation is one which naturally places the rhetor in a position of absolute dominion over his audience, for there is no chance for the audience to respond in the normal sense of dialogue. The spectator indeed expects to be enlightened or moved and struggles to attain the effects which the machine of film has been built to deliver. After all he has paid $2 to feel the effects which someone in Hollywood has created with $2 million. In addition, because the medium of film is technological, the spectator is even more disposed to accept his role as recipient of effect. A rhetor is speaking with the authority by means of a mysterious apparatus which confers on him special power.

Most of Eisenstein's early writings on cinema indicate that he accepted this situation and wanted to exploit it as fully as he could. He was appalled at how inefficient and dull most cinema was, especially cinema which sought to give its audience the impression of reality. Reality, he felt, speaks very obscurely, if at all. It is up to the filmmaker to rip reality apart and rebuild it into a system capable of generating the greatest possible emotional effects. The very sense of shock montage confirms this. In one of his most telling exclamations, one which he wrote toward the end of his career when he had greatly modified his ideas about Pavlovian shock treatment of the audience, Eisenstein still asserted an audience-oriented definition: "A work of art, understood dynamically, is just this process of arranging images in the feelings and mind of the spectator" (*The Film Sense,* p. 17).

Eisenstein's theory could readily be interpreted as a theory of propaganda. What is the purpose of propaganda films and TV commercials, other than cleverly to arrange images in the feelings and minds of spectators in order to give them the greatest possible emotional effect. The effect, mapped out in advance, becomes the *raison d'être* of the work of art. This situation subordinates art to its effect and encourages the view (though does not demand it) that a single effect might be rendered via two or more artworks. This would lead, naturally, to an evaluation of films based on their suitability in conveying an explicit effect.

A typology of films could be drawn up according to the importance and complexity of the message or effect conveyed and according to the suitability of the film for conveying those messages. Such a theory of the purpose of film seems apt for the major portion of cinematic texts. Many critics feel that all cinematic texts—the propaganda films of Nazi Germany, the Alka Seltzer ads of America, the films of Hitchcock and Bergman—are machines more or less successful in their task of driving home some pre-planned message or effect.

It is not easy to say to what extent Eisenstein might accept this view of cinema. It does seem fairly clear that he thought art was reserved for those kinds of effects and messages not available to ordinary speech. That is, art is first of all directed at the emotions and only secondly at the reason. It delivers an effect which is not available to ordinary language. Art, then, is similar to other rhetorical media, but it is of a higher order, capable of delivering fuller messages and capable of involving the entire human being. One might say that Eisenstein was arguing that film is the greatest possible propaganda tool. While he never discussed propaganda, he did suggest often enough that film is part of a world-wide revolution in consciousness. All this implies that the filmmaker exists in a state of knowledge and that the spectator is brought from ignorance to knowledge via the power of the film, a power which energizes the body of the spectator and through it his mind. In this rhetorical view, the process of knowledge is completed before the film is made. The film exists exclusively to channel the knowledge to a wider public, to disseminate it and to let its power work in the world.

Art

Ever since the Romantic poets of the early nineteenth century countless claims have been made for the importance of pure art. Art was said to exist in the object itself independent of any intention which the artist might have desired or of any effect the object might have on an audience. It exists solely to be beautiful, that is, to manifest itself. Art objects have a claim to a higher state of existence than other objects because they are, first of all, purposeless and, second, proper to themselves. They are said to be suitable to the aspirations they have for themselves. If the artwork is a baroque painting, it swirls its objects into the perfect arrangement for itself. If it is a Bach fugue, it organizes the notes and lines of melody into its properly intricate pattern. What is more, this pattern is not imposed on the work from outside, as an engineer imposes a design on a machine in order to make it function according to *his* wishes. No, the pattern somehow exists organically within the artwork. The artist labors until the form he creates exists as this pattern, releasing it from his control, allowing it to exist for our contemplation.

While this sketch of a theory of autonomous art is terribly brief, one can already see that Eisenstein would have little to do with most of its premises. But there are several elements, especially in his later writings, which indicate that the rhetorical model was too simplistic for his tastes and that he was ransacking Romantic art theories for a way to understand the full purpose of cinema.

Paramount is his meditation on the status of the image. In Eisenstein's later writing he defined the image as any global concept capable of animating a host of representations. His example of an image is 42nd Street. This image generated in him a total feeling which could be expressed through a series of individual representations (neon signs, crowds, certain buildings, theaters, and so on). Conversely, a properly organized series of representations could generate an image. From a strictly rhetorical viewpoint, the filmmaker begins with an image and then carefully calculates the best means to transfer that image to the audience. Invariably he must resort to a proper ordering of bits (attractions) which will build up in the spectator that total feeling or image. To a large extent Eisenstein seemed to hold exactly this view, but there are indications that he also felt the image to be something which develops almost spontaneously out of the representations which the artist is manipulating. The artist thus does not begin with a total view but arrives at one, something unnamable driving him to choose certain representations and to combine them in ways which emphasize certain relationships.

Eisenstein's ambivalence on this issue is transparent in his article "Word and Image." There, within the space of three hundred words, he seems to try to establish both possibilities (*The Film Sense,* pp. 30, 31). First he supports the rhetorical approach explicitly: "Before the perception of the creator hovers a given image, emotionally embodying his theme. The task that confronts him is to transform this image into a few basic partial representations which, in their combination and juxtaposition, shall evoke in the consciousness and feelings of the spectator . . . that same initial general image which originally hovered before the creative artist."

But only one paragraph later Eisenstein seems to modify the status of the image. No longer does it hover out of time. Eisenstein moves in the direction of the organicist camp when he says, "The desired image is not fixed or ready-made, but arises—is born."

Eisenstein never seems to have posed the problem in terms of rhetoric and art. He was far more likely to conceive of it in terms of *speech* and *inner speech.* All expressions affect the spectator but some do so through the clear public channels of speech while others invade the spectator's private mental world. While all films have a purpose, only the great films avoid a simplistic *rhetoric* which would proceed in the manner of speech, and in which montage is a simple theory of syntax. Great films affect their audiences in the manner of *autonomous art,* and these same montage theories this time promote the mysterious process of inner speech, that pre-linguistic patterning of phenomena which proceeds by the juxtaposition of bursts of attractions. Great films bypass conventional language which normally forces primal representations into a chain of deductive grammatical signification. In inner speech the only grammatical rule at play is association through juxtaposition. Like inner speech, film uses a concrete language in which sense comes not from deduction but from the fullness of the individual attractions as qualified by the image which they help to develop.

This kind of thinking is not entirely foreign to Marxism. Eisenstein was able to cite Lenin to help establish the claim of the strength of primal patterns. Lenin had said that the primary processes of nature, dialectic processes, manifest "recurrence on the highest level of known traits, attributes, etc. of the lowest" (*Film Form,* p. 81). This quotation comes alive when placed next to Eisenstein's later writings.

> Each montage piece exists no longer as something unrelated but as a given *particular representation* of the general theme that in equal measure penetrates all the shot-pieces. The juxtaposition of these partial details in a given montage construction calls to life and forces into the light that *general* quality in which each detail has participated and which binds together all the details into a *whole,* namely, into that generalized *image* wherein the creator, followed by the spectator, experiences the theme (*The Film Sense,* p. 11).

In art, as in inner speech, wholes determine, and are determined by, details. This process of coming to a self-justifying image is the process of art. We must recall here Marx's dictum that truth lies in the path as much as in the destination. And Eisenstein, in forcing the spectator to create the image by putting together all the relationships between attractions (relationships existing because of the interpenetrating theme), gives to the spectator not a completed image, but the "experience of completing an image." Such an experience yields an understanding of the theme more primal and more powerful than any appeal through normal speech and logic.

At this point it is even possible to see traces of mysticism in Eisenstein's thought. His constant curiosity about the mental processes of primitive cultures and of children stems from his belief that, by avoiding the chains of verbal logic to which we are doomed, they are naturally linked to a more *real* world, one in which the mind naturally patterns the stimuli it finds in the world. When all the members of a village aid the birthing of a child by opening their doors, they are, in his view, bound closer to each other and to this *natural* process than we, in our enlightened culture, can ever hope to be, except perhaps through the power of art and especially cinema.

In art we are led away from logic to re-experience our primary mode of understanding. Eisenstein, like Romantic theorists of art, believes that what is primary and natural will of itself be tied to the truth. For Eisenstein, both the method (dialectical juxtaposition of thematically interpenetrated representations) and the final image which that method creates will, in the proper film, join the creators (both artist and spectator) to the true processes and themes of life.[5] This, he was certain, would advance that state of life most consistent with the real processes of nature and history, the dialectical movement toward the Marxist millennium. Art, then, has a mission quite different from rhetoric. It exists to manifest the correspondence between basic human perception and the basic processes of nature and history. This cannot be accomplished by a carefully reasoned system, but by the nearly mystical showing forth of the artwork itself which, by being perfectly itself, mediates between man and nature.

In the Marxist state Eisenstein felt that art would reinforce the culture, since that culture is already based on proper dialectical principles, coordinated from the first with the processes of mind and nature. In pre-revolutionary societies like ours, true art must necessarily be an insurgent force destined to manifest, at the level of perception and imagination, the antinomies of a society not in tune with man and nature. Art, therefore, can still change behavior by changing perception, but it does so indirectly, as a natural byproduct of simply being itself. Rhetoric, on the other hand, exists for no other reason than to make specific changes in knowledge or behavior.

While Eisenstein desperately wanted such changes, he gradually thought of film art as something higher and more lasting. He thought of it not so much as deliverer of a truth (rhetoric) but as a general image of the truth (art). While an art machine built to rally the proletariat behind the 5-year plan of 1925 might today be ineffective, an art organism which grew into an image of the truth in 1925 can be rediscovered by every generation.

In a real sense Eisenstein's film theory has also embodied this dialectic of machine and organism. Most of his essays were written as part of an aesthetic war in Russia, as apologies for certain kinds of filmmaking and as attacks on other kinds. They were rhetorical in the fullest sense of the word. Yet his theory as a whole seems to have an organic life as well. Whenever his essays are translated into a new language one can trace their impact on the attitudes of still another group of theorists and filmmakers.

Perhaps the most striking example of the perpetual power of Eisenstein's theory comes to us from recent French film culture. Until the mid-1960s André Bazin's views were unrivalled. They dominated the film journals and they had an important effect on the most influential films of the New Wave. Bazin and his generation in France knew of Eisenstein only from secondary sources and from a few uncollected essays that had found their way into the French language. With the massive translation projects of the late sixties, Bazin's grip on the film theory of France was loosened. Eisenstein's ideas today are heard everywhere in Paris. They dominate the major journals, *Cahiers du cinéma* and *Cinéthique*. They are evident in the dynamic cutting style of recent French movies. In short they have been integrated into, and have helped foster, a new radical film consciousness. Because of the boldness of its formulation, Eisenstein's theory will always be instrumental to radical views of cinema, but because of the honesty of its constant self-qualification his theory will outlast every use to which it is put.

4

Béla Balázs
and the Tradition of Formalism

A SUMMARY OF FORMATIVE FILM THEORY

Béla Balázs's *Theory of Film* is one of the first and unquestionably
one of the best introductions to the art. It has been followed by
numerous imitators, each trying to provide a wide audience with a
basic grasp of the potentials of the medium. In this chapter the
whole enterprise of formative film theory will be put under a critical light so that we can understand the premises of such introductory film books and, more importantly, to see why Balázs's book
is among the very best.

The figures we have examined thus far are doubtless the most interesting and valuable members of the formative tradition. Munsterberg and Arnheim impress us because of the deep philosophic
heritage which actively supports their theories. Eisenstein stands
above even these men not only because of the diversity and origi-
nality of his writings, but also because he struggled all his life to
avoid the simplistic reductionism which formalist theory tempts
one to adopt. We saw that he had the courage to go beyond his
initial theoretical discoveries in order to seek solutions which
would account for more subtle aspects of the film experience.

In general the countless lesser figures following the general direction of formative thought have had neither the tenacity and

vision of Eisenstein nor the philosophic discipline of Arnheim and Munsterberg. Consequently most formative theory is predictable, often tiresomely so.

There have been two major periods of prolific formative theory. The first came between 1920 and 1935 when an entire intellectual class became conscious that cinema (especially silent cinema) was not merely a sociological phenomenon of extraordinary importance, but a powerful art form with the same kinds of rights and responsibilities as any other art form. These theorists wanted to make known the properties of this new medium in order to help explain the mysterious success of the great silent films and to help direct future cinema toward greater power and greater maturity. The second major period of formative film theory began in the early 1960s and is still growing today. This period draws its strength from the burgeoning academic interest in film. Our classrooms are teeming with students demanding to know the secrets of the screen, and introductory textbooks by the score, all of them necessarily in the formative tradition, have appeared to answer this student need.

Characteristically such books are divided into chapters based on the technical variables of film. There are always chapters on composition, camera, lighting, editing, sound, color, and often one on acting. Each chapter enumerates the various possibilities for artistic control in its domain, underscoring the "unnatural" (or specifically "cinematic") aspects of the medium. In one sense all such books are the offspring (desired or not) of Arnheim's *Film as Art*. Most make copious references to artistically successful films to prove the validity of the cinematic facets they are treating. Meaningful color is described in Michelangelo Antonioni's *Red Desert*. Artistic use of lighting is analyzed with reference to Fritz Lang's *M* or Carl Dreyer's *Day of Wrath*. In all cases we are shown the solution to a problem in signification which a director found by manipulating one or another technical aspect.

There is always something hollow about this kind of approach. Formative film theory is dangerous for the same reason it is attractive: it is centered entirely on the *technique* of film. When this focus is not supported by proper illumination of the issues pertinent to cinematic form and purpose, the result is a mere rubric for possible uses of the medium rather than a full and consistent theory.

Nearly all introductory texts of this sort give themselves ballast by drawing an implicit analogy between film and language. They deny being simple rubrics and claim instead to construct visual dictionaries and grammars, arming the student with the vocabulary and syntax necessary "to read" the various kinds of signification at play in the techniques of every film. The titles of many such books betray this intention: *The Grammar of Film, The Language of Film, The Rhetoric of Film,* etc.

Certainly cinema has some relationship to language and can be profitably considered a language in some senses: nevertheless, as Christian Metz, Jean Mitry, and others have shown, its relation to verbal language is not direct and is at best partial and complex. To draw an analogy between these media without confronting the limitations of the analogy is to fail to theorize.

Beyond the grave difficulty inherent in trying to discuss a liquid and physically multi-layered medium as if it were a digital, homogeneous system like language, there is the very dangerous implication in film language primers that film is a closed finite system, like a keyboard, on which the director plays whatever melody he has in mind. This turns the filmmaking process into a formula of "correct choices," choices proper to the message at hand. It was against this mechanical and digital tendency in his own thought that Eisenstein fought so long a battle. He knew well enough that a stringent formalism chains the artist and tends to dictate the look of films from the outside.

At its most simplistic, formative theory must inevitably place a premium on the sheer visibility of film language. Filmmakers whose techniques are striking are ranked above more subtle filmmakers,[1] for by itself a technically oriented theory can never differentiate the aesthetic value of a Robert Bresson film from any given TV commercial. There is in fact more technical "art" (visible techniques) in one Pepsi-Cola ad than in all of Bresson's films. Without a thoroughgoing sense of shape and purpose, formative theory provides us with nothing but a catalogue of film effects, and this is hardly sufficient for a theory of cinema.

To understand formative film theory in its full dimensions we have to go outside film theory proper, just as we went to neo-Kantianism to situate Munsterberg's theory and to Gestalt psychology for Arnheim's. To achieve the broadest view of the whole enterprise of formative film theory, to see its implicit world vision, we must look to Russian Formalist poetics.

RUSSIAN FORMALISM

Is it sheer coincidence that the dates of the Russian Formalist movement (1918-30) coincide so neatly with those of the first age of formative film theory? No doubt. But certainly Sergei Eisenstein was deeply influenced by their work and Arnheim and Balázs were well aware of them. More striking still, the Russian Formalist doctrines have been revived, widely translated, and openly celebrated since the early 1960s, precisely at the birth of film semiotics and the ascendancy of formative theory in our classrooms.

Aside from these intriguing historical relations, Russian Formalism gives to formative film theory the large philosophic context in which we need to see it. While not all formative theorists might accept them, the Russian Formalist positions are perfectly consistent with formative film theory. Primarily a theory of poetic language, Russian Formalism sets out an entire theory of human activity. What is it, the Formalists ask, which makes the artistic or aesthetic aspects of a man's life so different and so special? To answer this they first established a system of four categories of functions which, they claim, account for every possible human activity. Every action we perform belongs to one or more of the following functions: practical, theoretic, symbolic, and aesthetic.

The practical category concerns those objects or actions which serve an immediate use. (Highways and their construction enable us to get from one city to another.) The theoretical category comprises all objects and actions which function for general and unspecified uses. (Microbiology serves, and will serve, many purposes related to human health.) In the symbolic category a given object or activity functions in the place of another object or activity. (The marriage ritual stands for and objectifies the binding of two lives.) Last of all there is the aesthetic function which, oddly enough, includes those objects and activities which function for no purpose whatsoever. They exist for themselves, for pure contemplation and perception.

A single object or activity may serve various functions. For example, an Egyptian key coming from the XIIth Dynasty once served the practical function of opening a door. Today it is placed under a glass case in a museum as a purely aesthetic object. Our language, to take another example, generally serves a symbolic function, requiring that we go beyond it to that which it represents. In poetry, however, the Formalists contend that language exists for itself.

Now the aesthetic category operates in many areas of life, not all of which we call art. A mathematician may perform his activity for sheerly aesthetic purposes. A panorama in nature may be viewed entirely without motive, sheerly for itself. Art is the name we give to activities which fashion purposeless objects, objects which do nothing but exist for our intense perception and contemplation.

Victor Shklovsky, one of the most prominent Russian Formalists and a friend and biographer of Eisenstein, summarizes these ideas perfectly:

> Art exists that one may recover the sensation of life; it exists to make one feel things, to make the stone *stony*. The purpose of art is to impart the sensation of things as they are perceived and not as they are known. The technique of art is to make objects "unfamiliar" to make forms difficult, to increase the difficulty and length of perception because the process of perception is an aesthetic end in itself and must be prolonged. Art is a way of experiencing the artfulness of an object; the object itself is not important.[2]

Most early film theory neatly fits itself into this vision of art and life. The theorists whom I have labeled "formative" all believe that the cinema serves a symbolic function when it simply reproduces reality. It serves an aesthetic function when it forces us to attend in a special way (via its unnatural techniques) to that reality.

In 1926 the artist and exprimental filmmaker Fernand Léger

lamented the fact that most films waste their efforts in trying to build a recognizable world, neglecting all the while "the powerful spectacular effect of the object. . . . The possibility of the fragment."[3] Léger of course created the famous *Ballet méchanique* in which everyday practical objects, like knives and spoons, are set against one another to produce a rhythmic pattern of perceptual forms. As Shklovsky proclaimed, these everyday objects become unimportant while at the same time they impart to us the experience of their "artfulness."

A few years later the American critic Harry Alan Potamkin, who visited Russia during the period of the Formalist hegemony, claimed, "To make the material significant he [the filmmaker] must break the continuity of vision,"[4] must make us see the film not as a mere substitute for a real world but as an image existing for significant perception. Hans Richter, one of the great avant-garde artists of the twenties, summed up these notions: "The main aesthetic problem for the movies, which were invented for reproduction, is, paradoxically, the overcoming of reproduction."[5]

We have already noted that Eisenstein rejected the long take because its purpose is always "the continuity of vision," the impulse toward sheer "reproduction" scoffed at by Potamkin and Richter. And Arnheim, for his part, clearly stated,

> No representation of an object will ever be valid visually and artistically unless the eyes can directly understand it as a *deviation* from the basic visual conception of the object.[6]

Arnheim's vocabulary here corresponds exactly with that of the Russian Formalists for whom the technique of art was always based on deviation. "Make the object strange!" they cried. For them art was never a matter of significant content, inspiration, imagination, or whatever else people have put at the heart of the artistic endeavor. It was precisely technique; that is, the perception, the labor, and the sheer talent which can take an object or activity and wrench it from the flow of life. In stopping to regard this object we are struck by its visible shape, struck, the Formalists say, by the technique itself which stands before us.

The overall process whereby technique calls attention to the object is termed *defamiliarization*. The Formalists were quick to praise those artworks which emphasize this process. In one of the most notorious formalist articles, Shklovsky held up Sterne's *Tristram Shandy* as the paradigm of the literary object.[7] *Tristram Shandy* is a novel in which the reader is continually notified that he is involved in a literary experience. Sterne makes it nearly impossible for us to relate his book to the outside world. We are left with an aesthetic object, the enjoyment of which is a product of our perception of the literary process itself, of literary *technique* itself.

Boris Tomashevsky, taking his cue from Shklovsky, generalized this process by cataloguing various literary techniques and pointing out how each technique forces art away from the representation of reality.[8] He distilled plot (technique) from story (reality), motivation (technique) from general causality (reality), etc. He concluded that all literary techniques which we regard as artistic (irony, humor, pathos, figures of speech) function as conscious distortions of reality. One can see immediately how close this position is to Arnheim's.

A second wave of literary Formalism, which flourished in Prague in the late twenties and early thirties, further refined the concept of defamiliarization by introducing the notion of "foregrounding." Artistic speech, these Formalists said, is speech which lifts itself outside the readily understandable (the clearly codified) and stands solidly in front of the reader's eyes. He cannot avoid it because it is simultaneously different and difficult. They saw every artwork as a construction of various sorts of artistic speech and judged each by its success in foregrounding itself.

The relationship between these literary concepts and film theory is unmistakable at this point. Tomashevsky's emphasis on the exaggerated detail and Jan Mukarovsky's delineation of foregrounding have direct counterparts in the cinematic close-shot. Several film critics, most notable among them the East European Béla Balázs, establish cinema's claims to art in its capacity for the close-up, "for the pictorial forming of details."[9]

The spatial metaphor of foregrounding has its temporal counterpart in the notion of rhythm which is, predictably enough, another central concept of the Formalists. Just as we can associate the filmic close-up with foregrounding, so we can put montage together with rhythm. Allardyce Nicoll, when speaking of the Russian films of the twenties, said, "If cutting is prose, then montage is poetry."[10]

In the extreme, this view of cinema is one which feels that the artistic is that which works in direct opposition to the prosaic. This follows precisely Shklovsky's dictum that "poetry is *attenuated, tortuous* speech," and his conception of rhythm as a "disordering which cannot be predicted,"[11] but which continually invites mistaken prediction. Compare Shklovsky to film theorists like Dallas Bower for whom editing rhythms "break up the omnipresent flux . . . to produce a new artificial time superimposed as it were on real time"[12] or to Potamkin for whom rhythms are "repetitions, repetitions in variation, the progressive *deformation* of a theme."[13] And finally we have Jean Cocteau's epigram: "My primary concern is to prevent the images from flowing, to oppose them, to anchor them and join them without destroying their relief."[14]

There lies within these notions of defamiliarization, foregrounding, deformation, and deviation the possibility of a gross and dangerous exaggeration. Shklovsky to a great extent implied that only foregrounded material is artistic. Now this formulation can lead to some rather bizarre misconceptions. For instance, from this it could be asserted that a particular poem or film contains exactly thirty (or *n*) artistic moments built upon its prose background. Should a work of art be judged by its density of foregrounding?

Few Formalists have been willing to go this far because such a notion implies a quantitative notion of aesthetic value. Few would consider T. S. Eliot's *The Waste Land* a more poetic work than Alexander Pope's *The Rape of the Lock* simply because it breaks up the prose meaning more often and in more varied ways. Yet Formalists have always been tempted to rank artworks bearing ostentatious technique above more subtle kinds of artworks. In effect Formalism has been tempted to become a partisan of a particular style of art rather than a philosophy applicable to artworks of all styles.

In both film theory and literary theory there have been Formalists who have fought this temptation. Jan Mukarovsky, a major critic of the Prague school, was quick to see that the densest possible artwork would succeed in foregrounding everything, completely eliminating the background.[15] In this case all relief would be lost and nothing whatsoever would really stand out. For him foregrounding is that which makes the aesthetic object stand away from the *world* rather than the specific elements within an artwork which oppose themselves to the rest of the *artwork*. The style of the work depends upon the kinds of foregrounding employed in relation to a specific background, but sheer quantity of foregrounding can never make an object "more aesthetic." An object is either viewed aesthetically or not, and it is enough for an artwork to have one and only one instance of deformation within it to make us view it aesthetically as a whole.

It is possible, therefore, to believe that art separates itself from the world by techniques of defamiliarization without implying that "more deviation equals more art." Mukarovsky and his Prague colleagues developed the concepts of aesthetic "norm" and aesthetic "value" to deal with the specific situations of individual artworks. This more fluid Formalism allowed them to maintain a descriptive rather than an evaluative position and to deal with artworks of all sorts. When we study the kinds and amounts of foregrounding within various artworks we are studying and comparing styles. Style is nothing other than a specific strategy of technique; and technique, Shklovsky said, is art itself. Formalism, then, tempts one to set "highly visible" styles above more naturalistic ones but does not, I think, demand this hierarchy. While most formative film theorists have succumbed to this temptation, there have been from the first some writers who strove to avoid the reductionism which is its major pitfall. One of the very earliest and certainly most influential of such theorists was Béla Balázs.

BÉLA BALÁZS

Balázs's first writings on film appeared as early as 1922. In the thirties and forties he was to add thoughts he developed while lecturing in the Soviet Union. The volume of his writings popularly available, *Theory of the Film,* organizes both his early and later essays into a systematic whole. Unquestionably, Balázs's book today looks largely unoriginal because it covers the same technical ground as so many other introductions to film. But despite the historical fact that his was virtually the first such text, Balázs's work stands out for its clarity and caution. He surrounded his remarks on film technique with a host of ideas concerning film's origin and purpose, and he added to this broad perspective the passion of one who believes that a complete theory of the film is necessary to guide cinema to more fruitful paths.

Balázs opened his book with a look at the genesis of film. His purpose was to narrow his subject to that of film art, or what he called the "language-form" of cinema. In this he resembled both Munsterberg and Arnheim, but unlike them he went about his inquiry by analyzing the economic infrastructure of film which he, as a Marxist, insisted was at the basis of this new art.

Film art could grow, he stated, only when business conditions allowed it to. Because it was at the mercy of theater managers trying to fill a need for novel entertainment, cinema was in competition with vaudeville, music hall, and popular theater, and in order to compete with live entertainment, film promoters were forced to look for subjects which cinema alone could render. For this reason nature was quickly brought onto the screen as an active participant in film dramas. Even the stars of cinema were not the full-throated actors of the stage, but rather animals, children, and other "more natural subjects." In slapstick comedy, to use another example, multiple takes were used to produce spectacles of motion and magic impossible on the live stage. All these subjects were proper and natural to film, Balázs said, but they did not yet add up to a new art. Cinema was still primarily photographed theater, competing with theater only in the domain of subject matter. Balázs posed the next questions clearly:

> When and how did cinematography turn into a specific independent art employing methods sharply differing from those of the theater and using a totally different form-language? What

is the difference between photographed theater and film art? Both being equally motion pictures projected on a screen, why do I say that the one is only a technical reproduction and the other an independently creative art? (*Theory of the Film,* p. 30).

To answer them Balázs did a short comparative analysis of the two media. He defined the theatrical situation as one which always maintains its action in a spatial continuity separated from the spectator by a stable distance. Furthermore, the spectator views this action and this space from one unchanging angle. While photographed theater often varied distance and angle between the scenes of a drama, every event (or complete scene) unrolled without change. Hence, the film situation was essentially the same as that of the theater, until these conditions began to be questioned. It was D. W. Griffith, in Balázs's view, who created the new form-language of cinema by breaking scenes up into fragments, shifting the distance and angle of the camera from fragment to fragment, and especially by assembling his film not as a linkage of scenes but as a montage of fragments.

For Balázs the form-language of cinema was a natural product of the oscillation between subject matter and technical form. Economic factors made the cinema seek new subjects, but these subjects (chases, children, nature and its wonders) in their turn demanded the utilization of new techniques such as the close-up and montage. A form-language quickly emerged from these techniques and that language itself started to dictate the kinds of subjects and stories suitable to cinema. Like so many theorists after him, Balázs believed that cinema achieved full maturity in the twenties: in that era proper subjects were presented in proper cinematic form, all aiding the development of a rejuvenated popular culture, a culture no longer dependent on words, but sensitized to the emanations of a visibly expressive world.

THE RAW MATERIAL OF FILM ART

Like Arnheim, Balázs recognized that cinema has numerous functions, but it was only the *art* of the cinema, harboring as it does this revolutionary potential for cultural rejuvenation, which seemed worth his attention.

Balázs's awareness of the origin of the aesthetic use of cinema enabled him to elaborate quite rapidly his theory of its form-language and to make predictions and suggestions for the future. The cinematic process for him, as for all formative theorists, involves the creation of film art out of the stuff of the world. The raw material of film is not exactly reality itself but is instead the "filmic subject" which presents itself to one's experience in the world and which offers itself to be transformed into cinema.

This notion of "filmic subject" is both curious and unique. As a Marxist, Balázs had a firm belief in the reality and independence of the external world of sensation. Art never grasps reality in itself because art always brings to this world its own human patterns and human meanings. Reality, though, is multifaceted and open to many uses. Each art deals with reality in its own manner and takes for its subjects just those aspects of reality which can be readily transformed by its special means. A novelist, painter, and filmmaker may all be present at the same historical event but each will transform this event in his own way, dictated largely by his medium. No one of these media can claim to grasp the reality of the event, though all make use of it.

Balázs's view of artistic raw material is neatly revealed by his remarks about adaptation. The filmmaker who delves into another artwork for his subject matter does nothing wrong so long as he tries to reshape it via the form-language of cinema. (On this point Balázs couldn't be further from the position of André Bazin, who urged that filmmakers forget their precious form-language and put themselves at the service of the masterpieces they want to bring to the screen.) Balázs admits that the adaptation of masterpieces by his method has not proved fruitful. Think of the many versions of *Moby Dick*. They are disappointing not because adaptation in itself is impossible but because a masterpiece is a work whose subject ideally suits its medium. Any transformation of this work will inevitably produce a less satisfactory result. Balázs would never accept Bazin's solution to this problem because it amounts to a suppression of the "properly cinematic" and makes cinema merely a handmaiden of the other arts. Instead Balázs counsels the adaptation of mediocre works which are more likely to have within them the possibility of cinematic transformation. He can point to innumerable cheap novels and plays which have made magnificent films because the adaptor saw within them a truly cinematic subject, films like *Birth of a Nation, Touch of Evil, Psycho, The Searchers,* and *Treasure of Sierra Madre.*

So great is Balázs's respect for the proper selection of cinematic subjects that he gives to the film script itself the stature of an independent work of art. Just as we consider Shakespeare's plays fully realized even when they are not produced, so Balázs felt that the completed film script could, on occasion, be read as a full transformation of reality. In this he surely contradicts most other theorists. While this is by no means an important aspect of his overall theory, it does illustrate Balázs's unique belief that the raw material of cinema is not something which lies dormant for any man to use. Cinematic raw material exists only for those who have the talent and energy to seek it out in their experience.

THE CREATIVE POTENTIAL OF FILM TECHNIQUE

Compared to the other theorists we have studied, Balázs's sense of cinema's raw material is practically undeveloped. Saying that filmmakers should always go to properly cinematic subjects for their material simply passes the question on to a further level of generality: what indeed is properly cinematic material?

It was Balázs's sense of the continuity of the film process which allowed him to treat this question in so hazy a fashion. For him cinematic subject matter naturally produced, and in turn was produced by, cinematic techniques. Proper subjects are those which can most fully and revealingly be transformed by the various techniques of cinema. The Russian Formalists would have fully supported him here. Like them, Balázs was most comfortable in the domain of creative process.

Most of Balázs's ideas about film technique correspond quite closely to Arnheim's, for both feel that all vision is formative. Both see the screen as a pictorial frame within which the filmmaker organizes his subjects into significant and signifying patterns. And while Balázs was, unlike Arnheim, an ardent proponent of new cinematic inventions, he insisted that they be used for their formative rather than realistic potential. Many of his attacks on the gross representationalism to which sound was immediately put read as if they were written by Arnheim. But Balázs was as open to technology as Eisenstein. He knew that great filmmakers could make extraordinary use of the device which Hollywood merely slapped alongside its images. His prophecies about sound even pre-dated Eisenstein's:

> Only when the sound film will have resolved noise into its elements, segregated individual, intimate voices, and made them speak to us separately in vocal, accoustic close-up; when these isolated detail-sounds will be collated again in purposeful order by sound montage, then will the sound film have become a new art (*Theory of the Film,* pp. 198, 199).

Balázs's vision of film technique was completely based on the belief that films are not pictures of reality but rather the humanization of nature, since the very landscapes we choose as backgrounds for our dramas are the products of the cultural patterns within us. This notion, which has been taken up most recently by the extreme left-wing film journals of France, finds its source in Russian Formalism. Since all vision is in a serious sense cultural rather than natural, the artist does reality no great disservice when he distorts and deforms it. Through his distortion he may in fact physically stretch the visual patterns within the minds of his spectators until they are able to see reality anew.

> Only by means of unaccustomed and unexpected methods produced by striking set-ups can old, familiar and therefore never seen things hit our eye with new impressions (*Theory of the Film,* p. 93).

But when it came to applying the theory of visual distortion Balázs quickly became conservative. Over and over he insisted that distortion must always be used in relation to a naturalistic context of background.

> Distortion . . . must always be distortion of something. If that something is no longer present in the picture then the meaning and significance of the distortion is also gone (*Theory of the Film,* p. 102).

Balázs asked for strange angles only to the extent that the spectator can still orient himself in the picture and differentiate the familiar from the strange. For example he was eager to allow subjective shots, including entire dream sequences, as long as such narrative and visual distortion was set against an orderly plot which it commented upon or advanced. His position here can in some ways be related to that of Mukarovsky, mentioned above, for whom a superfluity of foregrounding reduces rather than enhances aesthetic perception.

One can begin to surmise Balázs's view of editing practices; nevertheless it would be hard to predict the extent of the support he gave to every effort to shape the subject through manipulative cutting,

> The shots are assembled by the editor in a pre-determined order in such a way as to produce by the very sequence of frames a certain intended effect, much as the fitter assembles the parts of a machine so as to turn these disjointed parts into a power-producing, work-performing machine (*Theory of the Film,* p. 118).

Eisenstein never came out for so openly a mechanistic theory of montage. Balázs went on to enumerate the kinds of editing possible in cinema and did not neglect the "inner-speech" ideal Eisenstein was striving for.

> Good editing . . . starts trains of ideas and gives them a definite direction. . . . In such films we can see a sort of inner film of associations running within the human consciousness (*Theory of the Film,* p. 124).

But when it came to the extremes of metaphorical and intellectual montage, Balázs pulled up, and he did so by explicitly attacking what he considered excessive in Eisenstein. Concentrating on the film *October* he decried visual "hieroglyphic picture-writing in which the pictures mean something but have no content of their own." Eisenstein, he said, had "fallen victim to the mistaken idea that the world of purely conceptual thinking could be conquered by film art" (p. 128). Here the nature of film technique prohibits the use of a certain kind of subject matter, for Balázs readily accepted those figures of speech in film which come naturally out of the images themselves. He appreciated Eisenstein's work in the last section of *Potemkin* where an unmistakable analogy is drawn between the men on the ship and the engines which power that ship. Both terms of the figure (the men and the engine) in this case arise directly from the subject and story. The mind apprehends the comparison in passing, seizing the relationship present in the world being filmed. But this is something else again from the willful joining of dramatically unmotivated terms, such as the fall of the Tsar and the crash of a statue, in a famous scene from *October*. While the mind may readily associate the statue and the power of the Tsar, Balázs decried this misuse of what he thought was an essentially visual and dramatic (rather than conceptual) medium.

Balázs's caution, however, only extended so far. He was certainly no proponent of some mystifying realistic cinema. He was in full accord with both Eisenstein and the Russian Formalists that the artist must be bold enough to display his techniques, so that the audience be not tempted to look through the work to a supposed "reality" behind it. Fades, dissolves, and other narrative punctuation graphically indicate that the images are of human construction, meant not to stand for reality but to criticize it or respond to it. Yet even here Balázs stopped short of a rigorously formalistic approach. He insisted that cinematic conventions, like the fades which open and close sequences, maintain a naturalistic relationship to mental processes. Dissolves and fades, in other words, are "like" the mental processes by which we move from image to image in our own inner worlds. Such techniques are conventions, to be sure, but rather realistic ones and preferable in his

Crashing statue in *October,* 1928. *Blackhawk Films*

view to such other conventions as the wipe, "those curtains of shadows . . . drawn across the picture, . . . an admission of impotence . . . contrary to the spirit of film art" (p. 153).

And so Balázs, while recognizing the conventional and formative nature of film techniques, nevertheless consistently appealed to filmmakers to use their techniques diligently and always in relation to our everyday vision, building filmic signification out of the normal world of sight and sound. He frequently used standard Marxist rhetoric to attack the indulgence of overly distorted films which obfuscate the primacy of normal perception and create strange visual and temporal universes. Such films, he said, are a "degenerative phenomenon of bourgeois art"; they have "peeled facial expression off the face and physiognomy off the object, creating abstract, floating 'expressions' that no longer express anything" (p. 108). Less committed to pure shape than were the Russian Formalists, Balázs wanted to retain the status of the object and lift it to signification by means of film technique. His interest continually returned to those original objects which for Shklovsky and the other Formalists ceased to matter the moment the artist touched them.

CINEMATIC SHAPE OR FORM

Theory of the Film was divided into two sections by its author. The first section, primarily a call to the understanding of cinema as a new language-form, concentrated heavily on film technique. Part Two began with a consideration of the various genres of film. It is in this section that Balázs examined the *formal* principles which shape the language of film into actual examples of cinema. The importance accorded cinematic form by Balázs cannot be overestimated.

> A stone on the hillside and the stone of one of Michelangelo's sculptures are both stone. As stones their material is more or less the same. It is not the substance but the form that constitutes the difference between them. . . . It is an old canon of art that the spirit and the law of a material manifests itself most perfectly in the constructed forms of a work of art and not in the raw material (*Theory of the Film*, p. 161).

Balázs proposed to study the forms of cinema by examining what he considered to be marginal genres. He hoped that by looking at its extremes, he would be able to see the laws and rules of cinematic shape. For Balázs the outer regions of cinema had been colonized on one side by the avant-garde or abstract film and, on the other, by the pure documentary. Between them lie the more conventional genres of fictional film, news and educational film, and personal documentary. It is, however, the outlying genres which always test our beliefs and it is to them that he directed his attention.

At both ends of the film spectrum Balázs found forms which intentionally avoid story. "On the one hand the intention was to show objects without form and on the other to show form without objects. This tendency led on the one hand to the cult of the documentary film and on the other to toying with objectless forms" (p. 174).

Balázs's very tone is indicative of his conservative formalism. The pure documentary, in trying to avoid a particular story, loses its voice entirely and is dumb. It is like the uncarved rock on the hillside, rude and virtually meaningless. The purely abstract film, on the other end of the continuum, had gone beyond story in its search for "absolute share," thereby losing touch with the reality it should interpret.

Balázs opened his argument by outlining with the greatest of sympathy the rationale of the "pure documentary." It hopes, he said, to "penetrate so deeply to the core of life, reproduce so vividly the raw material of reality, as to find sufficient expressive dramatic elements in it without a need for a constructive 'plot,'" (p. 156) let alone preliminary scripts and scenarios. But everything in Balázs's philosophy argues against such an ingenuous approach. For him, as for Eisenstein, reality wasn't something one could grasp naïvely. Filmmakers must find truth in the incomprehensibility and noise of reality; and they must set this truth free so that it can speak. This process requires both talent and energy; it almost always demands a plot and a firm control of film technique.

> In order that out of the empirical fog of reality the truth—that is, the law and meaning of reality—may emerge through the interpretation of a seeing and experiencing maker, such a maker must bring into play every means of expression available to the art of the film (*Theory of the Film*, p. 162).

Even granting that photography can capture reality (and we have seen that Balázs had serious reservations about this claim), bare reality was for him insufficient. Like Eisenstein and all formative theorists, he had a tendency to place editing far above photography. "Single pictures are mere reality. Only montage turns them into truths or falsehoods" (p. 162). Here Balázs took his stand against realists like Kracauer and Bazin. For both of them reality could never be termed "mere," and photography, they would have said, is its handmaid.

But of course Balázs's attacks were launched not against realist film theorists so much as against extreme tendencies in filmmaking. The Kino-Eye newsreels of Dziga Vertov, for instance, irritated him primarily because of their claim to superior objectivity. Balázs found such film thoroughly subjective, for the spectator is at the mercy of the cameraman's whims. This cameraman, for his part, tries not to render up truths about reality, nor even an objective view of it, but rather the continuity of vision which he himself supplies. It is only this personal continuity which joins the various images in such a film. How subjective can a movie get, Balázs asked! And how tyrannical.

While his argument may seem rather harsh, Balázs tempered his tone with characteristic equanimity and understanding. This time his understanding was personal, for he himself had made at least one "hero-less" documentary (*The Adventures of a Ten Mark Note*). He recognized the value of the desire to have done with the run-of-the-mill film which "strings the characteristic events of life on the slender thread of a single human destiny" (p. 159). The documentarist wants to avoid the appearance of the artificial so that his subject does not look like the "mere invention of some scriptwriter."

With some regret Balázs undermined this naïve desire, calling not only for scripted films but for films based on specific human dramas. Without particular dramas, human experience cannot be organized, for it never exists in the mass. Even films which strive to engender social awareness and action do best to couch their philosophies within small human dramas, showing social concern emerging in an individual rather than in a faceless crowd. Most likely it is the primacy Balázs always accorded to the facial close-up which led him to this conclusion. But we should never forget that he was writing during the age of Soviet socialist realism, a movement promoting simple personal social dramas and specifically condemning the "formalistic" mass epics of the early Eisenstein.

If Balázs was disturbed by pure documentary's tendency to edge cinema from its proper narrative path, he was outraged by the goals of avant-gardism. For here the technical capability of cinema absolutely dictates what should be filmed, what can be seen. Films of mere appearance result, whose principle of continuity lies in some abstract law. Such films try to "produce not the soul in the world, but the world in the soul" (p. 179). Balázs's vocabulary here has recently been taken up by avant-gardists like Stan Brakhage who turn it around to support their aesthetic. Abstract films to his displeasure and Brakhage's admiration are "like visions seen with closed eyes" (p. 179).

Surely Balázs's own prejudices weakened his theory. For both abstract films and fiction films succeed in transforming subject matter into significant shape, yet Balázs still praised narrative shape at the expense of plastic shape. Perhaps the lack of a clearly thought out notion of subject matter (raw material) hampered him, for isn't it simple willfulness to permit avant-garde techniques only when they serve, and are tied down by, logically constructed and humanly interesting plots? Wasn't Balázs making arguments analogous to those of early twentieth-century art critics who hoped to stem the tide of non-representational painting?

Balázs would not be subject to attacks such as these had he mapped out in some detail the importance of the representational and, more specifically, of the "human" to the subject matter of film. Whereas the Russian Formalists accepted the consequences of their theory, admitting that the subject matter of art does not matter once it has been taken up by technique, Balázs held back. He was a formalist to the extent that he believed art results only from the conscious and consistent transformation of reality into art; he was humanist when he asked that the subject matter be humanly interesting; and he began to turn toward the realist view when he decried avant-garde techniques and modernist film forms which neglect or undermine the human world which, to his mind, only drama can reveal. But with these thoughts and criticisms we pass to the purpose of film art.

CINEMATIC FUNCTIONS

Although I referred to Balázs's book as an introductory text, we should not mistake his purpose. Balázs no doubt was content to instruct the uninitiated in the language and forms of film, but his primary and lifelong goal was the advancement of the art itself. Balázs, like Arnheim, had a profound regard for the cinema of the late silent era. At that time the language-form seemed to confront proper subjects as a matter of course, producing stunning dramas of individuals in conflict with nature or culture. While Balázs was never so parochial as to assert that only this kind of dramatic film should be made, such films clearly form the core of the art in his estimation. They do so because they immediately perform the function of all great art by bringing us to an awareness of human meaning and human perception and by expanding that meaning and that perception.

For Balázs every artform exists like a search light pointed in its own particular direction. Cinema has thrown a light in a completely new direction, illuminating what was formerly enshrouded in ignorance or, more often, unconsciousness and disinterest. The belief which Balázs had in such "directedness" of artforms chiefly drove him to look for cinema's proper form, for its proper direction. The power source generating the light of an artform is akin to its technique or particular creative potential, and the mechanism which aims the light can be regarded as its form.

Cinema's first responsibility is to grow and change until it reaches its proper strength and is able to function as well today as other artforms have functioned in the past. It must, moreover, find its own direction so that it can illuminate the spiritual darkness of our culture just as that darkness has been illuminated by the other arts. Balázs had no belief in the progression of the arts; cinema would never be able to do more than what other arts have always done. At best it will be like the frescoes of the Middle Ages or the drama of Elizabethan England.

This does not mean that cinema must emulate the other arts. It must emulate only their success in illuminating life and perception. But to do this cinema must employ means radically different from those any other art has yet developed. In one of his most striking sections Balázs chided the stodgy Old World culture for trying to make cinema perform in the manner of classic art (with discretion, distance, and cold objective form). Europe, for once, had to learn from America that the true form of cinema is one of spectator identification in which the distance between vision and the visible falls away. In cinema as in no other art the spectator encounters not a self-sufficient artistic organism, but the world itself in the process of being formed by man.

> Hollywood invented an art which disregards the principle of self-contained composition and not only does away with the distance between the spectator and the work but deliberately created the illusion in the spectator that he is in the middle of the action reproduced in the fictional space of the film (*Theory of the Film*, p. 50).

Here Balázs has marked out a privileged power for cinema, but he has done so at the expense of consistency. Spectator identification and delusion are seen here in a positive light whereas they work against the concepts of defamiliarization and of art as formal technique, which Balázs struggled to establish.[16] How can one experience the "artfulness" of a work if he is caught up in that work's illusionary system? Put another way, who has ever been lost within the illusion of *Tristram Shandy,* the novel Shklovsky called "the most typical of all novels"?

This is by no means the only inconsistency to be found at the more general levels of his theory. Most disturbing of all are his direct flirtations with the very realism his theory denounces. At every level he hinted at the special ability cinema has to bring us into accord with nature. For instance, it is the close-up, he said, which gives cinema this power of revealing the secret movements and the laws of nature.

> The close-up can show us a quality in a gesture of a hand that we had never noticed before. . . . The close-up shows your shadow on the wall with which you have lived all your life and which you scarcely knew (*Theory of the Film*, p. 55).

A Day in the Country, 1937. The realm of "natural expression," gift of the close-up, vies with Balázs's theory of "expression through form." *Blackhawk Films*

Unquestionably Balázs is the poet of the close-up. Its power to him was infinitely moving, infinitely revealing. But this very lyricism before the close-up budged him inevitably away from the Formalists and toward the realistic positions of Siegfried Kracauer and André Bazin.

Even when he left the subject of camera position and discussed dramaturgy, Balázs emphasized cinema's affinity for "nature" and its powers of "revelation." These are terms which recur endlessly in Kracauer. For Balázs the cinema made nature the equal of man, for it both surrounds his dramas and plays an active role in them as well. While the filmmaker may manipulate these landscapes, there remain those films in which it seems as if "the countryside were suddenly lifting its veil and showing its face" (p. 97). There is nothing comparable to this tone in Arnheim or Eisenstein.

Balázs's penchant for, but theoretical denial of, the real and natural is what ratified his unshakeable love for what he termed *micro-dramatics*. If the cinema's chief power is in the close-up then its proper form must surely be the minute psychological drama which proceeds on the basis of details and which affects us by means of the intimate gestures of the faces of people and things. Balázs, like Bazin after him, compared the film to a microscope capable of revealing the hidden world of both nature and the psyche. These close-ups cannot be called a language of gestures (though a throughly formative theorist would call them just that) but a "radiating" source of meaning. Balázs specifically attacked attempts to treat gestural meaning in digital or linguistic terms. Modern formative thinkers would here have discarded Balázs as mystical and unscientific.

There are, finally, moments when Balázs contradicted his first principle that meaning and truth reside in man, not in nature. He said, for instance, "The camera may stress hidden meanings present in the object" (p. 114). From this it would appear that the filmmaker's task is not to create meaning by using film's technical arsenal on incoherent material but rather to explore and reveal the meaning inherent in objects in themselves.

No doubt Balázs was fully capable of arguing himself out of this apparent contradiction, but the curious and profound tension in his thought between the formative and the photographic approaches should be apparent. His book was organized to argue a formative aesthetic and his arguments were not only among the first but also among the best of formative texts on cinema. Still, his preferences and predilections (for the close-up, for micro-physiognomy, for small psychological films, for audience identification)—all these seem born from a realistic impulse he tried hard to suppress. When forced, he admitted that his penchant for the small and the natural was a shying away from the "whole truth," that reality sometimes interested him more than truth. The opposition which he tried hard to maintain between reality and truth was what finally landed him next to Eisenstein in the formative camp, despite his conservatism, despite the pull of the "natural" which is more evident in him than in any other formative theorist. While such tensions produce some obvious theoretical difficulties, they save Balázs from that impoverished reductionism which empties so many formative theories of interest and of value.

Realist Film Theory

While there can be no doubt that the dominant theoretical trend in the first decades of cinema was the formative one we have just examined, there remained an undercurrent, actually a counter-current which was the beginning of the photographic or realist tradition. In the chapter concerning realism in his *Esthétique du cinéma* (Paris, 1966), Henri Agel followed this current back to the first proclamations of Louis Feuillade in 1913 in which he advertised his films as showing life as life is. Anyone who has seen even a few episodes from one of Feuillade's serials will be startled by this, so fabulous is his melodramatic story-weaving. Yet these modern fairy tales did take place in a real world and, compared to the other film styles of that era, merited Feuillade's advertisement.

Well into the sound period of cinema, the only realist theory of note comes from men actually engaged in making films. Statements like Feuillade's come from the British documentarists Paul Rotha and John Grierson as they sought to bolster the prestige of their non-entertainment films. In France there were Marcel L'Herbier and especially Jean Vigo, whose famous remarks introducing his first film *A Propos de Nice* are a paradigm of early realist theory. Dziga Vertov in Russia loudly proclaimed the absolute realism of his *Kino-Eye* in order to compete with his formalist compatriots Pudovkin and Eisenstein.

These statements (and many other sources could be listed) convey the bitter belief that the dominant fictional cinema exists like a drug, created by sorcery (the magic of the formative methods of editing, lab processes, and, above all, fabulous script), destined to lull a paying public to sleep. We can see from the outset that realist film theory is closely linked to a sense of the social function of art. While Feuillade's advertisement was strictly an advertisement, trying to draw big crowds and big money with realistic spectacle, the statements of Vertov, Rotha, and Vigo shriek with a sense of political aspiration. Realist cinema should not compete with entertainment films, it should provide an absolute alternative, a cinema with a conscience true both to our everyday perception of life and to our social situation.

The linking in documentary film theory of an aesthetic of perception and an ethic of social concern has continued to this day. We find it in the important writings of Cesare Zavattini and other neorealists; since 1959 we find it in the statements of our *cinéma-vérité* filmmakers, like Ricky Leacock, D. A. Pennebaker, Arthur Barron, Fred Wiseman, and the Maysles brothers. Over and over we read or hear them say that cinema exists to make us see the world as it is, to allow us to discover its visual texture and to let us understand the place of man within it.

While the proclamations of these documentary filmmakers undoubtedly belong to the heritage of realist film theory, none of them is developed or elaborated sufficiently to be considered a theory in the sense of the theories we have looked at so far. Even Grierson's *Documentary Film* falls outside our investigation, since it is a combination of film history and social exhortation, albeit with a realist bias. His arguments lack the incisive logic or significant tradition which supports to a greater or lesser extent all the theories being examined in this book.

It is my own view that the social philosophy of many documentarists so dominated their conception of the medium that their writings are only minimally interesting to the student of film theory. One reads more about the social reality which cinema is able to expose and to help alter than about the *means* by which cinema is suited to this task. Strangely enough, the most rigorous and interesting film theory which might be termed "social revolutionary" has all come from the formative camp. Eisenstein is the most notable example. Followed today by the politically radical film theorists associated with *Cahiers du cinéma* and *Cinéthique*.

Realist film theory has been elaborated most fully by two men for whom cinema exists beyond practical political action. While by no means politically neutral, Kracauer and Bazin saw cinema in a vast context which very much included politics but which was not dominated by it. Their allegiance was first to reality. Their vocation was to bring mankind into harmony with it via the cinema. To both of them this meant a radical revamping of society, but to both such revamping had to follow rather than precede a proper rapport with nature; and this rapport, if it comes at all, will itself follow a renewed human perception, the product of a vivifying and harmonious cinema.

5

Siegfried Kracauer

Of the theorists belonging to the realist camp, Siegfried Kracauer is one of the most recent, his *Theory of Film* having appeared in 1960. It is helpful to examine his work before treating the earlier writings of André Bazin because *Theory of Film* is clearly organized, systematic, and utterly transparent. It stands before us a huge homogeneous block of realist theory: direct, self-consciously academic, thorough. It dares us over and over to refute it. It is full of self-clarifications and judiciously enumerated catalogues. More than any other realist theory, it presumes to be an exhaustive, carefully planned and patterned argument.

While little known in Europe, Kracauer's book has had incredible impact in England and America, in part because its appearance coincided with the advent of widespread film study in both countries. More telling than this, however, is the book's solid structure and broad scholarship. *Theory of Film* appears authoritative in its very format, especially when compared to its rivals. It is a big book, replete with references to a vast range of films, film theorists, and scholars from all fields, and written with incomparable self-confidence and an imposing Germanic seriousness.

Kracauer had been a leading reporter of Germany's most important democratic newspaper, the *Frankfurter Zeitung,* writing lengthy and detailed articles on many subjects, both political and cultural. In America during World War II he brought out his monumental study of German Expressionist film, *From Caligari to Hitler*. Even severe critics of this book cannot dismiss it, for it is at once theoretically audacious and extensively well-researched. Kracauer's other books (one on the composer Offenbach and one on the subject of history itself) are equally weighty, equally serious of purpose.

The critic Peter Harcourt once characterized Kracauer in a way which, while no doubt imaginary, still seems dramatically apt.[1] Kracauer, he suggested, is the kind of man who decided after forty years of viewing film that he ought to work out and write down his ideas about the medium; so he went straight to a library and locked himself in. There, reading widely, thinking endlessly, and working always alone, always cut off from the buzz of film talk and film production, he slowly and painstakingly gave birth to his theory. His book is full of the credits and debits of this kind of detached singlemindedness.

MATTER AND MEANS

It is deceptively easy to outline Kracauer's beliefs, for he continually drummed his essential concepts into the reader's mind. In the Preface to his book he distinguished his work from all previous theories, claiming that his was a *material aesthetic* founded on the priority of *content,* whereas all other theorists had been primarily interested in artistic *form.* His purpose was to examine various kinds of films to determine the richest lines of cinematic development. He planned to do this by plotting out, in the first half of his book, a full analysis and description of the medium. In other words, he began self-consciously with an exploration of the matter and means of cinema. Then, in section III, Composition, he turned to the heart of his study, a thorough critique of each form of film based on the criteria already developed. Finally, in an epilogue, he put the completed theory in the larger context of human activity and elaborated its purpose and possibilities.

The medium of film, in Kracauer's theory, is a mélange of subject matter and subject treatment, of cinematic raw material and cinematic technique. This mélange is unique in the aesthetic universe because instead of creating a new "world of art" the medium tends to turn back to its material. Instead of projecting an abstract or imaginative world it descends to the material world. The traditional arts exist to transform life with their special means, but cinema exists most profoundly and most essentially when it presents life as it is. The other arts *exhaust* their subject matter in the creative process; cinema tends on the contrary to *expose* its matter.

To take a simple example, an artist uses a building in his cubist painting, consuming that part of the building which interests him and making us forget it as a building once we have rediscovered it as a form for an artwork. The filmmaker, on the other hand, shows us the same building and commits our interest to the building itself. No matter how thoroughly he explores the visible aspects of the building, we always want to know more about it. The filmmaker throws us back on the model, while the artist makes us transcend the model and forget it in the face of the painting.

Kracauer's material aesthetic blends two domains: the domain of reality and the domain of the technical capabilities of film. While photography was developed (and is still being developed) to record visible reality, it records some aspects of this reality more readily than it does others. And, from the other side, physical reality is made up of many aspects, some of which are better suited to the camera than others. In Kracauer's view, it is the function of the filmmaker to read both reality and his medium justly, so that he can be certain to employ the proper techniques on the proper subject matter. Kracauer thinks of cinema as if it were a scientific instrument created to explore some particular levels or types of reality. His book hopes to elaborate the most appropriate uses of this instrument and the benefits derivable from it.

The meshing of matter and means here is reminiscent of Béla Balázs. Both men are in search of proper cinematic subject matter and both feel that film techniques exist only to operate on that matter. We found that Balázs was unable to define what proper subject matter was; Kracauer, confronting the same problem, turns to still photography, hoping to find the answer there. For Kracauer cinema is heir to the still photograph and to its unquestioned link to visible reality. The subject matter of cinema must therefore be the world which the still photo was invented to serve: the "endless," "spontaneous," visible world of "accidental occurrences" and infinitely minute repercussions.

The raw material of cinema is in all cases the visible, natural world qualified by its suitability for the photographer. Thus the technical aspects of the medium (photography) determine to some extent the subject matter of that medium. How can Kracauer possibly call such a system a "content-oriented" view? He is well aware of the problem lurking here and cleverly divides the means of cinema into two groups: the basic properties and the technical properties.

The basic properties of film are entirely photographic, cinema's capability of registering (albeit most often in black and white and in two dimensions) the visible world and its movement. While he is aware that every photograph is full of "unavoidable transformations" of reality (in Arnheim's sense), he feels they may be discounted because "photographs still preserve the character of compulsory reproductions."[2] The photographic base of cinema, then, is technical, but Kracauer opts not to take the technical limitations into account. The world exists for him *as photographed* or as photographable, and this world is the raw material available to the filmmaker. By refusing to question the basic (i.e., photographic) properties of cinematography, he irrevocably rejected formative theory which marks a world of difference (and a world of potential art) between visible reality and the moving photographs which grasp it in their peculiar way. For them photography is technique; for Kracauer it is nearly a given part of nature.

Kracauer associates the basic means of photography with cinema's raw material. He labels all other aspects of the film medium supplementary "technical" properties. These luxuries of the medium include editing, the close-up, lens distortion, optical effects, and so on. Kracauer makes it clear that the technical properties are only indirectly related to content. This gives the basic properties priority and he exhorts filmmakers to use the technical properties only to support the primary function of the medium: the recording and revealing of the visible world around us.

In sum, the subject matter of cinema is the photographable world, the reality which seems to give itself naturally to the photographer. Besides making possible the photographic record of the world and its motion, cinematic means can further transform the world through its supplementary technique. Some transformations support the photographic effort and allow us unique visual insights of the world; but many technical transformations make us forget the matter for the means, make us attend to the movie and not to the world. In this case cinema is striving to be like the traditional arts in going beyond its raw material. Arnheim approved of this enthusiastically; Kracauer had to decry it. While he granted that men can use their creations any way they choose, Kracauer couldn't help criticizing certain uses. Unrealistic cinema is like a scientific instrument used as a toy. It may be interesting, exciting, and fun, but it will always be a diversion.

Kracauer considered all art to be a battle between form and content. He saw in cinema the first "art" in which content has an initial edge in this battle. It is for this reason that he felt justified in developing a "material" rather than a formal aesthetic. If content is pre-eminent in cinema then an analysis of cinematic contents should be able to establish the essence of the medium. This he proposed to do in the body of the book (Section III), which he devoted to the various genres of films. But Kracauer felt compelled to argue first for the validity of his principle, to argue that the conscientious viewer can intuitively tell which forms of cinema are important and which forms are nothing but the economic ventures of producers, the vain distractions of a mindless public, or the pretentious games of would-be artists.

How can we differentiate that cinema which uses its properties to record and reveal, as best it can, certain areas of reality, from that cinema which records reality only to exploit it in the pursuit of trivial goals? Except for animated film and certain extreme forms of experimental work, which Kracauer felt free to disregard as outside the perimeters of his investigation, all cinema records reality via cinematic techniques. How did Kracauer dare single out central from peripheral cinema?

It is here that most of his hostile critics have taken exception and it is here that Kracauer returned to photography for support. Proper cinematography, he said, is based on an extension of the ideals and natural methods of photography. All other kinds or uses of cinematography (especially those analogous to theater or painting or music) are peripheral. This is so because photography is the first and basic ingredient of cinema, tying it forever to the natural world.

Kracauer was forced to admit that not every still photograph serves its subject. There has always been a debate between the formative photographer and the realist analogous to the debate we've been following in cinema. In appealing to photography, then, as the basic force behind cinema which dictates its subject matter, Kracauer was really appealing to his own view of photography, the realist view. In effect he said that since photography can serve visible reality, it ought to do so; and since it ought to do so, so also ought its son and heir, cinema.

The weaknesses of this argument are apparent and are further strained by Kracauer's sense of "visible reality." As a twentieth-century thinker he felt uneasy in making substantial claims about this raw material of cinema. Modern science has thrown the physical world into question and it is in part up to cinema to reveal to us the visible aspects of our cosmos. Man, Kracauer has said, no longer knows what reality is. Old beliefs in nineteenth-century materialism have crumbled before the discoveries and warnings of Einstein and Heisenberg. The high-speed and infrared camera can record a world which looks unrealistic, which is unpredictable to common sense, but which nevertheless is verifiably there.

This openendedness of nature would seem to block Kracauer from stating anything at all precise about cinematic raw material and the techniques which, by his own admission, cannot be justified except in nature's service. But Kracauer here was able to concentrate on the admittedly vague but undeniable "tendencies" associated with film. He found that nature from her side and man from his converge on the photographic process, and come into a new and intimate rapport. It is here that he brought into play and developed his famous, lengthy catalogues. He listed first of all those aspects of nature which have an affinity for photography and cinema: the endless, the spontaneous, the very large, the very small, and so on. These aspects of nature are available to man in no other form. Nature seemed to wait, as it were, for the birth of photography before expressing them.

Turning away from nature and toward the way certain human aspirations converge on photography, Kracauer meditated on the various virtues of what he began to call the *cinematic approach*. This of course is nothing other than the realist approach, the tendency in man to follow nature wherever it leads, to attend to the flow of life rather than to the fixed constructs of his own imagination. It is the special technology of cinema which gives substance to these human tendencies. Kracauer felt justified, then, in examining the history of the medium to show when and how the cinematic approach was best utilized or when it was bartered away for other, more trivial goals. He could examine the duties of the filmmaker as they are dictated to him, first by the tendencies of his subject matter, nature itself, and, second, by the tendencies within the tools he plans to use on that subject matter.

The filmmaker thus has two objects in mind: reality and the cinematic record of reality. He has two goals: the recording of reality through the basic properties of his tool and the revealing of that reality through the judicious use of all the properties available to his medium, including the more flamboyant ones. Kracauer sees two possible motivations available to every filmmaker, that of realism and that of formalism. The latter destroys the cinematic approach only when it operates unauthorized on its own. When used properly, it can help perform the second of the filmmaker's double duties: to let reality in, and then to penetrate it.

Kracauer tried to blur the sharpness of these omnipresent dualities by suggesting that the "either/or" become a "both/and." Thus, the filmmaker should be *both* realistic *and* formative; he can *both* record *and* reveal; he must *both* let reality in *and* penetrate it with his techniques. But in all these cases it is the first term which must dominate.

Seen in this light, Kracauer's realism is, in practice, not really so radical or absolute. He recognized that filmmakers must, and ought to, render their own views of reality. It is a human realism he demanded, a realism not of fact but of intention. The same scene may be praised in a film with realistic goals and condemned in a formalist "art" film. For example, Kracauer extolled the abstract forms in a scientific film showing the microscopic particles in a single drop of water, but he had to reject the use of the same abstract imagery photographed for its own sake or to serve in a psychological drama as a "subjective" shot or dream sequence.

Kracauer was prepared to follow this position out to its logical conclusion. The filmmaker is barred from nothing so long as his intentions are pure.

> He may feature his impressions of this or that segment of physical existence in documentary fashion, transfer hallucinations and mental images to the screen, indulge in the rendering of rhythmical patterns, narrate a human interest story, etc. All these creative efforts are in keeping with the cinematic approach as long as they benefit, in some way or other, the medium's substantive concern with our visible world. . . . Everything depends on the right "balance" between the realistic tendency and the formative tendency; and the two tendencies are well balanced if the latter does not try to overwhelm the former but eventually follows its lead (*Theory of Film,* pp. 38, 39).

Kracauer faced the consequences of this with real courage, standing up against all previous film theory. He put in question the primacy of "cinema as art." While Balázs, Arnheim, and Munsterberg searched for ways to prove that cinema could be an art, Kracauer concluded that in going the way of traditional art, cinema loses its unique character. Art is an expression of human meaning; it is unified and brought to a satisfying close; it succeeds by imaginatively transcending its material. Cinema fails its primary responsibility when it follows these ideals. On the contrary, cinema should be an expression not of man's but of the world's meaning, insofar as man can see it; it should be indeterminate, not unified; and open, not closed in structure; it exists not to transcend its material but to honor and serve that material. The filmmaker must be artful, to be sure, must have all the sensibility of an artist, but he must in the end turn both his imagination and his techniques back to the flowing and endless world rather than exploit his medium for its own sake or in pursuit of a subjective content.

Here Kracauer terminated his first section, his analysis of the matter and means of cinema. In Section II, Areas and Elements, he attempted to deduce some consequences of the cinematic approach, but his remarks were incomplete and arbitrary. They are, and must remain, merely selected ideas made from the standpoint of a realistic film theory, for he has already shown that "all means" are appropriate if used in the service of content, and that film content itself is not in the end specifiable. Section II is interesting, but logically unnecessary; and we must pass through or over it before encountering the crucial Section III, Composition. It is in this domain of composition, or film form, that we can observe the filmmaker following or betraying the cinematic ideals already outlined, and it is in this domain as well that we can look for the kinds of realities which stand by ready to be revealed through cinema.

COMPOSITIONAL FORMS

The filmmaker has two primary ways to engage his material formatively. The first is at the level of the image where he can either be true to the object or overwhelm it with his "artistic" photography. The second is at the level of construction where he places his images in a context and makes clear his intentions for them. The various genres of film make up the history of the use and goals of such second-level formation. Kracauer calls this process "composition."

Kracauer's classification of types of films, as well as his very interest in that kind of study, again reminds one immediately of Béla Balázs. This is all the more true since their judgments concerning proper film types are strangely similar. Like Balázs, Kracauer broke his subject down, immediately singling out story films as the central genre against which all other types of film must necessarily react and be measured. He too proposed to examine first the non-story film which he divided into the *film of fact,* and the *experimental film.* From opposite directions these genres have constantly harassed the fictional film which to them is "literature" and "mass entertainment" rather than a "pure" use of cinema.

Kracauer considered these claims, beginning with the experimental film which has always been most strident in its proclamations. He presented many declarations and manifestos by avant-garde artists, and he grouped them roughly into three categories. The experimental filmmaker, he stated, operates under three related "intentions" toward his material:

1. He wished to organize whatever material he chose to work on according to rhythms which were a product of his inner impulses, rather than an imitation of the patterns found in nature.
2. He wished to invent shapes rather than record or discover them.
3. He wished to convey, through his images, contents which were an outward projection of his visions rather than an implication of those images themselves (*Theory of Film,* p. 181).

The avant-gardists would agree with Kracauer's formulation of what they are doing and why; but they would disagree on the value of that work. They call it "cinematic par excellence," while Kracauer, on the basis of the definition he built up over the first half of his book, had to find such work utterly anti-cinematic. One lengthy citation sums up his impatience with this whole tendency:

It appears, then, that the experimental filmmakers, whether favoring rhythmical abstraction or surrealistic projections of inner reality, approach the cinema with conceptions which alienate it from nature in the raw, the fountainhead of its peculiar power. Their formative aspirations gravitate toward achievements in the spirit of modern painting or literature—a preference for independent creativity which smothers their concern with camera explorations, their curiosity about reality at large. Liberating film from the tyranny of the story, they subject it to that of traditional art. In fact they extend art into the cinema. "Help the development of film as a fine art form . . ." reads a 1957 leaflet of the New York Creative Film Foundation. But the artist's freedom is the filmmaker's constraint (*Theory of Film,* p. 192).

His aversion to the whole concept of art in the cinema will disturb many readers, but it is a logical consequence of Kracauer's whole position. Nor do his remarks really differ greatly from those of Balázs, a self-acknowledged champion of cinematic art. Balázs complained that the avant-gardists so reduced the impact of reality that their films were empty forms instead of full-bodied transformations of reality. It is true that Balázs argued for an artistic manipulation of reality which Kracauer could hardly accept, but he did insist that this manipulation still exhibit the reality on which it is based. Both theorists softened their condemnations of this type of film by pointing, as was their duty, to the profound historical effect of the avant-gardists. "One does well to remember," Kracauer concluded, "that the avant-garde's experiments in cinematic language, rhythmical editing, and the representation of near-unconscious processes greatly benefited film in general. Nor should it be forgotten that, like Buñuel, many an avant-garde artist became realistic minded and outward bound" (p. 192).

Between the experimental film and the film of fact Kracauer discovered an interesting genre which mediates the two. This is the film on art, architecture, and sculpture. Characteristically Kracauer praised those films which faithfully record objects of art in the creation of a new but related work, while he condemned those which make use of the images of sculptors and painters in the service of new, imaginatively transformed films. His disgust for this new kind of film avant-gardism intensified because it ransacks legitimate art. These films never give the audience a sense of the artworks they draw upon. For instance, they seldom show the frames of paintings, preferring to create a kind of collage or cartoon, albeit drawn by the world's greatest artists. He dismissed this trend first as a species of experimental film and second as an unseemly sycophant

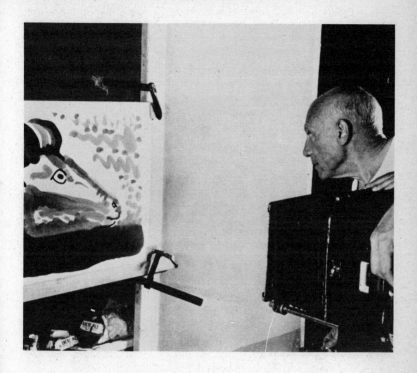

Clouzot's *Mystery of Picasso* (1956) inserts the space of the painting into a larger space. *The Museum of Modern Art/Film Stills Archive*

of fine art. He was much more sympathetic to films which are content to show the development of an artist's work or, better, as in the case of Clouzot's *Mystery of Picasso,* to chronicle the very genesis of a painting itself. These Kracauer gladly placed "nearer the center" of the cinematic ideal. His belief that when dealing with art objects, filmmakers should treat them as physical objects existing on their own in solid space, rather than as mental or spiritual objects, is strikingly close to Bazin's views on this subject.

Berlin, 1927: Behind this documentary lies an impulse to abstraction. *The Museum of Modern Art/Film Stills Archive*

While interesting, the problem of the film on art is at best a local and highly specialized problem. It leads us, however, to the true documentary of which we expect Kracauer to be highly supportive. Here a non-story genre has as its purpose the documentation and exploration of the world; here if ever, one would assume, Kracauer must find cinema in its true home. Yet in one of the most stunning paradoxes of the book, Kracauer refused to accord this extreme of cinema any special prestige. Indeed, he could find little at all to say about straight newsreel and educational films, the genres at the very limit of the realistic tendency.

The films in this area he did want to discuss are conventional documentaries, no doubt because here the human impulse to shape reality directly confronts recorded reality. Although cinema's basic photographic function is a cornerstone of Kracauer's theory, he seems much less interested in the bare use of that function than in the struggle between the imagination of the film artist and a reality he must somehow respect and bring out. Newsreels hardly exhibit this tension. They meet the basic characteristics of the medium but pose no further problems and, he implied, can go no further than themselves.

In the realm of the conventional documentary, Kracauer was only a little more tolerant. He lashed out against a number of films which mask as documentaries but surreptitiously exploit the visible world in the service of an abstract imaginative creation (Ruttman's *Berlin: The Symphony of a City*) or of a didactic, doctrinaire message (all propaganda films, including the great U.S. government documentaries of the depression like *The Plow that Broke the Plains*).

Certainly Kracauer had enormous respect for properly cinematic documentaries, those which seek out and present countless subjects or countless aspects of a subject without the strictures of a plot. But even these fail to measure up to Kracauer's ideal. Like the newsreel, they are appropriate but not optimal uses of the medium; they "suffer from a limitation in range. Confined, by definition, to the rendering of our environment, they miss those aspects of potentially visible reality which only personal involvement is apt to summon" (p. 212).

It is apparent that Kracauer's realism was as cautious and conservative as Balázs's formalism was. Both men pulled back from the extremes toward which their theoretical principles seemed to point. Balázs retreated from the absolute formalism of experimental cinema and Kracauer from the radical realism of newsreel and *cinéma vérité*.

Kracauer, then, like Balázs, wanted desperately to retrieve the centrality of the human drama in film because of the depth which stories by their nature usher in. Without stories, cinema is condemned to a surface view of life. Kracauer stated point blank:

> In the case of the film of fact, it opens only on part of the world. Newsreels as well as documentaries feature not so much the individual and his inner conflicts as the world he lives in. . . . The suspension of the story, then, not only benefits the documentary but puts it at a disadvantage also (*Theory of Film,* p. 194).

It is the story which gives cinema its chance at fullest development. For both Kracauer and Balázs, the story film is the aesthetic as well as the economic basis of cinema, because it brings into play a kind of subject matter and a kind of audience involvement which can make for the most complex of experiences. The best documentaries, Kracauer insinuated, always move toward the fabulous power of spectator participation.

Kracauer's whole thesis seems in jeopardy here. Is the documentary, the genre most closely tied to the exploration of reality, to be subordinated to the whims of plots devised by story-writers? In his predicament he called once more on the concept of balance. Just as in the first section of his book, when treating the film image, he demanded a balance between the realistic impulse which wants to record the object flatly and the formative impulse which tries to reveal its meaning, so in this section he saw the proper film form as a balance between the documentary which tries to follow the random flow of nature and the story film which strives to pull nature into a human shape. Kracauer's chapters on the story film set out to show how this balance can be attained.

We are told that story film can be most profitably broken into three sub-categories, the theatrical film, the adaptation, and the found-story or episode. These Kracauer treated in ascending order of acceptibility.

The theatrical film, with its origins in the Film d'art movement of the silent screen, goes against all cinematic principles. It is a closed form which surrounds actors and their stylized speeches with artificial or carefully chosen decor. It explores nothing and records only the playing out of an essentially cerebral game. Kracauer included among these films the bulk of Hollywood's products since these are generally dependent on "tight" scripts and artificial, if appealing, decor. Such factors make it impossible for nature to intrude upon the story. Instead of aiding the exploration of reality, the story has here become a substitute reality. Naturally the theatrical film has its power and its pleasures, but they are not those of true cinema. They consist in bringing to masses of people the classics of stage art, or in satisfying the multitudes with clever but "detachable" story lines.

Kracauer's remarks on adaptation are predictable. After some initial theoretical comparisons showing that of all literary forms the novel is closest to cinema, though still distinct from it, he reintroduced his familiar concepts of cinematic and uncinematic. Adaptations make sense only when the content of the novel is firmly rooted in objective reality, not in mental or spiritual experience. He found that realistic and naturalistic novels like John Steinbeck's *Grapes of Wrath* and Emile Zola's *L'Assomoir* are suitable material and have in fact been suitably, that is, "realistically," translated to the screen. On the other hand, a novel whose primary movement occurs within a character, such as Stendhal's *The Red and the Black,* is doomed at the outset of the adaptation enterprise. The filmmaker can render only the world around Julien Sorel, not his complex emotional reactions to it. This is all the more apparent, said Kracauer, in Bresson's heroic attempt to bring Georges Bernanos's *Diary of a Country Priest* to the screen. While the camera does properly engage the countryside parish of the priest, and while it also painstakingly explores the tribulations of the priest's soul as these are reflected on his face, Bresson was forced to resort to an off-camera voice to carry along this essentially spiritual drama. For Kracauer, the cinema is first and always a visual medium, and such introspective voice-over techniques are an admission of the failure of the visual imagination or of the impropriety of the subject matter. *Diary of a Country Priest* is, as we shall see, a crucial example, because it is a film hailed by André Bazin and his disciples who in most other instances agree with Kracauer.

Kracauer discovered his ideal cinematic genre at last in what he termed "The found story."

Diary of a Country Priest, 1950. The Museum of Modern Art/Film Stills Archive

When you have watched for long enough the surface of a river or a lake, you will detect certain patterns in the water which may have been produced by a breeze or some eddy. Found stories are in the nature of such patterns. Being discovered rather than contrived, they are inseparable from films animated by documentary intentions. Accordingly they come closest to satisfying that demand for the story which "reemerges within the womb of the non-story film" (*Theory of Film*, pp. 245, 46).

The filmmaker who creates a found story will never be guilty of allowing the plot to disengage itself from the earth in the way of the theatrical story. By definition found stories are dependent upon the chaotic and unpredictable whirl of life which spins them out. They are open-ended, unstaged, and indeterminate. The films of Robert Flaherty (especially *Nanook of the North* and *Man of Aran*) and the earliest examples of Italian neorealism (for example, *Paisa* and *La Terra trema*) are the finest films of this sort, for their stories arise out of the locale and culture being filmed. Never in these films does an individual initiate a plot, for the plot must come from reality itself. The individual exists in these films to bring out the human dimensions of a broad and objective situation, to make us as spectators view it deeply and passionately rather than for its informational content as we might view a documentary about the same problem. Vittorio de Sica's *Bicycle Thieves* makes us aware of an enormous and widespread social problem in Italy after the war, but at the same time it gives us that problem in all its pathos by focusing on one man and his plight.

With the "found story" Kracauer has arrived at the end of his exploration of formal issues. He ended with a deductive summary of his theoretical position, appropriately entitled, "Matters of Content." "It may be taken for granted," he said, "that the screen attracts certain kinds of content while being unresponsive to others" (p. 262).

Uncinematic content is best exemplified by "conceptual reasoning" and by what he terms "the tragic." For obvious reasons films which treat conceptual material are organized by closed systems of logic, illustrated by visuals. It is useful here to recall Eisenstein's proposal to adapt Karl Marx's *Das Kapital* to the screen; for Eisenstein the flow of juxtaposed particles could reach a level of abstraction comparable to, though not identical with, rational thought. Kracauer, who pays little attention to editing, focusing on film's material in its untampered state, could never accept this. In Eisenstein's hypothetical film, the images would lose their unique physicality as they helped create the complex patterns needed to render the hermetically logical system of *Das Kapital*.

"The tragic" is a more interesting taboo for cinema. Kracauer listed the major attributes of this mode, finding each essentially anti-cinematic. He dealt in succession with tragedy's "exclusive concern with human affairs," its presupposition of a "finite, ordered cosmos," its "elimination of the fortuitous" and accidental, and finally its comparative "remoteness from imagery." There is always something final and determinate about the tragic, epitomized by the endings which such stories necessarily have. In a rather amusing aside, Kracauer explained that happy endings are in fact more compatible with cinema than tragic ones, since they have about them a sense of continuance rather than of termination.

The conceptual and the tragic illustrate the negative side of his position. Kracauer found that of those story forms and motifs which are naturally and positively cinematic the "sleuthing motif" is exemplary. Here a conventional literary plot device (the detective seeking out the truth) drives both the filmmaker and the spectator back into the raw material of life in search of significant clues. It is a literary device which by its very nature upholds the importance of the world over the imagination. It forces us to use, not play with, our imaginations in seeking out the meaning of the world around us.

Kracauer's theory of the formal composition of cinema is the best section of the book, because it logically follows his initial speculations on the basic requirements of cinema, while at the same time it provides those empty speculations with the concrete historical evidence they need. This historical examination of types of films does not prove his initial thesis that only the realistic approach is cinematic. Instead it shows us the consequences of such a thesis and allows us to judge for ourselves. Do Flaherty's films indeed seem more cinematic, more true to the properties and possibilities of cinema, than German expressionist films, Hollywood genre pictures, or the latest avant-garde piece coming out of New York? For Kracauer, this is not a mere matter of taste but a proof of aesthetic principle.

THE PURPOSE OF CINEMA

Implicit throughout Kracauer's entire book is a teleology of cinema. In the Epilogue he finally turned his focus directly on this vision of the purpose of cinema in the life of man. Unquestionably this is the most exciting section of his book, providing a final intellectual flourish after the rather academic tone with which the theory proper has been expounded. In a ten-page synopsis of the state of modern man, Kracauer attributed the diffusion and emptiness he found in contemporary life to the disappearance and fragmentation of ideologies. Culture is no longer held together by belief, religious or otherwise.

While his is only one voice among countless to have decried the modern waste land, Kracauer, more uniquely, coupled it with what he claimed is the failure of science. In the nineteenth century the scientific attitude tore to shreds what was left of the Christian basis of our civilization. There remain Christians, to be sure, but now they wander side by side with remnants of other lost ideologies in a pluralistic, secular culture. Science made extravagant promises to replace Christianity with a modern and irrefutable system in which everyone could believe and profit. Science's claim rested on its alleged tie to the truths of nature. The broken and "unnatural" life we lead in this century is evidence enough of the disillusioning failure of that claim and those promises. But why has science been unable to fill the ideological void it created?

Kracauer insisted that the failure of science was a result of its incessant drive toward abstraction. Instead of helping us learn to know, love, and live in harmony with the things and beings of the world, science has consistently foresaken those things and those beings in search of the higher laws which control them. It has sacrificed intimate knowledge of the earth in order to allow us to "understand" more phenomena from more perspectives. Because it always regards things from an abstract point of view, science has enabled us to deal with phenomena easily (our technological gadgets are one obvious measure of this), but we have lost the sense of the "thingness" of things. The phenomena we encounter are not valued in themselves but only insofar as they participate in large patterns in our minds or in the "minds" of our computers. Without any unifying belief we are living in a fragmentary world of intersecting patterns barely touching on the physical universe those patterns are supposed to explain.

How can we reverse this ennervating trend? Kracauer cautioned us against retreating to old-fashioned pre-scientific ideologies and religions as a solution. We must, he claimed, go forward with science, working through its abstraction to the world itself. Only when we let the world of objects talk to us directly can we escape the solipsism of our patterns. Only then will we have the chance to create anything like a new ideology which can unite us as a culture by joining us intimately to the earth. This would be utopia, a spiritual culture based solidly on matter, responding naturally to matter.

To attain supremacy and unite us all, the new ideology will have to be qualitatively different from all world views which have existed in the past. It must not, like them, be a system worked out in the imagination and then applied, with greater or lesser success, to the earth and to our experience. To have a lasting effect on culture, such an ideology would have to arise out of the earth itself, not out of man. This can occur only if we re-attune ourselves to the earth and become responsive to its truths.

The task of re-attunement is an essentially anti-scientific task, in that it reverses the direction of human interest away from abstraction. Up to now this task has been given to art which supposedly heightens our experience of life. We have seen the Russian Formalists give voice to this project. But Kracauer felt that art failed and unconsciously played directly into the "abstractionism" of culture. Art always begins from the imaginative patterns which appeal to man and then works these patterns out in a physical medium. It begins, Kracauer said, from the top, from a high level of generality and works its way down to experience. No matter how realistic his intentions may be, the traditional artist overwhelms reality in creating his autonomous work. He necessarily makes reality conform to his vision of it. And while the spectator may believe that he is at last in touch with raw experience, he is in fact re-experiencing in a new way the same patterns which shape his ordinary life and action, keeping him forever deaf to the messages of the earth.

It is up to the photographer and, above all, the filmmaker to save us from this deadening narrowness. Far from ransacking reality to create their works, they exhibit it more fully than traditional art. Rather than forcing reality into a human pattern, they follow nature's own patterns. Film is a process (and a technological one at that) which works from the bottom up. It begins in the earth and shapes our imaginative patterns to the earth. It can rediscover for us the world we had bartered in return for general scientific knowledge.

Kracauer's sense of the purpose of film as well as his admonitions about the correct "cinematic approach" are closely related to his theory of the uses and methods of history. In a posthumously published treatise on historiography, Kracauer specifically related the historian's task to that of the photographer. He attacked from the first all ideological histories, be they Marxist or Christian. Then he condemned the twentieth-century attempts at grand evolutionary schemes, such as those of Oswald Spengler and Arnold Toynbee. Kracauer has praise only for the modest historian, for the scholar who painstakingly attends to the details and objective facts which are the stuff of life and of its history. The historian's task is to make the facts of the past comprehensible to the present. If until 1800 historians served great metaphysical schemes, it was only because science had yet to turn us forever away from such schemes. But science itself lives far above its facts in a world of abstract laws and cannot serve as a perfect model for the historian. No, the historian must hover near the facts of life and be mobile enough to come down for intimate scrutiny or to sail high enough to see them in their context. Certainly the historian uses his imagination, but he does so to serve the facts rather than to serve his own beliefs and lofty abstractions.

Kracauer goes on to compare large, general, synoptic history books to "theatrical" films, rejecting both in favor of smaller concrete histories, analogous to the "found story." These tend to rise out of the chaos and continuum of life only to fall back into it at the end. For Kracauer both film and history should serve philosophical ends though not be philosophical themselves. They are, he said, anterooms to the grand palaces of unified systems of culture. We must necessarily traverse them, though they are smaller and less exciting than the palaces themselves, if we are to enter into grandeur.

Kracauer was a traditional democratic and liberal theorist. He distrusted ideologies, yet he was confident that man, confronted with real experience, will shape his life in terms of the real. He was also a rationalist whose critique of science is anything but the critique a more poetic or mystical theorist might advance. He wanted us to use science to get to the proper understanding of things. Science has made us concerned with things, but only in an abstract way. It is up to those "mediating" processes of history, photography, and cinema, which are at once part art and part science, to make us live within a world of objects and things, to make us appropriate this earth "which is our habitat"[3] and only heaven. These mediating processes put man in his proper relation to life. They submit themselves neither to the tyranny of facts (for they always organize and compose) nor to the tyranny of the imagination (for they reject organizations and compositions which claim supremacy over facts). These processes, then, are truly human, for they let us live as men within a real world.

Kracauer closed his *Theory of Film* with the hope that men may find peace and communal friendship through their mutual experience and knowledge of the earth. If wars and human strife have in the past resulted from a clash of ideologies, we may hope that a common ideology, based not on schemes but on the facts of earthly experience, may bring us peace and harmony. Film, when properly used, is already helping us advance toward this dream.

REBUTTALS

Kracauer's *Theory of Film* cannot help but provoke arguments. Any theory which candidly proceeds by ranking films on the basis of their "cinematic" value will necessarily anger those who are drawn to films which do not comply with the definition given. In addition, Kracauer himself admitted that nothing will ever be able to completely obliterate the differences raging between realists and formalists since the birth of photography, for such arguments are largely the result of opposite points of departure. His theory, while finding a place for the formative impulse within it, comes down solidly, unmistakeably, even fanatically on the realist side.

Kracauer was probably aware that no matter how many examples he might bring to bear on the question, he would remain forever unable to prove his initial assertions: (1) that cinema is more a product of photography than of editing or other formative processes; (2) that photography is first and foremost a process tied to the objects it registers rather than a process transforming those objects; and (3) that cinema must therefore serve the objects and events which its equipment allows it to capture; that is, that it should be formally (his term is "compositionally") realistic because it is imagistically realistic.

The first two assertions are exactly that: assertions. Kracauer cannot prove them so much as point to them, meditate upon them, testify to their reasonableness. This he does with enthusiasm. The third assertion, however, is a conclusion drawn from the first two. When critics disagree here, they do so not simply out of an opposing, equally unprovable conviction but rather out of outrage at Kracauer's logic. This is important since critics of Kracauer's first two assertions are formative theorists who simply substitute for his assertions formalistic ones of their own; whereas critics of his third assertion come from all camps. It is this third assertion, then, which merits closer scrutiny.

Kracauer's belief that films should compositionally mirror reality is in the tradition of "imitation" theories of art. It is no coincidence that he frequently called upon the authority of Erich Auerbach, a fellow German expatriate, who has been this century's leading scholar in this tradition. Auerbach's profoundly influential *Mimesis: The Representation of Reality in Western Literature* has a conclusion much in accord with Kracauer's epilogue. There Auerbach argued for a serious literary realism which, in avoiding ideology and in imitating the plurality and variety of man's experience, may lead the way toward a lasting brotherhood.

Auerbach dealt with authors who compose a fictional world in a form which seems open to, and in imitation of, the real world of experience. Such writers, he found, begin with a record of human speech and an outline of human events. From this they build a world in language in which those kinds of events and those varieties of speech are transformed into a whole which gives them artistic power and resonance, while still retaining a focus on reality. Valuable realistic literature allows the reader to recognize his world and the world of his neighbor; in so recognizing it, he can criticize it in the pursuit of a better world.

Even this brief summary hints at several points of agreement between Auerbach and Kracauer. Most obvious is their passionate sense of the importance of realism to past culture and to the one which must emerge if we are to survive as human beings. Second is their mutual descriptions of the artistic method. Each saw his art as a kind of "mediating" process which begins in reality and which, in transforming it, never loses its "reality focus." Artistic transformation for both of them serves to clarify and amplify patterns found in experience rather than to create new experiences dictated by the inner patterns of the artist.

Artists in all media can create realistic works if they form their raw material (whatever that may be) into a composition which is structurally similar to that of the empirical world. There are, of course, countless other ways to shape raw material and Auerbach, for instance, never even hinted that all literature ought to be imitative. He carefully suggested that a great strain (to him the greatest strain) of Western literature has indeed been written within this tradition. He succeeded in *Mimesis* in showing this strain at work and in exposing its importance and glory, but he didn't in the least try to set it off in competition with other forms of literature such as lyric poetry or the didactic essay.

Kracauer, on the other hand, used the great history of realism in cinema to try to extinguish other strains of cinema. It is this which understandably alarms his critics. Certainly he has shown how one might use film realistically as literature has often used its medium realistically. More, he has shown the glories of realistic films in film history and his hope for them in the future. But he has not thereby proven that *all* films must be realistic to be cinematic.

The task which Kracauer assigned the filmmaker seems to differ hardly at all from that of Auerbach's literary realist. The filmmaker here appears equal, not superior, to the writer. What has happened to cinema's *special* realism? The filmmaker fashions moving pictures, not words, but he does so like any other artist. Kracauer's beliefs notwithstanding, the realism of the film artist is akin to, not different from, the realism of the writer, the painter, the librettist.

Kracauer justified himself by repeating that cinema differs from the traditional arts in that its very raw material is realistic. But even if this be so, is there a binding link between the forms of an art and its material? Wasn't Kracauer himself guilty of that very abstraction he so detested? Isn't his "system" in fact a huge filter which sifts all the films which have been made into a convenient hierarchy of categories? Didn't he give up the close attention to the texture of films which should be the critic's primary concern, just as the close attention to the texture of things is the filmmaker's first duty and final goal?

These questions become more poignant in the light of the writings of the *Cahiers du cinéma* critics of the fifties. André Bazin and to a lesser extent his disciples, François Truffaut, Alexandre Astruc, and Eric Rohmer, all managed to combine a phenomenal catholicity of taste with basic principles not at all different from Kracauer's. They saw nothing wrong with believing in the essential realism of the film image, while at the same time approving countless uses of that image. The realism of the *raw material* of cinema is not, in their view, a restriction on the kinds of cinematic *form* that material may take.

The difference in practical criticism between the work of these French realists and Kracauer is enormous because of their opposite feelings toward cinematic form. Take, for instance, the question of adaptation. In a notorious *Cahiers du cinéma* article[4] Truffaut had roundly attacked the work of Jean Aurenche and Pierre Bost for their cinematic reworking of such literary masterpieces as *Symphonie pastorale, Devil in the Flesh,* and *The Red and the Black* and for their proposed adaptation of Bernanos's *Diary of a Country Priest.* This last project had been rejected and given instead to Robert Bresson. Truffaut compared the methods of Aurenche and Bost to those of Bresson, just as Kracauer did, and came to opposite conclusions. For him, Aurenche and Bost stereotyped French literature in adapting it all according to perfect studio methods. The precise psychological acting styles are true to French film style of the 1940s and 50s but are certainly not true in equal measure to Gide, Radiguet, Stendhal, and especially Bernanos. The "studio look" of all the sets, even in their exact historical reconstruction, does not really do justice to the atmospheres created by these authors, although it does show up the decorative ability of the film architects. Finally, the altered scenes and dialogues which Aurenche and Bost contrived certainly visualize these novels but in doing so they make them over into something they are not: French films.

For Truffaut, and for Bazin to whom most of Truffaut's ideas on this matter are indebted, it is Bresson's slavish, visually murky adaptation which is true to the novel and therefore most cinematic. The voice-over narration, which so appalled Kracauer, is seen by Truffaut and Bazin as the perfect answer to the problems posed by such a text. At the end of his *Cahiers du cinéma* essay Truffaut rammed his point home by reproducing several scenes from the rejected adaptation script written by Aurenche and Bost. True, these scenes are highly visual; true, they clarify the motivations of the characters; true, they allow for expressive histrionics. But it is exactly these qualities which would have reduced the Bernanos to the level of conventional French film productions. Bresson, in retaining the visual and psychological ambiguity of the original, in reducing acting gestures to a minimum, and in adding a reflective narration taken verbatim from the priest's diary, has given us a film unlike other French films but very like the reality it wanted to be faithful to, the reality of the Bernanos novel itself.

The Bresson film will never appeal to the massive film audience which Aurenche and Bost always reach, but this is only because a massive film audience would (perhaps could) never respond to the subtleties of Georges Bernanos.

Kracauer's vast bibliography includes not one reference to Bazin or his followers. Had he been familiar with Truffaut's essay and Bazin's theories, Kracauer no doubt would have argued that cinema is basically a "visual medium" and that Aurenche and Bost have excellent visual imaginations. But the realists at *Cahiers* were not convinced that "realistic" cinema is equivalent to "highly visual" cinema, for reality is not equal to the visible. In the decade before Kracauer's theory appeared, and somehow unbeknownst to him, they had been seeking the forms of reality cinema could illuminate. On a realistic basis, not very different from Kracauer's own, they had been asking not "what is cinematic?" but "what is cinema?"

6

André Bazin

The writings of André Bazin are unquestionably the most important of realist film theory, just as those of Eisenstein are the most important of formative theories. Like Eisenstein, Bazin never constructed a clear deductive system, but his ideas do have a solid logic and consistency running through them, and their very diversity and complexity give them a richness and cultural impact rivalled only by those of Eisenstein.

We have seen that theorists advocating a formative cinematic tradition were practically unopposed until the end of World War II. This was the case because the formative theory of film was consistent with traditional theories of art and most of cinema's earliest aestheticians (Munsterberg, Malraux, Arnheim, Balázs, and Eisenstein) had been involved with other arts. While Marcel L'Herbier, Dziga Vertov, and the Grierson school of British documentary filmmakers were influential advocates of the "photographic" properties of film, André Bazin was the first critic to effectively challenge the formative tradition. He was without question the most important and intelligent voice to have pleaded for a film theory and a film tradition based on a belief in the naked power of the mechanically recorded image rather than on the learned power of artistic control over such images.

From 1945 to 1950 Bazin's voice was more and more evident in continental film criticism. His theoretical espousal of realistic cinema coincided precisely with the ascendency of Italian neo-realism. Bazin's theories rose to popularity with these films and at the same time guided them to their proper audience. In 1951 he, along with Jacques Doniol-Valcroze, began *Cahiers du cinéma,* the most influential single critical periodical in the short history of cinema.

Cahiers du cinéma gave Bazin the home base he needed to set a critical trend in film. To him came young critics seeking a new and revivified cinema. Such men as François Truffaut, Jean-Luc Godard, Pierre Kast, Eric Rohmer, and Claude Chabrol listened to Bazin and wrote under his tutelage. Later, of course, they created the influential New Wave cinema in France. As Chabrol and Truffaut were preparing the pioneer films of this movement late in 1958, Bazin died. He was forty years old.

As is widely known, Bazin himself never left a systematic book of theory, though his English translator, Hugh Gray, is quick to point out that this in no way indicates a lack of system in his thought. It illustrates instead an important aspect of his personality, the sociability of his scholarship. Unlike Kracauer, who spent years alone in a library generating his *Theory of Film,* Bazin seems always to have been with people who were making films or discussing them. His writings appeared in journals more often than not as part of an implicit dialogue with a filmmaker or with another critic. It has been suggested that the best of his criticism has been lost because it occurred in the form of oral presentations and debates at such places as I.D.H.E.C. (Institut des Hautes Études Cinématographiques), the French film school. In any case Bazin displayed little concern for the future of his ideas. He seemed satisfied that his thoughts could be of service in particular situations.

The most important of his essays Bazin began to collect in 1957 under the title *Qu'est-ce que le cinéma?*. This collection posthumously reached four volumes comprising some sixty essays. Nearly half of these essays have appeared in English under the title *What Is Cinema?* and *What Is Cinema?, II.*[1]

From 1954 until his death Bazin strove to complete a book on the filmmaker, Jean Renoir. His notes and fragments for this book have been published recently in France and translated into English. While this work is fragmentary, it remains a formidable critical treatise containing some of Bazin's most important ideas. The rest of Bazin's work—a short book on Welles, a collection on Chaplin, and several hundred articles—have not been translated. Even so, the core of Bazin's theory and the method of his mind are fully evident in the three translated volumes currently available.

While the fragmentary method of his writing may have prevented him from organizing a fully elaborated system like Kracauer's, it gives to his writing both a density of thought and a constructive dependence upon his examples which are absent from Kracauer. Bazin's usual procedure was to watch a film closely, appreciating its special values and noting its difficulties or contradictions. Then he would imagine "the kind" of film it was or was trying to be, placing it within a genre or fabricating a new genre for it. He would formulate the laws of this genre, constantly reverting to examples taken from this film and others like it. Finally, these "laws" would be seen in the context of the whole theory of cinema. Thus Bazin begins with the most particular facts available, the film before his eyes, and through a process of logical and imaginative reflection, he arrives at a general theory.

Unquestionably the most striking instance of this procedure is the essay "The Virtues and Limitations of Montage" (*What Is Cinema?*, pp. 41-53). Here Bazin begins, not with questions about film language, but with a discussion about the possibility of a truly "fairy tale" cinema. This discussion was preceded by his viewing two children's films, only one of which seemed to develop into its proper form. From such a seemingly humble and particular start Bazin somehow leads us into one of the most profound and important treatments on film language yet written.

This method makes reading Bazin exciting but it makes summarizing him extremely difficult, for no summary can capture that style of theorizing and writing which may be the most valuable thing we can learn from Bazin. As we did with Eisenstein, we must assemble Bazin's consistent but widely scattered viewpoints, trying not to discard his special approach in our search for order. In fact this situation is worse with Bazin, for many of his most revealing arguments and statements are vitally attached to the films which provoked those thoughts and which provide him with a wealth of examples. Often, as in the case of "The Virtues and Limitations of Montage," Bazin's articles have outlived the insignificant films which occasioned the writing.

To gather, organize, and compare his scattered and engaged ideas we will have to content ourselves with investigating his theory under the four controlling categories of matter, means, form, and goal, all the while realizing that much of the "quality" of his theorizing will escape this approach. It is no coincidence that the most fertile theorists, Bazin and Eisenstein, markedly resist easy description.

THE RAW MATERIAL

As we have seen, Kracauer's *Theory of Film* seems a model of research and scholarship, but his vast bibliography somehow neglects altogether the writings of André Bazin. Nowhere is this more apparent than in Kracauer's attempt to show that photography and film exist to explore and expose a raw material of brute reality. Kracauer's discussion of this most basic issue is fraught with problems and is at best simplistic. Bazin, some fifteen years earlier, had engaged the same issues with much the same attitude. His results, while problematic, are denser and more thought-provoking than Kracauer's.

From the first, and in nearly every essay, Bazin proclaimed the dependence of cinema on reality. "Cinema attains its fullness," he said, "in being the art of the real."[2] Unlike Kracauer, Bazin constantly strove to clarify what he meant by reality. We talk about many kinds of reality, but cinema depends first upon a visual and spatial reality, the real world of the physicist. Thus cinema's core realism is "not certainly the realism of subject matter or realism of expression, but that realism of space without which moving pictures do not constitute cinema" (*What Is Cinema?*, p. 112). Bazin here moved beyond Kracauer's material aesthetic, the aesthetic of realistic content and technique, to an aesthetic of space. Cinema is

first of all the art of the real because it registers the spatiality of
objects and the space they inhabit.

This basic thesis of cinematic realism is not very fruitful in practice because it cannot tell us why cinema *seems* realistic. It is a
physical realism which doesn't take the spectator into account.
Bazin's second thesis aims directly at our experience of cinema and
might be termed a psychological thesis of realism. He began with
an analysis of the psychological realism of photography which he
differentiated absolutely from painting:

> For the first time, between the originating object and its repro-
> duction there intervenes only the instrumentality of a nonliving
> agent. For the first time, the image of the world is formed auto-
> matically, without the creative intervention of man. . . . All
> the arts are based on the presence of man, only photography
> derives an advantage from his absence. Photography affects us
> like a phenomenon in nature, like a flower or a snowflake whose
> vegetable or earthly origins are an inseparable part of their
> beauty (*What Is Cinema?*, p. 13).

In numerous passages such as this Bazin's claim about the
realism of cinema is based not on a physicist's notion of reality but
on a psychologist's notion. We view cinema as we view reality not
because of the way it looks (it may look unreal) but because it
was recorded mechanically. This inhuman portrait of the world
intrigues us and makes of cinema and photography not the media
of man but the media of nature.

In a psychological sense, realism has to do not with the accuracy
of the reproduction but with the spectator's belief about the origin
of the reproduction. In painting this origin involves the skill and
mind of an artist confronting an object. In photography it involves
an indifferent physical process confronting a physical object. The
fact that the photograph is of the same nature as the object (purely
physical and subject only to physical laws) makes it ontologically
different from traditional types of reproduction:

> The objective nature of photography confers on it a quality of
> credibility absent from all other picture-making. . . . We are

forced to accept as real the existence of the object reproduced, actually represented, set before us, that is to say, in time and space. Photography enjoys a certain advantage in virtue of this transference of reality from the thing to its reproduction (*What Is Cinema?*, p. 13).

With cinema, then, we are struck by two kinds of realistic feelings. First, cinema records the space of objects and between objects. Second, it does so automatically, that is, inhumanly. For Bazin every photograph begins to affect us with a primitive psychological impetus derived from the fact that it is linked to the image it represents by means of a photo-chemical transference of visual properties. If we notice that the photo has been touched up after the fact or that the objects represented were tampered with before the fact, some of the psychological impetus will be lost.

Now Bazin was not naïve. He realized that this photochemical transference, which makes of cinema nature's work rather than man's, requires an enormous, complex technology: it requires celluloid, emulsion, a proper camera, exact development, and a projector, not to mention focus and light control. This technology is the invention and work of men. Bazin was arguing, though, that man had created these inventions and works with them so that nature will ooze onto the celluloid where it can be preserved and studied. The technological history of film can be told as the story of man seeking ways to let nature work its magic more and more fully. If Arnheim were correct and cinema derived its power from its unreality, then we would have to agree with him that such realistic developments as sound, color, 3-D, and Cinerama are superfluous. But these inventions were demanded, Bazin claimed, by the underlying spirit of what cinema is, by the desire for perfect representation of reality.

While technology may be bringing cinema to closer and closer approximations of visible reality and while the human mind may be ready to give to the photograph a kind of blind faith in its realism, the film image is obviously not exactly the same as the reality it stems from. In a series of striking and thought-provoking metaphors, Bazin tried to account for the difference between the photograph and its object, and difference he claims the mind is disposed to erase. He called the photograph "a mould in light" (*What Is Cinema?*, p. 96). The photograph takes an "impression" of the object, like the "casting of a death-mask."[3] It is not the real object but rather its real and verifiable *"tracing,"* its "fingerprint." We are psychologically stunned by such tracings because they have been actually left by the object they make us recall. Thus Robinson Crusoe is terrified by the footprint of Friday, not because it looks like Friday, but because it was really made by him. In his most lyrical and evocative style Bazin said that we love the crude pictures taken by the mountaineer Herzog at the summit of Everest because "The camera was there like the veil of Veronica pressed to the face of human suffering" (*What Is Cinema?*, p. 163). There may be accurate and beautiful pictures of Christ but none of them will have for us that eerie sense of his presence which Veronica's veil claims. Similarly Hollywood has made in its studios exciting and visually stunning films about mountain climbing but none has the authentic thrill of the clumsy Herzog photographs clicked off in moments of real crisis, for these moments and these crises have thus been preserved.

To sum up, Bazin like Kracauer felt that brute reality is at the heart of cinema's appeal; but unlike Kracauer he tried desperately to show in just what way it functions. He concluded that the raw material of cinema is not reality itself but the tracings left by reality on celluloid. These tracings have two absolutely important properties. First they are genetically linked to the reality they mirror, as a mould is linked to its model. Second, these tracings are already comprehensible. They do not have to be deciphered in the way a fingerprint does, or an electrocardiogram or even an X ray. These other tracings of reality are at second removed from their object. But photographs are as accessible as our everyday vision. Not only has the world made a tracing of itself in cinema, it has nearly duplicated its visual reality for us. Cinema then stands beside the world, looking just like the world. While it is incorrect to speak of "reality" appearing on the screen, Bazin provided a more exact term borrowed from geometry. Cinema, he said, is an *asymptote of reality,* moving ever closer to it, forever dependent on it.

While this definition of film's raw material is more precise and richer than Kracauer's simple equation of film and reality, it is, nonetheless, even in Bazin's system, a principle rather than a deduction. The filmmaker Eric Rohmer, a close associate of Bazin's, called this principle "the objectivity axiom," suggesting that it is at the very heart of all Bazin's thinking.[4] Axioms are not proved; they can only be held up as self-evident. Once they are accepted the theorist (whether mathematician or aesthetician) is free to use them to derive a system, but his system will never "prove" the truth of the axiom. In the case of Kracauer, we saw that no matter how much he wrote about film from the realistic perspective, his basic tenets about realism always remained in question. Bazin, realizing this difficulty, continually tried to demonstrate the adequacy of his axiom. He did so, as we have just seen, first of all by narrowing the scope of his axiom as finely as he could. The concepts of tracing and asymptote are more subtle than Kracauer's undifferentiated reality. Then Bazin called on our belief in this axiom through his endless store of metaphors and analogies. If one accepts his premise that a death mask carries its model with it in a special sense, then one is forced to believe in cinema's basic objectivity.

We will see that this raw material can in the hands of artists, be shaped into countless varied forms. "Art is what artists do" and sculpture is what artists do with solid materials. In the same way, film art is what filmmakers do with these tracings of reality.

Bazin did have a prejudice which it is only fair to emphasize in concluding this section. Just as many art critics place highest value on those abstractions in oil or marble which return us to the material from which they arise, so Bazin felt that cinema at its highest will always press us back to its raw beginnings, to the crude mold of reality and through its technical genesis, to reality itself.

CINEMATIC MEANS AND FORM

Bazin versus Traditional Theory

We have seen that Kracauer, after determining that the raw material filmmakers must shape is reality itself, urged those filmmakers to limit themselves primarily to realistic means in producing films which have a realistic form. This restricting position has annoyed many critics who feel that filmmakers should be allowed to do anything they please with their raw material, even if this material be reality itself.

Hostile critics often attempt to link Bazin with Kracauer because of his lifelong praise of realistic films. Bazin's belief in the realistic nature of the photographic image led him, to be sure, to a predilection for realistic films but only in these respects: he felt that most films conform to their material rather than against it and that every filmmaker, no matter what his intentions, must take into account the realistic nature of his material, even if he wants to deform or distort that material. Raw material, then, exerts a compelling but not a final influence on the medium. Bazin had a horror of prescriptive aesthetics which dictate what is cinematic from what is not. Always the existentialist, he believed that "cinema's existence precedes its essence" (*What Is Cinema?*, p. 71) that theorists must describe and explain what has been done in cinema instead of deducing what should be done from some abstract system.

Bazin's many remarks on the objectivity of film's raw material, then, stand to the side of his consideration of the work of the filmmaker. In his abstract jargon, the ontology of cinema stands to the side of the language and function of cinema. It exerts a pull or force on that language but it does not absolutely dictate how cinema is to be used.

Most of Bazin's writing investigates the style and form of actual works of cinema. He was basically a genre critic, deriving his theories about cinematic means (language) from his meditations on the purpose and shape (form) of films. Bazin perceived a necessary causal link between a film's form and its means. In practice this came down to a relation between genre and style. For instance, the city symphonies of the twenties (like *Berlin* or *Rien que les heures*) were characterized not only by their subject matter, but by rhythmic editing on matched forms, by hide and seek cameras, and by the frequent use of natural dollies like escalators and trollies. In this example even the name of the genre signalled the style which created it. Bazin had an unequalled talent for discerning the genre of a film (its form and the psychological impact of the form) and then discovering the stylistic laws which govern that form and deliver its psychological rewards.

The raw material of cinema, then, is made "to signify" through various cinematic means and it achieves its proper "signification" when it finds its forms. It is up to the theorist to study the various processes (means) by which a filmmaker can make reality (the raw material) significant and, more particularly, to make it significant in a certain humanly valuable way (form). Most of the major essays Bazin wrote can be best seen in the light of this terminology: how does a filmmaker make his material signify and what kind of signification has he formed? These were the crucial questions for Bazin and he seldom separated them.

Signification is the result of style; significance, the result of form. Both style and form in cinema can be determined by paying attention to the kinds and amount of abstraction which the filmmaker employs or creates in dealing with his raw material. Realism in the use of cinema is opposed to abstraction (i.e., symbolization and convention). Bazin saw in realism a kind of style which reduced signification to a minimum. In other words, he saw the rejection of style as a potential stylistic option.

While all films exhibit empirical reality lifted to some degree of abstraction, the ratio between the two determines the primary interest and purpose of any given film. For instance, if a director is trying to tell a complex story in cinema, he is likely to use pictures of empirical reality to create the abstract relationships which form the story. In such a case, he "has subordinated the wholeness of reality to the 'sense' of the action; [he] has transformed this reality without our knowledge into a series of 'abstract signs.' "[5]

It is precisely this process of the transformation of empirical reality into abstraction that in the eyes of traditional film aesthetics constitutes the art of the cinema. Munsterberg, Eisenstein, Arnheim, and Malraux are all on record as having condemned cinema's crude appeal to actuality. All of them claimed that cinema became an art when man began intelligently to shape this mute material, to transform it. Eisenstein and Arnheim went furthest in this direction, the latter seeing in silent cinema a symbol system as conventional as, but more evocative than, verbal language.

There are two major ways in which cinema can speak a conventional language. First, the filmmaker has the ability to manipulate several formal aspects of the image in order to give to the image of reality the shape he desires. Second, the filmmaker can give to his images any context he desires through the formative editing process known as "montage." In the first case he manipulates the light scale, the grays, the composition within the frame, the foreshortening of the third dimension, the isolation of the sense of sight from the other senses, and so forth. In the second case he "builds" the discursive or narrative meaning of the already "stylized" images by controlling their rhythm and the context in which they appear. Both Malraux and Eisenstein assign to montage the full artistic capability of cinema, because it confers on images a purely mental design in the same way that rhythm confers on sounds a design which we distinguish as music.

Until Bazin, virtually every theorist was at pains to indicate the similarity between either the film image and the plastic arts or between film continuity and music. Bazin was the first to see that because of its natural origins, the unadorned mold of reality has its own aesthetic validity, if by this we mean a rendering of the given in such a way as to focus attention upon it as if it had intrinsic value. In writing of a medical film, Bazin asked:

> What cinema of the imagination would have been able to conceive and convey the fabulous descent into the inferno of the bronchioscope where all the laws of "dramatization" of color are naturally implied in the sinister bluish reflection of a cancer which is visibly mortal? . . . The camera alone [i.e., the crude mechanical reproduction] possesses the sesame of this universe in which supreme beauty becomes identified, at one and the same time, with nature and chance: that is to say identifies with everything that a certain traditional aesthetic considers the contrary of art.[6]

In this case, "There is nothing aesthetically retrogressive about simple cinematographic recording, on the contrary, there is progress in expression, a triumphant evolution of the language of cinema, an extension of its stylistics" (*What Is Cinema?*, II, p. 26).

The director of the medical film has no thought other than to render what he sees in as simple and unadorned a manner as possible. Expressive composition may have artistic merit, may be a cornerstone of cinematic language, but Bazin could conclude that in this film such manipulative techniques would have worked against the form of the film whose purpose was to make visible a drama created by nature, not by filmmakers.

This example of the pure documentary is a typical case which can stand for a host of different kinds of films whose subjects or purposes can be attained only by a conception of cinematic art not subordinate to "symbolic transformation." Films which have "realistic" pretenses and still employ "symbolic" styles are fraudulent; they have chosen conventional means which are not suitable to their realist goals. The realist pretense in film can be defined as the disposition to seek and present the significance one finds in objects by means of the objects concerned rather than by using these objects to body forth an idea not already implicit in them. Of de Sica's work, Bazin said, "The events are not necessarily signs of something, a truth of which we are to be convinced, they all carry their own weight, their complete uniqueness, that ambiguity that characterizes any fact" (*What Is Cinema?*, II, p. 52).

For Bazin the situation was clear: either a filmmaker utilizes empirical reality for his personal ends or else he explores empirical reality for its own sake. In the former case the filmmaker is making of empirical reality a series of signs which point to or create an aesthetic or rhetorical truth, perhaps lofty and noble, perhaps prosaic and debased. In the latter case, however, the filmmaker brings us closer to the events filmed by seeking the significance of a scene somewhere within the unadorned tracings it left on the celluloid.

Bazin, then, differs from conventional film theorists in two important respects. First, he posed a goal for cinema which is outside the realm of our usual conception of art: cinema as a "sesame" to universes unknown; cinema as a new sense, reliable like our natural senses, giving us knowledge of empirical reality otherwise unavailable. The other major difference which distinguishes Bazin from other film theorists is his belief that cinematographic language is more than a list or dictionary of potentials for abstraction, that it includes all the possibilities of the unadorned image and the un-edited scene as well.

To investigate his remarks concerning the limitations of the abstractive capabilities of cinema is to focus on the bulk of his writing and at the same time to see him sharply defined against a backdrop of traditional film aesthetics. Bazin characterized the conventional understanding of cinema language as

> . . . very broadly speaking, everything that the representation on the screen adds to the object there represented. This is a complex inheritance but it can be reduced essentially to two categories: those that relate to the plastics of the image and those that relate to the resources of montage, which, after all, is simply the ordering of images in time (*What Is Cinema?*, p. 24).

Thus Bazin saw the problem very simply: in trying to make a significant film the filmmaker must confront the raw reality of his material with his own abstractive abilities. The style and form of the film is the outcome of this confrontation. We can watch this crucial confrontation at two places: in the plastics (i.e., quality) of the image, and in the montage (i.e., ordering) of images.

Bazin felt that film theory up to his time had been able to account for only the most obvious kinds of style and form. The most abstract techniques and forms were consistently praised as being the most cinematic or the most artistic. It was his purpose to show that cinematic signification is a continuum from the most unadorned realistic films to the most abstract. He went about his task in two ways. First, he continually debunked and discredited the view that only abstract techniques and films are truly cinematic. Second, he brought to light and praised numerous types of films and techniques which had been neglected by formative film theory. We can see this dual approach at work both in his scattered remarks about the plastics of the image and also in his continual references to montage.

The Plastics of the Image
Bazin wrote comparatively little directly dealing with the aesthetics of the image. He did, however, consistently advocate technical de-

velopments which would render screen perception closer to natural perception. He praised Gregg Toland's 17mm lens, which in *Citizen Kane* provided an angle of vision similar to human vision and which, with the help of refinements in lighting and filmstock, rendered objects in focus from seven to three hundred feet. Similarly he found in Cinerama a size of visual field that measured 146 degrees, from periphery to periphery, and by this technical fact reduced the power of artistic stylization. The spectator is no longer glued to a small box, a slave to the changing shapes through which a director may try to affect his response. He is no longer hypnotized by a kaleidoscope which the director controls. He is at last freed by the realism of the screen size itself. As Bazin said, the spectator "is not only able to move his eyes; he is forced to turn his head."[7]

We should recall here that definite geometrical framing had been a cornerstone of Arnheim's belief in film as art. But film history challenged this technique as it had previously challenged the black and white film and the silent cinema. For his part, Bazin gladly anticipated an age when even the two-dimensional screen would be filled out in full relief, striking down the major difference between screen perception and actual perception.

While praising naturalistic techniques, Bazin also debunked, as old-fashioned and immature, crude unrealistic conventions such as the superimposition. As in Victor Sjöstrom's *Phantom Chariot* (1920), the superimposition "meant" that the supernatural was present in many early films. But as film history and technology matured, ways were found to insist on this fact without shattering the realism of the image.

In general, then, technology has been at work not in creating new kinds of conventions but in perfecting the complete realism of the image. Thus man's technological impulse has often been an embarrassment for traditional film theorists like Arnheim. Of course technically faithful images of reality can be used in the most abstract of ways. We need only look toward the work of the Soviet montage filmmakers for proof of this. So Bazin's discussion of technical realism is an aside at best and must give way to a more substantial topic, decor.

The Phantom Chariot, 1920. The Museum of Modern Art/Film Stills Archive

Bazin's conception of plastic values in cinema is best seen in relation to his view of theater decor. Bazin believed that stylization and convention are the essence of the theater, marking it off at the outset from cinema. He isolated cinema from theater in numerous ways. First of all, film was born of a different psychological need, the need for representation. Second, the very locus of its presentation has deceptively little in common with that of theater. Although both film and play audiences exclaim, "Tonight we are going to the theater," they are in one case going to a place of ritual (theater) and in the other to "a window on their dreams" (cinema).

Bazin offered us many long passages showing that the architecture of a theater together with its decor focuses our minds and eyes on the drama being played out within it. Costume, language, footlights, etc., all put us in an abstract and absolute universe. By contrast in cinema the screen appears as a window. Like many theorists since, Bazin distinguished the frame of a painting from that of a movie. He called the outer edges of the screen "a piece of masking that draws only a portion of reality." When a character walks out of sight, "he continues to exist in his own capacity at some place in the decor which is hidden from us. There are no wings to the screen" (*What Is Cinema?,* p. 105) as there are in theater, for an actor to wait until he is needed on stage.

Bazin's lengthy reflections on these differences of theater from cinema coalesce into one of his most elaborate and beautiful analogies. The force of theater is centripetal, with everything functioning to bring the spectator, like a moth, into its swirling light. The force of cinema is, on the contrary, centrifugal, throwing the interest out into a limitless, dark world which the camera constantly strives to illuminate.

> "The theatre," says Baudelaire, "is a crystal chandelier." If one were called upon to offer in comparison a symbol other than this artificial crystal-like object, brilliant, intricate, and circular, which refracts the light which plays around its center and holds us prisoners of its aureole, we might say of the cinema that it is the little flashlight of the usher, moving like an uncertain comet across the night of our waking dream, the diffuse space without shape or frontiers that surrounds the screen (*What Is Cinema?,* p. 107).

Clearly it would be a mistake for cinema to try to emulate theater decor, theater costuming, and theater staging. Yet this was exactly the project of the German Expressionists whose work is so often cited as exemplary by theorists like Arnheim. Bazin, then, at first belittled the universality of the formative aesthetic. He claimed that plastic values in cinema must take into account its essential realism. He then turned more positively to establishing the importance and beauty of several genres which refuse plastic manipulation and remain true to realistic decor. The films of Jean Renoir and the genre of theatrical adaptations are the most powerful examples of such films.

Henry V, 1944: Shakespeare's words in their centripetal space. The Museum of Modern Art/Film Stills Archive

Bazin wrote many articles on adaptations of all sorts (films based on fiction, theater, architecture, painting, music). His remarks on theatrical adaptation may serve to show his general attitude. Consistently Bazin advocated filming the artificiality of the play rather than transforming it into a cinematic artificiality through stylized decor. In a notable example, he praised Olivier's *Henry V,* which opens by showing us the theater, the stage, and the props of a Shakespearean Production, in contrast to the London about them. Shakespeare's words, then, reverberate in their natural centripetal stylized space instead of being lost in a false attempt to transform reality into a setting for them. This film in fact moves through several layers of setting, Shakespeare's verse providing both its continuity and unity. Appyling Bazin's Baudelairean analogy to the problem, we can see the reasons for Bazin's firm disapproval of total transformations of plays into the "art of the film." His solution was to turn the "flashlight" of cinema onto the "crystal chandelier" of theater, to film the abstract reality of the play and to learn to film it faithfully.

While the film of a play should look stylized, this stylization will be seen as coming from the original rather than as being given to the original by a "cinematic interpretation or reworking." If the purpose of this genre or form of film is to retain that very special reality of the original masterpiece, then cinema must employ none of its own formative plastic tricks; it must let the original shine through as purely as possible.

Those of us who have never seen the Taj Mahal or Michelangelo's David are grateful to the photographer who uses his most objective lenses to bring these masterpieces to us in pictures. Why praise the "creative" photographer who shows off his photographic techniques and talent by offering us "arty" pictures whose filters, distorting lenses, obscure lighting, or unnatural perspective transform these originals into mere pictures. It is all a question of genre. Bazin never condemned outright the genre of creative experimental cinematography. But if the purpose of a genre is the replication of artworks taken from other media, then such plastic deformation is silly and in error. The form demands realistic means in order that we can marvel at the stylization of the original.

Utterly different from adaptation is the case of Jean Renoir, whose work provided Bazin with his most illuminating insights into stylization in cinema. Bazin wanted desperately to establish the mastery of Renoir even though it is difficult for audiences to decipher the impact of his style. With other directors, one can simply disregard the objects represented in characteristic images and be left with a style; for example, Eisenstein generally employed diagonal composition and placed his subject slightly to the left of screen-center. Of the many books and articles devoted to this kind

Jean Renoir's *A Day in the Country,* 1937. *Blackhawk Films*

of study, Lotte Eisner's *The Haunted Screen,* a marvelous explanation of the graphics of German Expressionist films, is unquestionably the finest.[8]

Such stylistic examinations reveal practically nothing, however,
when applied to a director like Jean Renoir. We are disappointed
because we expect to see in his work a legacy of pictorial values
passed down from his father, Auguste, but Renoir works with
other values in mind. To take one example, Bazin recalls that all of
Renoir's many boat scenes avoid the use of the rear projection.
Nearly all other directors of that era would employ studio techniques in such scenes both to be able to record dialogue with
higher fidelity and to allow them to create the precise pictorial
image they want. But,

In *A Day in the Country* (1937), the opening of a shutter ushers in both joy and desire. Renoir's lens allows this to happen naturally, without disturbing the space or time of the scene. *Blackhawk Films*

153

this technique would be unthinkable for Renoir, for it necessarily dissociates the actors from their surroundings and implies that their acting and their dialogue are more important than the reflection of the water on their faces, the wind in their hair, or the movement of a distant branch. . . . A thousand examples could illustrate this marvelous sensitivity to the physical, tactile reality of an object and its milieu; Renoir's films are made from the surfaces of the objects photographed.[9]

If one looks with the careful eye of Renoir, one does not need to shape appearances into meaningful relationships, for the world will begin to radiate its own meaning. This is why Renoir, even before Welles, employed a lens capable of keeping as much of his subject in focus as was technically feasible.

In what sense is such neutrality "style"? Bazin likened this negative film style to the literary style of Gide, Hemingway, Camus, and other modern novelists. He spoke of style as the "inner dynamic principle of the narrative, somewhat like the relation of energy to matter . . . which polarizes the filings of the facts without changing their internal chemistry" (*What Is Cinema?*, II, p. 31). This image, characteristically drawn from the physical sciences for which Bazin had a continual respect, no doubt has its limitations. Nonetheless it serves to reinforce Bazin's insistence on a cinematic art which should exploit to a maximum degree, but without trickery, the impressions made by the empirically real alone. From this follows a central conclusion of Bazin's theory that an artist's vision should be ascertained from the selection he makes of reality, not from his transformation of reality.

This aesthetic of the "neutral style" which finds its epitome in Renoir demands of the audience not that it comprehend the significance which the filmmaker is creating but that it recognize the levels of significance within nature itself. Recall again the example of the medical film wherein nature obeys all the laws of dramatization of color and the filmmaker records them as faithfully as possible.

It appears, then, that Bazin demolished the symbolic and abstract use of cinema only to be able to rebuild it in a new way. While he rejects arbitrary symbols, Bazin allows "correspondances" (a term he borrows from Baudelaire) and sensual meta-phors if they arise from reality itself. He claims that the neorealist directors, for instance, while they seemed to abandon style, actually "reinstated the conventions of style no longer *in* reality but *by means of* reality."[10] Such statements help Bazin avoid the *cul de sac* into which the other great theorist of realist cinema, Siegfried Kracauer, wanders.

Kracauer assumes that cinema must record the everyday occur-rences of life because of its affinity for empirical reality. Bazin, on the other hand, has a far more complex view of reality, conceiving of it as multi-layered. For him empirical reality contains corre-spondances and interrelationships which the camera can find. In addition, man has created a political and artistic world atop "natu-ral reality" and this, too, is available for the camera. Thus while Bazin distrusted abstract and painterly compositions in films, he wholeheartedly supported documentaries on paintings and paint-ers. Similarly, while his theory, like Kracauer's, has no place for German Expressionism, Bazin defended a Czech film on a concen-tration camp which had the precise look of German Expressionism because this horrible decor, this "world of Kafka, or more curi-ously, of de Sade" had an internal fidelity which made it clearly not a whim of an artist but a result of the logic of a political ma-chine.[11] Expressionism here exists not in cinema but in history. Cinema merely records it.

To sum up, then. In regard to the "plastics of the image," true cinematic expression is not a product of a considered use of the idiosyncracies of the medium but instead a value attained when the medium is used realistically, though selectively. Style need not alter reality, but may choose to present certain aspects of it. This notion leads directly to the second category of abstraction.

The Resources of Montage

Without question Bazin's remarks on montage are the best known of his theories. When we discussed the plastics of the image our basic unit was the "object." How should any given object of em-pirical reality look in representation? To take up the question of montage is to assume that the basic unit of film recording is the "event." How should any given event be rendered? An event implies a relationship between terms over a definite period of time. Editing decisions are merely decisions concerning the status of the event filmed and its significance.

Classical film theory conferred on editing the ability to interpret events in the same way that stylization can interpret objects. Malraux, Pudovkin, and Eisenstein all say explicitly that without montage cinema is not an art. Early in his career Bazin made his position clear, that this "celebrated aesthetic judgment of Malraux . . . has been momentously fruitful, but its virtues have been exhausted. The time has come when we have rediscovered the value of brute representation in cinema."[12]

Bazin conceives of two different orders of montage. The first is that associated primarily with the silent cinema whereby images would be conjoined according to some abstract principle of argument, drama, or form. Pudovkin provides the best examples of this. He himself points out the thrill of creating an explosion by editing together several segments of film, none of which were recorded together. No explosion ever occurred, yet Pudovkin has created one from bits of reality. A more famous and abstract case is his claim of having created "joy" by editing together shots of a baby's laughing face, a bubbling brook, and a prisoner whose release is imminent. Any television viewer, today, can quickly confirm the heritage of such "atmospheric" montage. A flood of different images gives us the sense of "Young at Heart" and makes us want to drink a Pepsi. Pudovkin explicitly claimed that his purpose in editing was to lead the spectator step by step into accepting his dramatic understanding of an event. In a simple scene in *Storm over Asia* (1928), the wounded Mongol hero stumbles across a room toward a fishbowl and falls, knocking the bowl onto himself. Generally such a scene might require two or three changes in viewpoint. It could even be done in one uninterrupted take. Pudovkin, however, broke this scene into nineteen fragments to energize the event with the kind of dramatic intensity (and, one might say, ideology) which he had preconceived. The event therefore serves a prior logic. Indeed in the examples here cited, none of the events occurred in nature: there was no explosion, no joy, no fall of a Mongol. In each case fragments gave us the "sense" of such events, more powerfully, Pudovkin believed, than could the bare events themselves.

A second type of montage has been far more prevalent since the coming of sound. This is a psychological montage by means of which an event is broken into those fragments which replicate the changes of attention we would naturally experience were we physically present at the event. For instance, a conversation is given in shot/reverse-shot montage because as a real spectator to such a conversation, our attention would shift from speaker to speaker. Psychological montage merely anticipates the natural rhythm of our attention and our eyes.

Bazin opposed to these types of montage the so-called "depth of field" technique which permits an action to develop over a long period of time and on several spatial planes. If focus remains sharp from the camera lens to infinity, then the director has the option of constructing dramatic interrelationships within the frame (this is termed *mise en scène*) rather than between frames. Bazin prefers such depth of field shooting to montage constructions for three reasons: it is inherently more realistic; certain events demand this more realistic treatment; and it confronts our normal psychological way of processing events, thereby shocking us with a reality we often fail to recognize.

The terms *depth-of-field* and *montage* are stylistic terms referring to potential renderings of events. Bazin, always interested in the relation of the film image to the reality it deals with, asked if one style can be said to be essentially more faithful to the actual event than all other styles. What is perceptual reality, he asked, and what cinematic style (or creative means) reproduces it regardless of the expressive purposes (or created forms) it may serve?

Perceptual reality is, for Bazin, spatial reality: that is, visible phenomena and the spaces which separate them. A realistic style of editing, at the most basic level, is a style which would show an event developing in an integral space. Specifically the realistic film style is that style which preserves the autonomy of objects within what Bazin called the undifferentiated *homogeneity of space*. In general, spatial realism is destroyed by montage and preserved by the so-called *shot-in-depth,* where universal focus pays tribute to the space between objects. The long take and depth-of-field emphasize that primary fact of cinema, its relation, its photo-chemical bond, to perceptual reality and specifically to space. Montage, on the other hand, substitutes for this an abstract time and a differentiated space seeking to create a mental continuity at the expense of perceptual continuity. Given Bazin's notion of reality, montage is essentially a less realistic style.

What gain is there in such realism? Eisenstein claimed that the long take showed a lack of artistic intelligence, a lack of economy, and an uncertainty of meaning. Bazin would agree with this last point, for to him, unity of meaning is a property of the mind and not of nature. Nature has many senses and can be said to speak to us "ambiguously." For Bazin such ambiguity is a value and cinema should preserve it, making us aware of its possibilities. He attacked Eisenstein's method of pruning a fecund reality until one is left with only one's own "unity of meaning."

Bazin argued that reality itself is meaningful, even if ambiguous, and deserves to be left alone in most cases. The first aesthetic emotion attending a film is the bare power of the image traced by real objects. Jean Renoir best exemplified service to this aesthetic:

> [Renoir] alone . . . forced himself to look back beyond the resources provided by montage and so uncovered the secret of a film form that would permit everything to be said without chopping the world up into little fragments, that would reveal the hidden meanings in people and things without disturbing the unity natural to them (*What Is Cinema?*, p. 38).

When Boudu falls from the boat at the end of *Boudu Saved from Drowning,* a single shot keeps him in view, exemplifying Renoir's attitude and technique. The camera must pan to take in the change of situation, but we see a boat actually tip and Boudu actually swim away. A plenitude of metaphors attends this shot (baptism, Lethe, revolution, etc.) but the primary interest, Bazin claimed, is still the physical one—a man swimming into a beautiful river, or better, Michel Simon swimming in the Marne. How different this example is from Pudovkin's Mongol whose symbolic fall occurs only in the spectator's mind and only as Pudovkin dictates. Whereas Pudovkin

Boudu Saved From Drowning, 1932. The Museum of Modern Art/Film Stills Archive

continually cut from shot to shot to give the correct view of the action, Renoir reframed, doing his best to *follow* what is of interest, not to *create* it. Together these techniques of the long take, of reframing, and of shooting in depth sanction not only a unity of place and of action, but also a potentially rich ambiguity of meaning.

As with his inquiry into cinema's raw material, Bazin supplemented the technical or "scientific" side of realism with a meditation on the psychological realism of editing styles. He asked to what extent the technical realism of integral space corresponds to the realities of perception. If realism consists not in fidelity to objects but in fidelity to the normal human perception of objects, then the technical realism of deep focus photography may not be a true or complete realism after all. Considered in relation to the psychology of the spectator, a certain amount of montage may very well be realistic. Obviously the classical editing techniques of Hollywood are designed to present events precisely in the way the mind would naturally understand them. The editing in conventional narrative films follows either a line of logic (Bazin gave the example of a close-up of the murder weapon lying next to the corpse) or the mental preoccupations of the main character or the audience (the cut to a close-up of the doorknob turning). When this kind of editing proceeds with precision the audience is unaware of the manipulation at work. Hollywood films of the thirties were remarkable in this regard and serve as a paradigm for the virtues of this technique. Bazin suggested that the memorable films of this period move along with such logical precision that the effective outcome always seems inevitable. The American filmmakers in this era found that if space were broken up according to the logic of the narrative, it would pass unnoticed as integral or real space. Editors learned to cut a scene into its narrative components and thus follow the line of curiosity of the audience. The film thereby mirrors the perceptual process of the spectator to such a degree that he barely notices that time and space are being fragmented, because he is concerned with the relationships between events not with the intrinsic value of the events themselves.

A story may be defined as a temporal relationship between carefully chosen events. These events are often spatially discontinuous. One sees the wife at home with a lover. Cut to the husband ringing the doorbell of his mistress. When the narrative demands spatial unity, when, for example, the husband returns and finds his wife and her lover together, then the scene's narrative content can be broken (spatially) into discrete bits in order to lead the spectators logically from one narrative image to the next, creating in their minds a seamless story. So, a scene among three characters in a single room would be broken into smoothly integrated shots, each providing a comment on the situation. In a conversation, this is epitomized by the shot/reverse-shot rhythm. In more active scenes, we can think of the movement from long shot to medium shot to close-up, or the use of significant cutaways (the hand turning the doorknob, etc.), all of which interpret the room for the sake of the narrative.

The psychological realism of Hollywood editing is opposed, then, to the technical realism of the long take. An event may be represented as a *physical* whole or it may be analyzed according to its *psychological* wholeness. Spectators rarely watch an event with the disinterestedness corresponding to the single take, which after all, is merely an effective mechanical mold of the event. Instead, they see it in terms of its logical, dramatic, or moral ramifications. This psychologizing of events is the very purpose of most films. They hope

> to give us the illusion of being at real events unravelling before us as in everyday reality. But this illusion conceals an essential bit of deceit because reality exists in continuous space and the screen presents us in fact with a succession of fragments called "shots," the choice, order, and duration of which constitutes exactly what we call the "decoupage" of the film, If we try, by an effort of attention, to perceive the breaks imposed by the camera on the continuous development of the represented event, and try to understand why we are naturally insensible (to these breaks) we understand well enough that we tolerate them because they give us the impression all the same of a continuous homogeneous reality. The insertion of a doorbell in closeup is accepted by the mind as if this were nothing other than a concentration of our vision and interest on the doorbell, as if the camera merely anticipated the movement of our eyes (*Orson Welles*, p. 51).

What Bazin described in his passages concerning *découpage,* or shot breakdown, is a system of conventions which pass unnoticed, leading us to the acceptance of a certain order of things. Psychological montage is an abstraction, but one we readily assent to as being equivalent to the abstractions we generally make.

> Under the cover of the congenital realism of the cinematographic image, a complete system of abstraction has been fraudulently introduced. One believes limits have been set by breaking up the events according to a sort of anatomy natural to the action: in fact one has subordinated the wholeness of reality to the "sense" of the action. One has transformed nature into a series of "signs" (*Orson Welles,* p. 57).

Narrative editing, he said, presupposes that a piece of reality or an event at such and such a moment has but one sense, a sense entirely determined by the action. Such narrative structuring is the antithesis of true realism to Bazin's mind. Because it specifies the meaning of the raw material, it doesn't correspond with man's normal relationship to objective reality. Bazin suggested that while we usually do deal with only one aspect of an object, we recognize that the object extends beyond any single use of it. It may be true that we most often use reality like a box of tools as we work on our personal lives. Nonetheless reality is "always free to modify [our] planned action" (*Orson Welles,* p. 57) and we are always aware that this reality transcends our designs for it.

Bazin was positing here an element of free interplay between man and perceptual objects as an essential aspect of reality. While psychological montage may organize objects as we are in the habit of organizing them, it rules out the freedom which is at the base of our power to organize and the autonomy of the objects which exist for other organizations as well.

> Classical editing totally suppresses this kind of reciprocal freedom between us and the object. It substitutes for a free organization, a forced breaking down where the logic of the shots controlled by the reporting of the action anesthetizes our freedom completely (*Orson Welles,* p. 58).

There is, then a deeper psychological reality, which must be preserved in realistic cinema: the freedom of the spectator to choose his own interpretation of the object or event. Certain directors have employed depth-of-field photography to retain for the spectator this privilege. Bazin found that William Wyler in his early films provided the spectator with a vast amount of information to see and he encouraged that spectator to choose to a large degree his own perspective on what he saw. Proponents of montage claim that Wyler is weak and that his films lack authority, but Bazin found that "the depth of field of William Wyler wants itself to be as liberal and democratic as the conscience of the American spectator and of the heroes of his films."[13] While depth-of-field shooting allowed Wyler to grant the audience a privileged position, other directors have used it to insist on the priority of the world in front of the spectator.

Orson Welles is the perfect example. He used this style so flamboyantly and successfully in his first two films that they gave prestige to what was formerly considered uncinematic. Yet his use of depth-of-field was utterly unlike Wyler's. No one has ever made the mistake of calling Welles democratic. He unnerved the spectator with his depth-of-field because "it forces the spectator to make use of his freedom of attention and forces him at the same time to sense the ambivalence of reality" (*Orson Welles,* pp. 58, 59). Welles's depth-of-field created a threefold realism: ontological realism, giving to objects a concrete density and independence; dramatic realism, refusing to separate actor from decor; and, most important to us at this point, psychological realism, putting "the spectator back into the true conditions of perception in which nothing is ever determined a priori" (*Orson Welles,* p. 60).

Bazin consistently implied an opposition between narrative realism and perceptual realism. If perceptual space and time are rendered with honesty, a narrative will lie obscured within the ambiguities of recalcitrant sense data. If, on the other hand, narrative space and time are the object of a film, perceptual space and time will have to be systematically fragmented and manipulated. In the realism controversy, Bazin has opted for "respect for perceptual space and time." Montage is always in some sense a *telling* of events, while depth-of-field shooting remains at the level of *recording.* Just as Bazin would call the picture of an event more realistic than its description in a newspaper, so he could claim that depth-of-field photography is more realistic than classical editing, no matter how invisible. Bazin's position here may come down to a moral disposition: the spectator *should* be forced to wrestle with the meanings of a filmed event because he *should* wrestle with the meanings of events in empirical reality in his daily life. Reality and realism both insist on the human mind wrestling with facts which are at once concrete and ambiguous.

Despite the possibility of Bazin's moral commitment to depth-of-field, it remains merely a technique which places the film image in close relation to its object. Like other such technical developments (color, sound, widescreen, etc.) the development of depth-of-field filmmaking by no means ensures that realistic cinema will result from its use. Patently surreal or abstract films could be conceived and shot in deep focus. Bazin's point can be taken only so far: in the history of film up to this time, montage is construed as an abstract way to present an event. Deep focus, on the other hand, allows the event to unfold of its own accord and thereby signals to us that the image we are watching is closely linked to the event filmed. Bazin was at his best when he considered particular editing problems and the issues of realism which they raise in relation to specific genres or forms.

THE USES AND MISUSES OF MONTAGE: CINEMATIC PURPOSES

Bazin never condemned montage outright. He did, however, reduce it to a more humble position in the hierarchy of cinematic techniques. He wanted the long take to resume its place as the standard mode of vision in cinema and he praised neorealist films especially for making it once more aesthetically viable. These postwar films composed their stories in real time, rejecting the swiftness and inevitability of classical editing. This does not mean, however, that they denied the value and potential of montage. As Bazin said, "far from wiping out the conquests of montage, this reborn realism gives them a body of reference and a meaning. It is only an increased realism of the image that can support the abstraction of montage" (*What Is Cinema?*, p. 39). *Citizen Kane* is an example Bazin was fond of citing in this regard. Its long takes and ostentatiously deep focus give it a feeling of solidity which compensates for, and indeed suggests, the imaginative flights of its young creator. In other words, the clever tricks of the "boy genius," epitomized by the five-year breakfast scene accomplished through grossly interpretive montage, are abstractions as attempts to impose a meaning or explanation on the life of Kane. They are doomed to failure, Bazin claimed, because the structure of the story demands mystery and ambiguity, and this mystery is present in nearly every image because of the depth-of-field:

> *Citizen Kane* is unthinkable shot in any other way but in depth. The uncertainty in which we find ourselves as to the spiritual key of the interpretation we should put on the film is built into the very design of the image (*What Is Cinema?*, p. 36).

Deep focus, then, adds to the stylistic store of cinema language, permitting a director to choose from several methods of rendering an event and permitting even the resources of stylistic mixtures which twentieth-century literature has found fruitful. Whereas deep focus in most cases is one of several stylistic alternatives, in some scenes it is demanded by the nature of the subject matter. Bazin would go so far as to suggest that some events exist in cinematographic reproduction only to the extent that their spatial unity is preserved *via* depth-of-field and long take.

The nature of certain events demands a cinematic form based on the shot-sequence (uninterrupted camera-take). Examples of such events are numerous in Bazin. The most famous was his praise of the long take in Flaherty's *Nanook of the North* (1923) which renders Nanook struggling with the seal through the hole in the ice. To split this scene up into dramatic fragments "would change it from something real into something imaginary." By this Bazin meant that our interest is in the actuality of the event, attained through its tracing on celluloid. To manipulate this tracing for the purpose of drama would be to shift our interest from the event *qua* event to the drama or meaning of the event.

Bazin pointed to the alligator fight in another Flaherty film, *Louisiana Story* (1946), as an instance in which this latter approach was taken. The scene is rendered in shot/reverse-shot montage and achieves a rhythm which can only be described as exciting. But this rhythm, like the rhythm of the music which accompanies the scene, is really a comment on an event which we never really see. It tells us to be excited and does its best to tell us why, while the event remains on the level of the imagination, constructed in the spectator's mind by the filmmaker, just as Pudovkin's explosion was so constructed. In certain films, indeed in Pudovkin's films, this choice is merely stylistic. The film is an imaginative story and the imaginative resources of montage are surely legitimate. But in the cases of the Flaherty films, we are dealing with an event whose main interest is its actuality. *Nanook of the North* thrills us because Nanook really lived in the Arctic and the camera captured something of his life. To treat this film as a fiction or as an imaginative drama is to reduce its latent power. The film could no longer move us as a record of a fact.

Bazin's respect for the power of factually based films was deeply held. Many of his greatest essays deal with the importance of deep focus for Italian neorealist films. The stated goal of this movement was to pictorialize as far as possible the interlacing structure of physical and social reality. The general method employed to accomplish this goal was to show multifarious causes of any event filmed. Clearly such films must avoid techniques which necessitate the "unity of meaning of the dramatic event." To gain the complexity of meaning which is presupposed by their theories, neorealists are "determined to do away with montage and to transfer to the screen the continuum of reality" (*What Is Cinema?*, pp. 34, 37).

Indeed any filmmaker whose goal is realistic, in the sense that he would like to erase as far as possible his own formative presence from his material, must employ deep focus. Bazin never stopped promulgating that such conventionless style is as artistic as the most carefully devised montage masterpiece. We need only look at slapstick comedy for proof of this, for it exists cinematically only to the extent that its spatial continuity is maintained:

> If slapstick comedy succeeded before the days of Griffith and montage, it is because most of its gags derived from a comedy of space, from the relation of man to things and to the surrounding world. In *The Circus* Chaplin is truly in the lion's cage and both are enclosed within the framework of the screen (*What Is Cinema?*, p. 52).

Imagine a Chaplin film shot with conventional editing. The comedy would no longer exist because the space would be destroyed. Bazin here has debunked one aspect of the commonplace notion that Chaplin was an unimaginative director because he failed to change his shots or come in for close-ups.

Liberty, 1929. Laurel and Hardy suspended in a space at once deep and comic.

To sum up, montage is one element in cinema's handbook of possibilities. It is an abstractive device which works effectively when grounded in a spatially real situation. In most fictional situations it offers the filmmaker an alternative way to represent a scene. But because "it is the aspects of this (filmed) reality that dictate the cutting," certain kinds of situations need to be rendered in the more realistic mode of deep focus and long takes. Such situations may be specific or general. A specific and local case would be the filming of a magic act. Montage techniques would sever our relation to the trick; we would believe in the film and not in the magician. Only if the filmmaker wanted to explain the trick would montage become the appropriate style. A general case would be that of neorealism, a genre comprising many films all purporting to transfer the complexity of social reality onto celluloid without artistic transformation. Depth-of-focus techniques are demanded by situations and theories which thrive on realism—that is, on the spectator's trust that what is given on the screen has not been put there by one man for one purpose, but exists beyond any film of it and beyond any one interpretation.

While Bazin can be seen as a realist because of his special beliefs concerning the raw material of cinema, his realism also can be seen to stem from considerations of the use of cinema: specifically, how must a film look to be realistic, and what gain is there in a realistic use of cinema? Bazin believed that most films benefit from a respect for their raw material and he advocated such respect in the two stages of filmmaking: in the plastic stage and in the editing process.

In propounding a realistic use of the medium, Bazin genuinely believed that he was advocating something far more universal than a mere stylistic trend or reversal. Realism in painting or drama is just another set of conventions, destined to appeal to some artists and some audiences and to be repellent to others, designed for some eras and not for others. As we have seen, cinematic realism for Bazin lies in the absence of convention, in the self-effacement of the artist, in the inchoate virginity of the raw material. This difference from the other arts is possible because photographs, unlike lines and colors, speak to us prior to their context, prior to their formation by an artist.

The realistic filmmaker is not an artless man, though his film may appear devoid of artiness. He is skilled in the arts of self-effacement which are first of all human virtues and secondly aesthetic choices. Such a filmmaker can use the interpretive powers of cinema when he needs them, but he is acutely aware of the primary and primitive powers of the bare image. While it takes artistry to construct significance through the interpretive powers of film, it takes artistry as well to reveal significance through the unadorned image.

Bazin felt that in all this he was not calling for a parochial type of cinema, but was instead expanding our awareness of the vast range of potentialities available in cinematographic language. The poetics of cinema before him had valued only one kind of technique, the birth of new abstract meaning from the deformation or the clever juxtaposition of pieces of raw material. Such techniques are analogous to the metaphor in language. Bazin, while never totally rejecting metaphor, felt that it was time to pay attention to the virtues and capabilities of other kinds of figures in cinema. In poetics there exist also the figures of ellipsis and metonymy in which a part of a whole signifies that whole. In Bazin's theory these figures predominate. The images on the screen for him ordinarily should not signal another totally new imaginative world but rather should signal the world to which they naturally belong. The artist must be primarily a very good observer, selecting from the whole of an event or of a given world just those parts of it which perfectly express it.

It is finally not a question of eliminating one kind of style in order to assert another. Rather Bazin would have us see that the universal prestige of montage and formativism is inadequate for many forms of films. The metonymic use of cinema serves all genres which depend on some kind of realism for their impact. Metaphor is the figure of the mind. Ellipsis and metonymy are figures of the world. We have seen that Bazin believed that the world has a sense, that it speaks to us an ambiguous language if we take care to attend to it, if we silence our own desire to make that world signify what we want it to. This opposition between *signification via* the world and *sense within* the world came to Bazin from Sartre. Cinema more than any other art is naturally able to capture and suggest the sense of a world which flows around and beyond us. It is the art of nature first because it comes to us automatically through a photo-chemical process and second because it reveals to us aspects of the world which formerly we were unable or unwilling to see. Not only do we encounter the world's sense in scientific films which show us micro-close-ups of cells or galaxies, we meet it as well in realist films of all sorts which make us look at a reality which through habit we had ignored or through selfishness we had assigned a signification to. It is the purpose of realistic genres to make us discard our *significations* in order to recover the *sense* of the world. In doing this we retrace the path of the truly realistic filmmaker himself who, like Flaherty, Roberto Rossellini, and Renoir, was always more interested in discovering the world through cinema than in creating a new cinematic world (or worse, speaking their minds) in images taken from reality.

Bazin's nearly religious faith in the power and sense of nature made him champion realistic forms and means. But we must guard against dismissing him as merely a realist. His practice of defining a film form first by its intentions or effects and secondly by the cinematic means necessary for those effects can be applied to all types of film. True, most of his writing does slight formalism and does support realistic film forms; but this can be seen as a corrective necessary at a certain point in film history. Perhaps Bazin's main concern was with the establishment of a broad and supple cinema capable of achieving countless human goals through diverse film forms.

THE FUNCTION OF CINEMA

What were the underlying beliefs Bazin held concerning the importance of the cinema? Why did he devote his life and ruin his health in its service? It has been claimed that his love for the medium was founded on his deeper love for the reality it mediates; but the opposite has also been suggested: that the cinema was always first in Bazin's life, and that his incessant references to reality are, like an art critic's references to pigment, necessary for the understanding of the medium but not the final focus of that understanding.

There are many reasons to suspect that Bazin was first and always the student and ardent lover of the earth which he felt could offer us untold revelations. His lifelong passion for geology, zoology, and botany make it seem as if he wanted cinema to aid our discovery of nature. Similarly his association with the Christian socialist journal *Esprit* and with the communist dominated organization *Travail et culture* point to his commitment to the reorganization of social reality, a commitment served by cinema. In both these areas, cinema appears as a unique and valuable *tool* for knowledge, perception, and, ultimately, action.

However, there is much evidence to support the other view, one which suggests that Bazin's love of cinema was self-sufficient, that he saw cinema as an intrinsically valuable entity. His creation of *Cahiers du cinéma* is a testimony to this value. True, he never stopped insisting on the fundamental role reality plays in cinema; but this view insists that his interest remained with cinema, with the refractions of reality it produces, not with reality itself. His advocacy of a "styleless" approach can be understood, we have seen, not as a desire to do away with cinema in the face of a reality which it usually distorts, but as a way to create a new kind of cinema, a cinema which engages its raw material intimately but which remains forever cinema. After all, he frequently supported his ideas by referring to writers like Hemingway and Dos Passos who had divested themselves of an overwrought literariness to achieve not reality itself but an immediacy to reality which remains literature all the same. Bazin wanted cinema to achieve new styles too, to surpass itself; and he was convinced that "realism" was the major avenue toward such progress.

It is my own view that Bazin held both these conceptions simultaneously or, better, dialectically. His love of the natural world, for which he was often called "a modern St. Francis," no doubt energized his vision of cinema. But this vision of cinema in turn became sufficient unto itself; Bazin appreciated film not as a *tool* with which to view nature but as a remarkable *product* of science and nature. His desire to see cinema expand into new areas was nurtured, then, at one and the same time by his concern for the future of cinema and by his concern for the future of reality, or at least of our relation to reality.

In this latter concern his attitude is of course similar to the one promulgated by Kracauer in the Epilogue to *Theory of Film*. Both men felt that cinema can provide a common non-ideological understanding of the earth from which men can begin to forge new and lasting social relations. Fed by the philosophy of Henri Bergson, André Malraux, Teilhard de Chardin, Gabriel Marcel, Maurice Merleau-Ponty, Emmanuel Mounier, and Jean-Paul Sartre, Bazin's aspirations for man's life on earth went well beyond Kracauer's.

Taken together these writers paid tribute to the creative energy of man directed at the ambiguous mystery of nature and the future. From Teilhard Bazin adopted the belief in the evolution of the earth itself and of all forms of life on earth. From Malraux he learned to read in the arts of the past man's developing spirit in the face of "the human condition." From Sartre and Marcel he imbibed the sense of adventure which both men associated with the "authentic" life. The cinema was for him a light which "man the traveller" (Marcel) could shine into the darkness that surrounds him as he projects himself toward the future and a destiny to be created.

Cinema always had for Bazin this status of sixth sense or privileged tool within the world view sketched above. But cinema went far beyond this status for Bazin, especially toward the end of his life. It became for him something to be studied like any natural or human process. It began to appear to him as an organism developing out of its own seeds and in a variety of environments. Cinema, in other words, could be studied as an "object" in itself.

Bazin was fascinated by the hypothesis that the cinema responds to the forces of growth and increasing complexity which govern other processes, and by the equally intriguing belief that cinema has certain inherited traits. He felt that this process, which has been with us for only three generations, could be understood only by taking into account its genetic "givens" and the history of its development within specific environmental forces. Bazin's existentialism kept him from trying to seek or formulate an essence which cinema ought to be or become. Instead, he hoped to do for cinema what Sartre had done for man: to make it aware of its freedom and possibilities, to unshackle it from old theories which tie it to particular self-conceptions or ideologies. "What is cinema?" Bazin ceaselessly asked without ever wanting or hoping to arrive at a definite conclusion. Cinema is that which it has been and can become; it is the story of its evolution, a process always growing, always becoming and revealing itself more.

This attitude explains the historical orientation of Bazin's theories. To understand cinema it is essential to take account of its origins and observe the directions of its growth in a changing milieu. Bazin saw cinema as the product of two parents and of two genetic strains. In this he was not at all original. On the one side is realism and on the other, institutionalism. Its realism comes first from painting which had carried with it since the Renaissance the desire for the duplication of the concrete world which Bazin had so forcefully shown in his essay entitled "Ontology of the Photographic Image" (in *What Is Cinema?*). From literature as well it received an impetus toward realism. Since the development of the novel in the eighteenth century, literature had been moving steadily toward a journalistic ideal culminating in the various movements of "realism" and "documentism" at the end of the nineteenth century. Cinema seemed to step right into the wake of these impulses, possibly freeing both literature and painting to some extent from what might be called their mimesis neuroses. Another factor is the scientific spirit which led to the invention of the very apparatus necessary for cinema. Of all the figures involved in the discovery of motion pictures, Bazin preferred Jules Marey, because he spent his life trying to understand the motion of birds and animals. Cinema was necessary for him; his curiosity about the world demanded its invention. Marey can stand as an emblem for his generation, a generation displaying in countless ways an incredible popular surge of interest in the way the world looks and works. Cinema came by means of this surge to serve that curiosity.

Popular culture played the other seminal role in the origin of film. Cinema immediately served, and was fostered by, an industry of entertainment. Bazin frequently pointed to its rapport with music hall, the dime novel, and the melodramatic boulevard theater. Bazin believed that it is as impossible to avoid the sociological function of cinema as to ignore its congenital realism.

Many of Bazin's most impressive articles trace the struggle between these tendencies. He wrote about the evolution of both cinematic language and cinematic content. His views here are well known and I would like simply to point to their most far-reaching implications in summarizing them.

In 1895 no one could say what films should look like or how they should go about the business of communicating and mediating reality. The gradual formulation of a language of cinema came about during the first twenty years of its existence. By 1915 the original freedom of the art was vastly restricted while its powers of expression had miraculously developed. Cinema bartered variety for a standard form and gained eloquence as a result. It chose a few of its infinite options and these few became the "Cinema" we all recognize. The fact that virtually all films run 80-120 minutes was a convention established around 1915. This is an inseparable part of our notion of cinema and it is a product of the institutionalization of the art. There are innumerable such "facts" and together they form the classic cinema which reigned supreme from 1915 to 1938 and which is still influential today.

During the era of the classic cinema people could justly say that they were going to the movies because any particular film they might see would be of less importance to them than the re-enactment of the cultural and aesthetic ritual which was "the movies." Every film was an example, good or bad, of the standard language at work. Bazin might well have said the same of our attitude toward television today. We turn on the television for the most part not to see a particular show but to see a series, or, more often, simply to watch TV. The homogeneity of today's TV language ensures that we will feel at home with the story and the images. For example, the dramaturgy is carefully worked around a framework of obligatory commercials, and it seems as if a single composer laid his upbeat score over every show. Even the credits can be reduced to a few styles. The case of the "film formula" of the twenties and thirties is even more striking considering that in America alone 50-70 million people went to the movies each week. They watched a language which had triumphed over all other possibilities and which reinforced its supremacy with every new film.

Bazin was convinced that this dictatorial language, even more than social convention, determined the kinds of subject matter available to the classic screen. Genres developed which could most readily respond to and display the machinery of cinema. In his penetrating examination of the genre of literary adaptations ("In Defense of Mixed Cinema," in *What Is Cinema?*) Bazin implies that the masterworks of world literature were cut down like so many redwoods to be fed to the sawmills in Hollywood and elsewhere. William Shakespeare, Charles Dickens, and Victor Hugo necessarily came out looking exactly like one another; worse, they looked like every other film of the period. Classic cinema, to sum up his position, has an official look which depersonalizes every film and treats every subject alike.

Some fascinating advantages attended this era. The ceaseless repetition of style allowed for an increasingly subtle system of film conventions. A natural rapport grew up between the public which went to the movies weekly and the producers who needed to supply the people with a variant of what they liked and were used to. Moreover, there was the possibility for social cohesion through cinema seldom available to any art. Cinema seemingly had an opportunity to unite the members of a culture with a traditional style and a network of traditional messages like the epic poems of Homer's Greece which every schoolboy memorized and every citizen heard year in, year out. Such a blatantly official art had been effectively unavailable in our culture since the Renaissance. The actualization of this potential is not nearly so exciting as the potentiality itself. Instead of epic poems or Gothic cathedrals, the money factories in Hollywood and other film capitals supplied, on the whole, a middle-class ideology. In fact this tells us more about our culture than about the power of the medium. In Russia, to take another culture, we can point to the use of this art to spread both a revolutionary style and message. In all cases, Bazin would say, the classic film was official; that is, it came down to the spectator from the mysterious land of Cinema, bedecked with a mystifying and self-assured style. It was, he would insist, a presentation of a spectacle to a passive audience hypnotized by the magic of film technique.

For clarity's sake, I have overstated the case. There were always films which resisted the pull of classic cinema toward the popular culture direction. There were always pioneers of personal realism (Robert Flaherty and Erich von Stroheim were Bazin's favorite examples) who conformed neither to the official look nor to the official message of the cinema of their day. Their films differ in many ways from the classic. First of all, they were largely made on location (*Greed, Nanook, Man of Aran*) giving them a graphic appearance at once more crude and more spontaneous than the studied spectacles we call classic. Second, they were scripted more in conformance with their material than with some higher dramatic logic. Von Stroheim filmed virtually every scene of the novel *Mc-Teague,* refusing to "cinematize" it by means of conventional cuts and changes. Flaherty, shooting miles of film with only a vague idea to guide his eye, made up his loose stories after the fact. Third, their editing exhibited a primary concern for the material shot, making the whole filming venture appear as an "investigation" of a phenomenon rather than a "presentation." All this adds up to a personal approach to the material, one in which style is not an *a priori* factor but is arrived at in the course of the film.

These few realistic vagabonds of the twenties and thirties were vindicated after 1940 by a general shift in filmmaking practice toward the more realistic principles they relied on. *The Rules of the Game* and *Citizen Kane* are for Bazin films which mark this new stage of cinema, forever breaking the absolute shackles of the official look. While most films today may still be content to satisfy the culture with a conventional style and message, the way is now fully open for multiple styles exposing and expressing multiple aspects of reality. Alexandre Astruc, a follower of Bazin, proclaimed in his famous 1948 article "La Caméra-Stylo"[14] that the filmmaker can be considered the equivalent of the novelist, letting his style be dictated by the exigencies of his material and his personal attitude toward that material. There is no longer anything we can label "cinema," he implied; there are only films and each film must find its proper style.

Despite the brevity of this summary, I hope to have outlined the synoptic view of cinema hidden beneath Bazin's numerous short articles: The apparently unalterable institution which cinema became in its first half-century had within its very core the seeds of its own destruction; from the first, and with progressively greater efficacy, the realistic impulse was eating away at its marvelous but impersonal edifice. While Bazin had a genuine and seldom-recognized love of much within the classic cinema tradition, he wanted desperately for the medium to evolve into more varied forms, more personal expressions. At Bazin's death the day had already come when we, as spectators, could follow the spontaneous and quirky styles of a Truffaut or a Rossellini as they struggled to explore and express aspects of the world never available to the cinema before. We can experience through their films both the reality they address and their own inner realities more intimately than was ever possible in the classic age of film. We can look at their films as free and direct responses to the world rather than as modifications of an official response to a given world.

Bazin saw in this a gain both in human sensibility and in the forms of art. He was excited by the prospects of the evolution of the cinema even though he felt it impossible to predict the direction of that evolution. New forms and new species of film will necessarily bring us even further gains in understanding ourselves and the world. In the end Bazin's vision of cinema is well reconciled to his passion for natural processes and human morality. Cinema, man, and the earth are, to him, all moving toward greater and greater self-revelations and self-expressions. All are in the process of becoming themselves, of discarding what no longer is germane and of creating themselves as they move into the future. In the philosophy of Sartre, such self-creation is the purpose and excitement of existence.

Bazin hoped that his theories would participate in this evolution, would drive cinema toward its eminently reasonable but necessarily hidden future. His wonderful good fortune lay in a catholicity of taste which allowed him to fully love films in themselves while, at the same time, to see them as links in an evolutionary chain. To him cinema, like man, is best itself when it recognizes its unfinished quality and strives to go beyond itself. This is why the humblest documentary and the meagerest western could so fascinate him. They perfectly fulfill themselves in the functions they perform, yet their blatant limitations make us look past them.

To love and to try to comprehend all stages of a process for themselves while continually looking beyond them into an undecipherable future—this is the spirit of Bazin's thought and of the age which fostered him.

At Bazin's death in 1958 there was no one to effectively challenge his film theory. In the years since his death that theory has had a variable fate. It was carried triumphant onto the screen by the New Wave films created by Bazin's colleagues at *Cahiers du cinéma*. It has more recently been openly reviled by the structuralists and semioticians who have characterized it with their most lethal epithets. Bazin, they sneer, was a "humanist" and his theory is "idealist."

No matter how it is characterized, Bazin's film theory will continue to have enormous impact because of its strength and variety. Its strength results from the consistency of his views and from the sophisticated philosophical tradition supporting those views. The variety, rarer and more special, comes from the fertility and energy of a man who was drawn to investigate everything he encountered and for whom every encounter inevitably revealed some new truth. These characteristics can be felt in nearly every essay he wrote. Whether the positions these essays propose are rejected or honored by future generations, the theorist behind them will always be revered for his astonishing brilliance and for the generous, unpretentious use he made of that brilliance.

Contemporary French Film Theory

Current film theory is healthy and internationally visible. There are theoretical cinema journals not only in France and England but in Italy, Spain, Germany, and most East European countries as well. Universities in virtually every nation offer courses and often entire programs of study in film theory.

But it can be agreed that France has been the seed-bed of current theoretical trends. The reasons stem back to Bazin and to his successful efforts to incorporate film discussion within the general cultural dialogue which had previously been hostile to the cinema. Through film clubs, the Cinémathèque française, the national film school, I.D.H.E.C., the serious criticism written in influential journals, and the birth of a succession of film journals crowned by *Cahiers du cinéma,* the post-war French populace was bombarded with fragments of film theory.

Bazin, leading this revival, brought to cinema the methods and often the findings of recognized disciplines like philosophy, art history, literary criticism, and psychology. Barred from becoming a professor by a life-long stammer, Bazin operated entirely outside the conservative university system. Many of his disciples at *Cahiers du cinéma,* most notably Jean-Luc Godard, saw themselves as alienated intellectuals disenfranchised because of their passion for an unrecognized subject of study.

Even before 1950 an attempt was made by several Sorbonne professors to adopt and legitimize the study of cinema. Under the leadership of the noted aesthetician Etienne Souriau, the "Institut de filmologie" brought together professors from various disciplines who shared an interest in cinema. One can find in their journal, *La Revue internationale de filmologie,* scholarly essays on such subjects as the physiology of image reception, the psycho-sociology of cinema, the economic context of film production, and the phenomenology of the viewing experience.

The "Institut de filmologie" gave cinema great prestige and hastened the time when courses in film study would be officially sanctioned in the French university system. But it is important to realize that Bazin and his followers had little to do with this organization. They found its members to be ransacking the virgin land of cinema, taking whatever plunder their particular methodologies enabled them to grasp and then returning post haste to their traditional respected homelands in sociology, philosophy, and the like. While it is true that Bazin brought philosophy to the cinema, he never did so patronizingly. Indeed, he more often chastened philosophy by the contact. For him and for the generation which was to become the New Wave, film study was not a new playground for scholars to romp in when they tired of the noisy marketplace their own fields had grown into. Cinema was for them a consuming vision and a way of life.

At Bazin's death in 1958, the university system, through the "Institut de filmologie," had given the serious study of film at least tacit approval so long as it was carried on within the tradition of more established disciplines. At the same time, through *Cahiers du cinéma* and other journals, a horde of students who were also devotées of film stood poised and ready to study film in a central way, not as a peripheral interest of traditional fields. In addition, the New Wave films began to spread a definite theoretical conception of the medium, a conception argued about in critical journals of all sorts.

The flowering of Bazin's theory, then, can be seen in new styles of filmmaking and in the development of an educated public willing to support these styles. The enthusiasm he generated for serious film discussion inevitably began to reach the classroom, though he did not live long enough to see it and perhaps would not have been pleased.

In contrast, the flowering of contemporary theory can best be seen precisely in these university classrooms, in doctoral theses, and in highly specialized journals and film books. The transition from the era of the film club to that of the university was effected largely by Jean Mitry. Although born well before Bazin, Mitry clearly belongs to a newer impulse in film theory because he became essentially the first recognized film professor at the University of Paris. Revealingly, his books have been published through the scholarly Editions Universitaires.

The synthesis Mitry has attempted between the ideas of Bazin and the more traditional formalism he instinctively prefers is the effort of a dedicated scholar. All the other theorists we have studied can be said to concern themselves primarily with the past, present, and future of film. With Mitry one feels that "ideas about film" have replaced "film" as the central focus of investigation. While this drier approach has never attracted excited disciples in the manner of Bazin's thought, indeed while his theory has yet to receive the wide attention it merits, most serious film students in the French universities have studied it and have grown sophisticated in the process.

Christian Metz is the most influential product of the growing university concentration on film. While pursuing advanced studies in linguistics, Metz kept in touch with cinema via film clubs and journals. It was his hope, as it had been the fruitless hope of many before him, to write his thesis and dissertation on cinema. In part because of the thaw of the French university system in the sixties, in part because of the mushrooming of the scope of modern linguistics, and for the most part because of sheer personal tenacity and ability, Metz composed a series of major papers culminating in *Language and Cinema,*[1] his book-length thesis which merited him the degree of *Doctorat d'Etat* and gave him the right to direct further dissertations in his field.

Since the conferral of this degree and the wide translation of his essays, Metz has become the center of an organized, international, quasi-scientific approach to film theory. It would be impossible to try to summarize the directions, both scholarly and political, into which semiotics has branched, but all these directions owe much of their original impetus to Metz. True, today he has more dissidents than disciples; but it is undeniable that his arduous and exact studies in the late sixties have made possible the current gush of "materialist film theory" and have given that theory a procedural model.

While Jean Mitry has been effecting a synthesis between Bazin and formative theory, and while Christian Metz has led a wave of revolt to replace Bazin's idealist existentialism with a materialist structuralism, not all reactions to Bazin's position have been negative. For a decade after his death, *Cahiers du cinéma,* under Eric Rohmer, Jacques Rivette, and François Truffaut, published criticism and fragments of theory directly derived from Bazin's positions.

In other countries this kind of positive response to Bazin is equally visible. Charles Barr's famous essay on the virtues of Cinemascope[2] is the high point of a British trend in criticism which eventually clustered around the short-lived journal *Movie,* a journal rather self-consciously modeled on *Cahiers du cinéma.*

In America, Bazin's ideas and preferences have been promulgated primarily through the controversial criticism of Andrew Sarris. Although he never constructed anything like a theory himself, Sarris has had immense impact on film theory in America through the presuppositions his criticism rests upon and through his sponsorship of *Cahiers du cinéma in English.* During 1966 this magazine printed translations of some of the most important essays of Bazin, Leenhardt, Rohmer, Truffaut, and others, preparing an audience for Hugh Gray's booklength translations of Bazin's essays in 1968 and 1971.

Recently two ambitious theories strongly echoing Bazin's approach have been developed in this country, Stanley Cavell's *The World Viewed*[3] and George Linden's *Reflections on the Screen.*[4] Neither of these books has had much impact largely because of the isolation in which each was written. Both could be said to be phenomenologies of film in that each tries in its own way to investigate not the structures of the medium or its products, but the very experience of watching films. Such reflective and interior theorizing has had a following in France and Germany over the last forty years, but it is still somewhat foreign to American criticism, and neither of these books is able to link up with the European tradition.

If we may hope to find a systematic challenge to structuralism in film theory, we must once again look to France and to the heritage of that country's phenomenology. Bazin was not the only film theorist influenced by Sartre, Marcel, and Merleau-Ponty. Each of these philosophers composed essays on the cinema and discussed this art in courses and at *ciné*-clubs. During the fifties their impact could be seen in the writings of many theorists, most notably Edgar Morin, whose *Cinéma ou l'homme imaginaire* (Paris, 1956) is perhaps the most sustained attempt to treat film through a reflective description of its psychological functioning.

Although phenomenology has been officially displaced by structuralism in French intellectual life, many film theorists are among those who still cling to its methods however unfashionable they may seem. There is more than a little phenomenology in Mitry's writing and in the early Metz. It is explicitly present in the essays consecrated to the cinema by the noted aesthetician Mikel Dufrenne and by the Belgian psychologist Jean-Pierre Meunier, whose book *Les Structures de l'expérience filmique* (Louvain, 1969) explicitly applies the methods of Merleau-Ponty to film. But unquestionably the most influential phenomenological film theory has been written by Henri Agel, Amédée Ayfre, and Roger Munier. Their works will be singled out for examination in the last chapter of this book, in part because each has consciously tried to expand the theories of Bazin but more because they have provided a visible alternative to Metz and to Mitry.

As we move into the era of post-structuralism, thinkers in all fields are talking about the emergence of a fruitful dialogue between a scientific, external structuralism and an internal, reflective phenomenology or hermeneutics. In the cinema this dialogue would be to a great extent a refinement and development of the interaction we have followed between formative and realist theories. There is little reason to believe, then, that the contemporary scene in film theory differs radically from that of the past. And as in the past the existence of a number of positions can only be a sign of health and of energy.

7

Jean Mitry

Jean Mitry has ushered in a whole new era of film theory with his immense two-volume treatise, *Esthétique et psychologie du cinéma* (1963-65). It is ironic that contemporary film theory should have its start in this man who was himself the contemporary and associate of figures like Jean Epstein, Abel Gance, and Jean Renoir. Indeed Mitry's first film book was a study of the actor Emil Jannings, who was at that time (1928) in mid-career. Mitry lived and labored in that golden age of silent cinema so beloved of Arnheim, Balázs, and countless others. Somehow his critical mind has conquered what must be a nearly irresistible pull toward nostalgia and a film theory based on the supremacy of those wonderful films of the twenties, for he has indeed written a remarkably modern theory.

Three aspects of Mitry's life have contributed to his critical distance. First, he began by actually working on films during the French avant-garde era. Even after the fall of this movement he has stayed close to film production, editing such films as Alexandre Astruc's prize-winning short "Le Rideau Cramoisie" (1953), filming and editing his own prize-winners in "Pacific 231" (1949) and "Images pour Debussy" (1952). These projects all have something of the experimental about them and forced him at the very outset to bring to bear on his own work some sophisticated ideas about

editing, music, the status of the image, and adaptation. The closeness of Mitry's film theory to filmmaking practice arises from these
kinds of working experiences. Only Eisenstein, of all the theorists
studied here, exceeds him in time and energy spent in editing
rooms.

The second aspect of Mitry's life and personality which suits
him so perfectly to his task is his penchant for history. Even during
his years in the French avant garde he was busily collecting data
and notes which might be of use to him later on. His files, already
sizeable in the 1930s, were immeasurably augmented when he,
along with Henri Langlois and Georges Franju, founded the Cinémathèque française in 1938. Of course this has since become the
greatest storehouse of films and film data in the world. During the
war Mitry devised the notion of writing a truly scientific history of
the cinema, a history which would document the art and which
would pose the most important questions raised by it. In the past
decade he has at last begun publishing this *Histoire du cinéma,*
now three volumes long and yet to reach the thirties. Anyone
thumbing through the 900 pages of his theory books will instantly
recognize the historian behind the theorist, for there are countless
precise examples on every page. This attitude toward his subject
has made Mitry the entomologist of cinema Bazin always wanted
to become. Who is better able than Mitry to trace Bazin's famous
"Evolution of the language of cinema," better able to classify genus
and species or to thoroughly dissect and analyze any specimen of
cinema? Bazin had to rely on his memory of screenings at *ciné-*
clubs, while Mitry has had the films at his fingertips, the documentation in his files. Bazin seldom saw films more than once and never
took notes on his reading. His brilliance was intuitive, his criticism
a reflex action of a perfectly cultured and attuned sensibility. Mitry,
on the other hand, has never had an instinct for practical criticism,
so his insights show the strain of long mental and bibliographical
labor.

Mitry must be the greatest living fund of information on cinema.
He was immediately called on to teach this field when I.D.H.E.C.
was founded in 1945. This third aspect of his career, the pedagogi-
cal, has forced him to tailor both his private creative experience

and his encyclopedic knowledge so that he can address key issues and respond to current problems and questions. Teaching in France, Canada, and the United States, he has been one of the first university professors of cinema.

Mitry's theory reads like a well-organized campaign. He tries to employ something of the working styles of all the authors we have discussed. His detailed table of contents manifests the considerable attention he has paid to the strategy of his theory. In this he resembles Munsterberg and Arnheim. But the sheer bulk of his writing and its fascination with what are, by themselves, minute problems in physical aesthetics remind one of Eisenstein, Balázs, and occasionally Kracauer. Mitry tries to make all his subsections play a role in his argument, but his table of contents often seems like a desperate and frequently unsuccessful attempt to yoke these subsections together. They have a life of their own on many occasions. Each section can be likened to a carefully researched classroom lecture. The ensemble forms a clear progression, but many of the lectures seem to have been included because the lecturer had a fund of information or research which somehow demanded to be spoken.

Mitry's scholarly approach to his subjects is felt in the weight of citation with which he compulsively bolsters every new subject. His readings in philosophy, psychology, linguistics, logic, and aesthetics help him come to grips with film problems at a level one step deeper than that of the theorists who preceded him. His synoptic view of the problems a film theory must encounter, a view less available to the theorists we have studied thus far, enables him to marshal helpful evidence and opinions. Typically Mitry embarks on a problem by summarizing the opinions of earlier theorists on the matter. Then he tries to solve their differences, often by appealing to the proper extra-filmic source. Piaget helps him mediate a dispute about audience participation; Bertrand Russell enables him to disentangle the image versus word controversy which has provoked so much theory but so little sense. Finally Mitry will illustrate as best he can the importance of a problem in the overall theory of film, preparing a proper entry into the next problem.

Now in this very method lies a new spirit of theorizing, a more academic spirit, one which distrusts and avoids easy or far-reaching solutions. In Mitry's view all previous theory had sought a key to the understanding of cinema. Mitry rejects this approach, demanding instead that each problem in film be treated in and of itself. The theorist must not lose himself in defense of a single important insight. To him Eisenstein's theory suffered from its obsession with his admittedly remarkable insight into editing. Similarly Bazin's views on reality and the shot-in-depth are brilliant and invaluable, but they weave themselves into all his writings, limiting his overall insight. Mitry, from his academic tower, hopes to avoid such oversimplification. And this is one of the major reasons for the length of his study. Every aspect, every problem in film deserves careful independent scrutiny, not the application of a favored formula.

Esthétique et psychologie du cinéma consequently lacks the passion for discovery and conquest which so often exalts the styles of all the other theories we have looked at. It hasn't the illusion of quickly and neatly accounting for this new medium. It is painstaking and measured like a treatise on the human body or on the life of insects. In this, Christian Metz has called it a watershed book.[1] It has organized all the theoretical problems which arose in the first fifty years of film theory and carefully delineated the major positions taken on those issues. In its coolness and readiness to look for aid from such fields as linguistics and logic, Mitry's work has brought film theory into the modern classroom. Cinema is not something to be understood instantly or argued about ideologically. It is an enormous field of inquiry which only patient and controlled study can progressively illuminate. This is the spirit of modern film study.

THE RAW MATERIAL

Volume I of *Esthétique et psychologie du cinéma* is subtitled "Les Structures" and purports to study those aspects of cinema which necessarily pertain to every film. Volume II, "Les Formes," is concerned with the theoretical issues brought up by particular styles and genres of film. Mitry's work thus falls into the organizational schema we have been using all along. Indeed Volume I, after a section called Preliminaries, is subdivided neatly into two major sections: the filmic image and montage The discussion of the filmic image corresponds to our category of the raw material of cinema; that of montage corresponds to what we have called creative means. Volume II just as neatly treats first the forms and shapes of film and then the powers, potentialities, and purposes of the medium.

If his overall logic is easy to comprehend, Mitry's specific inquiries are much less tidy. Added to the reader's problem of following digressions (usually digressions of great interest), which his penchant for citation continually leads him toward, is the more basic problem of discerning a middle view. Mitry's theories inevitably seek a middle ground between the extremes of earlier thinkers. The reader will quickly discover that it is far easier to sort out the theories of extremists like Eisenstein or Arnheim, on one side, or Kracauer, on the other, than to firmly grasp the mobile and self-qualifying assertions which Mitry tries to lay ever so delicately between them. This is never more evident than with the question of the basic material of cinema, where Mitry is eager to uphold simultaneously certain aspects of Bazin's realism and certain aspects of Arnheim's transformationalism. For Mitry the qualities of the bare film image synthesize the realist and the formative camps.

Images, he says, can hardly be discussed outside of their relation to the objects they are images of. True, they have an independent physical existence. One can destroy the film of a building without destroying the building; but it is specious to talk about images without talking about their objects. For Mitry, this fact instantly puts cinema into a different category from verbal language. Verbal language is composed of arbitrary particles which deliver a mental image to us, allowing us to think about the world "out there." But film images are already "out there" and incorporate within themselves many actual visual aspects of their objects, including the real movement of those objects. They are not, in his view, "signs" which allow us to call the objects to mind, but "analogues" of the objects, "doubles" of it.

The bare cinematographic image can, therefore, have no significations other than those which are virtual in the object it represents. The raw material of cinema is the image which gives us an *immediate* (unmediated, untransformed) perception of the world. The film image exists alongside the world it represents, not transcending it. Nothing human or artistic lifts the image (at this first level) into higher levels of signification or meaning. The film image designates nothing (unlike the word to which it has so often been falsely compared); it simply shows us itself, an analogue of the world, partial, but of the same nature as the visual nature of that world.

Mitry's position here is seemingly identical to Bazin's conception of cinema as "asymptote" to reality. But as has been pointed out,[2] Bazin spent his life discussing the importance of the "snugness" which the filmic analogue fits the world, whereas Mitry has spent his life investigating the crucial differences which keep this asymptote forever distinct from the world it runs beside and so faithfully mirrors.

What are these differences? Most important is the fact that the images on the screen have been put there by someone else. It is not our attention which brings this or that visual image into view but someone else who keeps saying "voilà!" by the sheer fact of having taken, developed, and screened these images for us. For Mitry, reality exists as an inexhaustible source of meaning for humans. We invest it with significance by choosing to deal with it in this or that way. In the film theater somebody else is telling us to look at this or that part of the world, telling us in addition that we should give it a "significant" look. While in one sense it is the world which is still speaking to us in its usual manner, the fact that someone else authorizes this significance is enough to tell us that we are not in reality but in someone else's version of the world.

Thus far we have been considering the analogic properties of the film image and Mitry has always emphasized them. The film image also has some life of its own, some peculiarities to which reality must submit before leaving its analogic imprint. These have been fully discussed by earlier theorists, by Arnheim above all. Mitry concentrates most fruitfully on the frame of the screen which is necessary in film but unnecessary in life. Always the mediator he finds that the frame at once hides reality from us (as

Bazin believed) and at the same time organizes the objects it contains (as Arnheim held). The spectator inevitably feels that reality lurks just to the side of the screen and if the cameraman would only turn a little we should certainly see it; simultaneously, however, that same spectator is caught in the visual tensions established by the frame. The framed image begins to strike us as an ordered image which we must look at purposefully and in relation to other framed images; but all the while it never ceases pointing to the world it represents.

Mitry clarified this notion by analyzing the difference between film and painting. Like Bazin he found that in painting the object represented surrenders its reality and is entirely incorporated into the new reality of the artwork. In film, however, no matter how significant a certain framing composition looks, it always tells us that it is but one way to look at the world there represented. The world outlives any framing of it. We note the framing of the image but remain involved in a real world it can't use up. In painting, a single aesthetic reality remains. In cinema this *aesthetic* aspect exists, to be sure, but it does so only in dialogue with the continual *psychological* realism the analogue can never slough off. Hence the title of Mitry's book. The film image transcends the world by giving it an aesthetic frame (by choosing to actualize one aspect of it), but the world reasserts its "virtual" transcendence by reminding us that there are countless other possible ways to see it.

Mitry's discussion of the screen as both frame and window is the key to his entire film theory. His beliefs about editing, about story, and about the very purpose of cinema flow directly from this position about the ambivalent status of the film image. It is here too that Mitry for the first time becomes evaluative. He outlines the "imagistic" tradition in cinema from the Film d'art movement through the Italian spectacle and German expressionist films culminating in the last films of Eisenstein, and he finds that their excessive concern with the aesthetic world they hope to create within the frame overshadows the reality to which these images, as analogues should naturally point to. Instead of a tension between the aesthetic and psychological aspects of the image, we get the aesthetic aspects pure and simple as in painting. These films nullify cinema's special and basic power by throwing over that tension for some supposed aesthetic advantage.

This assault on expressionistic cinema concludes Mitry's consideration of the bare cinematographic image and shows once more how close he is at this point to Bazin. The difference between these theorists begins to be felt more strongly as Mitry turns his attention to the problems of editing and the sequencing of images.

CREATIVE POTENTIAL IN FILM

Throughout Mitry's discussion of the film image as raw material he never ceases suggesting that as spectators we watch not raw material but fully formed films. Film images exist not simply as chosen by someone else but as organized into a filmic world by them. The bare image has a natural sense about it simply because it exists to be viewed; but the sequenced image, the image in a completed film, has more than a sense, it has a significance, a definite purpose conferred upon it by the role it plays in the "imaginary" but representational world the filmmaker constructs.

The most crucial characteristic of the film image, so obvious that it hardly needs mentioning, is that unlike the world it represents, the film image can be "played with" and arranged according to the mental schemes of the filmmaker. It can be combined with other images in innumerable ways, each time forming not simply a new aesthetic series (like some series of frescoes or stained-glass windows which give us an aesthetic narrative) but a new, psychologically real world. The psychological energy which makes us perceive the object through the film image also demands that we see any sequence of images as components of a continuum. We turn the flow of images into a continuous world. According to Mitry, not only do our senses constitute the objects they perceive by giving them a real status, they also spread these objects out in space and in time to build a world in which these objects are interrelated. The editing process is the filmic analogue of this mental operation.

Mitry is obliged at this point to define the editing process, or montage, more broadly than had early theorists, even Eisenstein.

Montage comprises all methods of giving context to individual images, of making a filmic universe out of the raw material, of making human signification out of the natural tendency of things and their analogues to have sense. He first defuses the dynamite on Bazin's critique of montage by claiming that even when a scene is shot with a moving camera instead of broken into small scenes, the montage effect is still at work interrelating the various image-objects which come into view. Mitry goes so far as to insist that montage can occur in a single scene filmed from an unchanging angle. If a character is reading a newspaper seated in a study and then is interrupted by a flaming arrow which suddenly sets fire to the curtains behind him, we have a montage effect without editing, for we have two images which together deliver a level of significance greater than themselves.

This level of significance one step beyond the composed film image is, in Mitry's mind, always associated with narrative. By interrelating the objects which his senses build for him, man gives to reality an order and a logic. Space, time, and causality put man at home in the world and allow him to understand it rather than simply perceive it. Objects don't merely exist for man, they play roles, and these roles change as his own needs and desires change. Hugo Munsterberg first recognized this psychological basis of the narrative film and Béla Balázs elaborated it when he spoke of a "current of meaning" running beneath the images, joining them together in the creation of a motivated, human world.

A filmmaker cannot withhold this human significance from his film. By merely putting together a series of images, he demands that we look for a motivation. Why these shots rather than others? Why does this follow that? The spectator on his own will try to give to these images some kind of meaning and human significance. He will not stop until each film image plays a role in the human drama created out of the perceptual world. The term "human" does not demand that all films be plot oriented. A series of images in a documentary about a desert may be motivated by the "human" desire to understand some aspect of nature; or a series of images of the sea and the sand may be motivated by the filmmaker's poetic reflections. Most often, of course, film images are motivated by a narra-

tive in which each finds its proper place contributing to our understanding of the story at hand. While we look through the images
to reality itself, we realize that those images and that reality are
speaking a higher language to us, a human not a natural language.
The filmmaker cannot rid himself of reality, but he can and must
insist on his own use of it.

Mitry finds, then, that at the first level, the level of perception
and of the film image, reality cannot be avoided. At the second
level, the level of narration and image sequencing, he finds that it
is man who cannot be avoided, man with his plans, his desires, his
meanings who makes these analogues of nature submit to his own
unquenchable need to signify. A new world is created by the filmmaker with the aid and complicity of the real world of sense. No
other art has done this.

Cinema is capable of a further level of signification beyond that
of creating a new kind of world. Since every sequence of images
(from that put together by a ten-year-old to an ad for deodorized
soap to the latest film by Fellini) must necessarily signify its world
to us, how can we discern artistic from ordinary signification? The
great and artistic films Mitry claims are those which somehow construct an abstract meaning beyond the obvious story meaning
which holds them together. At this abstract level the film is released from its link to sheer perception, released also from the
specific story it tells, and allowed to play freely with our highest
imaginative faculties.

Mitry's classic example illustrating how all three levels function
is taken from Eisenstein's *Potemkin*.[3] During the insurrection on
board the ship, the arrogant and effete Tsarist doctor finds himself
in a serious predicament. After showing the doctor brutally tossed
overboard, Eisenstein inserts a single shot of his pince-nez dangling from a rope. Mitry distinguishes three levels of signification
in this shot. First, the pince-nez presents itself to our attention as a
type of "glasses" in the real world. We recognize immediately that
it is a pince-nez and that the filmmaker is showing it to us in this
dangling position. Second, we motivate this object by seeing it in
the context of the film. We realize its human significance (that the
offensive doctor has been jettisoned). Third, because of associa-

tions built up earlier, because of the composition, the rhythm, and other resonances, the pince-nez becomes a symbol for the frailty of the doctor's social class and this specific shot represents the downfall of that class.

Mitry associates the higher levels of cinematic meaning with pure poetic meaning. While any child can speak intelligible phrases and tell an intelligible story, it is the poet who makes the language transcend the story and implicates our highest faculties. He does so primarily by means of rhythm, figures, and internal associations of all sorts. The great film artists too create poetic effects as they construct their film worlds out of the raw material of film images. The history of film art is not the history of subject matter (new images) nor even the history of film stories but the history of poetic techniques which reach beyond the stories they spring from.

Mitry is anxious to formulate the aesthetics of film by laying down the rules for the proper use of "poetic devices" in the construction of a film. Characteristically he arrives at these rules of editing by examining the history of artistic editing, cataloguing approaches as he goes along. He begins by looking at the extremes, those periods of hyper-aestheticism in which filmmakers sought to ignore the normal cinematic process which goes from raw images to a sequenced particular story to abstract meaning. He finds that in the 1920s a certain optimism about film led enthusiastic theorists and filmmakers to tug at this cinematic essence trying to pull it in one case into the realm of pure magic, and in another case into that of conceptual thinking.

Mitry himself was a close associate of many of the French avant-gardists who demanded that cinema discard its burdensome literary heritage in search of a new musical essence. Naturally he gives a firsthand summary of the proclamations and provocative films of Louis Delluc, Abel Gance, Germaine Dulac, Hans Richter, Viking Eggeling, and so on. These people realized that in every film, even a conventional narrative one, certain movements within the shots create abstract patterns; they also realized that these patterns could become the dominant factor in the film, if the editor so chose, for editing confers an external movement on the film, one that can amplify this inner movement or flow contrapuntally against it. By attending exclusively to the shape and movement of the image, rather than to either its status as analogue of a real object or its function in some story world, the filmmaker could build, it was thought, a piece of visual music which would bypass all literalness and appeal directly to our higher faculties.

In countering this movement Mitry aligns himself with Balázs and Kracauer; we have seen that these theorists had philosophical and even moral reservations about such an abstract use of film; Mitry's rebuttal, on the other hand, is characteristically drawn from science. He proves that the ear is, and must remain, our dominant rhythmic sense because of its unmatched ability to discern and catalogue minute fragments of sound. The mind confers "gestalts" on these catalogued sounds and we perceive the stimuli rhythmically, that is, as goal-directed wholes. The sounds act as nearly neutral material which the mind can pattern as it pleases. Our sight is not nearly so detached, nor so sharp. Mitry cites experiments showing that the duration of a shot is dependent to a large degree on its content. One cannot simply edit a film without regard to its psychological or narrative factors because these play essential roles in our perception of the movement and duration of the shot. There is no such thing as a pure shot or pure form in cinema, nothing to compare to the mathematically clean functioning of the ear. The most telling scientific fact is the eye's refusal, unlike the ear, to distinguish a null state, a vacuum. In modern terminology the eye works in an analogue fashion (proportions, relations, similarities and differences) whereas the ear works digitally (in an on-off manner).

Mitry doesn't want to dismiss cinematic rhythm completely. He simply wants to eliminate the improper rapport between film and music, the misconception that cinema is in any sense a digital art form. Mitry replaces the music analogy with one from literature. Filmic rhythm has many of the same powers and problems as prose rhythm. Both are dependent first on their representations rather than on a finite series of mathematically pure tones, as in music. Film and prose rhythms must always function *ad hoc* in response to the conveyed images. The film spectator, like the reader, while attending to the subject at hand, will be sensible as well to the movement and balance of the presentation. These can in some cases lead to overwhelming and nearly abstract effects: they can easily produce a tone and feel within the film itself, but they can never direct that film or dictate the shot. As Mitry so often points out, a film develops *in* a rhythm, not *from* a rhythm.

Another excess which appeared in the twenties is that of the conceptual abstraction or literary trope. As we have seen, it was the Russians who pushed this capability to its limits, and in Mitry's eyes, beyond its limits. They had discovered the effect which shot juxtapositions inherently create by watching the films of D. W. Griffith, Thomas Ince, Henry King, and others. They reasoned that not only could montage create a story logic, it could as well create a true logic, a language of images.

Once again theorists hoped to bypass narration in order to appeal directly to man's highest and most general faculties. If two distinct images always generate a concept beyond themselves, why not flood the screen with a carefully chosen series of images, whose interrelation is only abstract? The content of these images need not have anything in common for the film would create meaning directly via the rapports between the images. Recall Eisenstein's discussion of Japanese writing wherein a verb such as "to sing" is generated by two static images (a bird and a mouth). There is certainly evidence in Eisenstein's early writing that film is capable of a new kind of "ideogrammatic" language, a hieroglyphic code which would speak directly to the spectators.

Mitry needs to deflate this hope in order to preserve for cinema its special status as a concrete art. In his remarkable critique of the Kuleshov-Mozhukhin experiments, he shows that the supposedly purely abstract rapport existing between two distinct images (in this case, Mozhukhin's expressionless face and a nude woman) is mediated by the spectator's narrative sense.[4] The spectator must already be equipped with certain preconceptions (in this case, sexual ones) for him "to create" the meaning (desire) between the shots. The spectator must have a "logic of reality" which he recognizes in the image sequence. Without this logic and this experience the images would remain isolated. Mitry insists that a young child, for instance, would see each image perfectly well but

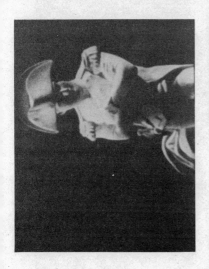

[Above] October, 1928. A statue in the decor of the palace crowns Kerensky. Mitry approves of this figure, but rejects the insertion of a peacock into the sequence. *Blackhawk Films*

[Right] October, 1928. A statue is made to speak through conceptual editing. *Blackhawk Films*

October, 1928. Statues exert meaning in their natural space. *Blackhawk Films*

wouldn't give to them a deeper inference. A truly abstract language (our spoken language) can manipulate concepts independent of our experience. In film, Mitry asserts, we must first recognize a world before abstractions can take on meaning. A series of ideograms purporting to be a visual language has nothing to do with cinema. It could only function to render local and familiar meanings like the flag codes of navigators at sea.

Mitry classifies the consequences of this fact about the medium. He lists the various kinds of montage and, much like Bazin at the end of his essay on children's films, differentiates legitimate uses from those which work against the medium. For Mitry, every abstract meaning in cinema must be grounded first in our concrete feelings. This is the reverse of the literary process in which abstract signs (words) generate concepts in our minds which are only then capable of producing feelings. Mitry can now attack metaphors such as those Eisenstein attempted in *October,* where at one point he intercut shots of a peacock with those of Kerensky. Since the peacock does not belong to the logic of the world unravelling before us, the comparison is purely abstract and leaves us unmoved if not confused.

On the other hand, Mitry praises the intercutting between Kerensky and a bust of Napoleon because that bust is part of the palatial decor around Kerensky. Only when the bust shatters of its own accord at the downfall of Kerensky does Mitry object, for here the "logic" of the world before us has been bartered for a literary trope.[5] In a poem or essay we might read "And so Kerensky's pretenses to power were overturned and shattered like an impervious but fragile bust." The very abstraction of the reading process authorizes this kind of figurative speech. But in filming the same moment, one must discover ways to imply the sentiment through a heightening, not an abandonment, of the real.

Mitry's attack on intellectual montage is amplified to include all films which use physical reality to argue a logical position. Film sequencing depends upon local juxtaposition, so it cannot hope to weave a subtle "verbal" logic over the whole course of a film. It cannot qualify or control the meaning released when two images explode into a concept. It cannot put meanings into hierarchic orders. Verbal language does this easily by means of an array of adverbs, conjunctions, and a whole system of syntactic relations whereby clauses and phrases depend one upon the other. In film, Mitry claims, we have but one instrument, the montage effect. To try to make it do the task of language and deliver conceptual arguments is to misconstrue the medium's powers. And so, Mitry alleges, Eisenstein's desire to film *Das Kapital* is doomed from the outset.

Except for his interdiction against these extreme uses of the technique, Mitry is eager to promote an understanding and respect for all kinds of montage. He cites Hollywood narrative editing as the discovery of the method of constructing a perfectly fictional world. So great has Hollywood's mastery of this process been that one is often completely lost within the film world because its logic is identical to the perceptual logic of our daily lives.

Mitry sees Hollywood editing as a "status quo" against which other kinds of montage programs have asserted themselves. First he isolates "lyrical montage" as a variant of conventional narrative editing. Here the filmmaker gives up the overwhelming illusion of verisimilitude by concentrating on the moments of greatest dramatic intensity. In the chapter on Bazin we discussed the scene in Pudovkin's *Storm over Asia* in which the Mongol hero stands up, walks across a room to a fishbowl and falls, bringing the bowl down on him. Pudovkin, as master of the lyrical process, makes this scene vibrate out of all reasonable proportion by cutting it rhythmically into some 18 to 20 fragments. The whole film is really a series of such high points, culminating in the "storm" finale with its collage of over a hundred shots. While Bazin was annoyed at such manipulation, Mitry finds it perfectly acceptable, not to say powerful. It is a process based precisely on the heightening of a real situation.

Mitry moves furthest from Bazin and closest to Eisenstein when he supports what he calls "reflexive montage." Here the filmmaker, while telling his story and respecting its world, manages to build another line of meaning "to the side" of the narrative. He may set up symbolic interdependencies between objects in the story; he may play their shapes off against each other; he may cut his film in response to the lighting or movement of the images. All these effects will propel the film forward if they have a literal base, that is, if they respect the story and the perceptual world which that story organizes.

Mitry here calls attention to the point, elaborated by Eisenstein, that all shots have numerous overtones in addition to their dominant sense. If a film is edited along lines dictated by the overtones, it will accumulate a wealth of meaning because this "subtext" cannot help but be seen in relation to the ever-present dominant. Mitry says that reflexive editing is the mark of nearly all great films. I find that certain passages in Dreyer's *Day of Wrath* illustrate this very well. For instance the lovers' meetings are photographed in a series of outdoor tableaux edited mainly for the mottled texture of lighting they exhibit. There were surely other, more logical ways of rendering these scenes, but Dreyer chose to build this sense of light. The impact is overwhelming in this case because these lyrical scenes alternate with the stark death of Master Laurentius and the whole sequence is imbedded within a film whose lighting is otherwise utterly severe. Not only do we recognize the *facts* of the story (that the lovers have at last come together), we see and nearly touch the *quality* of that love. Dreyer delivers more than a story; he gives us an experience by attending to the overtones of the images and the logic those overtones progressively dictate in his film.

Mitry accepts all kinds of extremes in reflexive editing, since by definition it bases these extremes within our perception of the world. The filmmaker is free to combine shots even according to some distant implication which unites them, so long as these shots are natural parts of the world being filmed. Here he is at odds with Bazin. For Bazin, such reflexive montage, when overused, belittles the natural power of the image because it makes us look at that image for the implications which the filmmaker is straining to make. The natural sense of the world, its multi-layered ambiguity, is subordinated to the abstract whim of the filmmaker. Mitry responds directly to Bazin's argument. There is no natural sense of the world, he claims, only those senses which men have given to their perceptions. While some uses of reflexive montage do build a rather thin and tendentious meaning, the filmmaker has every right to pre-

Day of Wrath, 1943—the subtext of lighting.

serve this possibility in case he needs to express just this sort of meaning.

Mitry praises Bazin for dethroning "king montage" forcing it to take its place alongside more natural approaches, giving the filmmaker a wide range of possibilities. His complaint is that in the rest of his writing Bazin consciously attacks obvious misuses of montage, never discussing or analyzing legitimate montage. Similarly, Mitry agrees with Bazin that filmmakers can and have ruined their films by using an abstract montage process in the heart of an otherwise "realistic world," but such misuses, he emphasizes, don't condemn the process altogether.

Mitry wants to retain for the filmmaker every style possible, but this does not mean that he feels all styles are equal. Far from it. Every stylistic choice implies a separate cinematic world, and in the first half of Volume II of *Esthétique et psychologie du cinéma* he outlines those possibilities and the worlds they generate. Mitry discusses the mobile camera, depth-of-field photography, Cinema-Scope, methods of creating various levels of subjectivity, the possibilities of dialogue, music, color, and rhythm. His philosophy refuses to accord priority to any of these techniques. It refuses as well to allow any one world to dominate completely. Bazin ran aground, Mitry feels, when he attributed to neorealism a closeness to the sense of the real world. For Mitry, reality has only those senses we give it. All versions of reality are human attempts at thrusting human meaning back on the inchoate sense perceptions which we encounter.

THE FORM AND PURPOSE OF CINEMA

Mitry's extreme pluralism in matters of style might lead us to expect a similar pluralism in the area of cinematic structure. After all, if no one stylistic device can claim natural priority over the rest, then shouldn't all the cinematic worlds such styles create be of equal value too? Mitry's resounding No to this question puts him among traditional film theorists like those discussed in this book and separates him from recent semiological approaches which otherwise owe him a great deal.

As a historian of cinema, Mitry has seen and studied at close range the whole gamut of film forms and he cannot help but decry certain forms as anti-cinematic. In matters of style, we have already encountered his disdain for overly expressionistic films or those based on some abstract rhythm. These films refused the stylistic possibilities natural to film and tried to create a kind of cinematic painting in the first case and music in the second. Cinema's third major "temptation" has come from the theatre. Even in the first decade of its existence, cinema went the easy road of copying the dramatic structures of plays, and it has never entirely conquered its obsession with this older and more respected rival. As Christian Metz notes, Mitry's attack on the theatrical influence on cinema is double-pronged, aimed at film style and film structure.[6] First he buries the heritage of theatrical *mise en scène* in cinema, showing, as Béla Balázs had, that cinema became an art only when it overcame the theatrical aesthetic of unchanging angles and continuous time within scenes. Mitry establishes this point concretely in an incredible display of scholarly virtuosity. He makes us feel the historical struggle of a new art-language to wrest itself from the simple and conventional solutions theatre gave to directors. Mitry's attack on this aspect of the theatrical influence is not unlike his refusal of expressionism and abstract cinema. In each case a close analysis of historical cases reveals the cinema trying to achieve the *style* of another art, thereby forfeiting the natural method and power of cinematic style. Mitry accepts any style which proceeds from bare images and the objects they represent to the creation of a humanly interesting world and beyond that to higher and more general meanings. In each of these three cases, however, this process of cinematic signification is confused and the images are made to function in the manner of other arts.

The second attack on theatricality in film comes at the level not of style but of *structure* or what he calls "dramaturgie." Here Mitry guards cinema against the unacceptable film worlds built in imitation of theatrical works. His discussion of this problem reflects and systematizes the writings of Bazin and Kracauer on the same subject. The theatrical world is seen by all these theorists as abstract, a world dominated by metaphysical speech, in which men play out their roles before other men or God. Theater decor is a key to this. It is always partial and privileged, a few special objects being lifted out of the undifferentiated mass of nature to aid man in his dramatic ritual. Mitry notes that classical Greek tragedy is quite conceivable as a sequence of voices with no decor at all. The true action of theater is its text, a play of voices in which men sort out and test their values, their condition. As such it is essentially timeless and works itself out through a series of autonomous scenes built up against the next. The outcome is characteristically final and absolute, for nothing impedes the naked battle of voices and values from struggling toward a definitive resolution.

Mitry opposes cinematic dramaturgy to this in nearly every respect. Most fundamentally, film integrates man and his speech within the natural world. Balázs and Bazin before him had often pointed out that theater renders the drama of man against man or even man against God, but cinema renders the drama of man and the world. This fact has enormous consequences. Not only does it call for a reconsideration of the role of dialogue in films; it suggests a dramaturgy based on very real historical and material conditions, moving from an initial situation to a significantly altered, but not absolute one at the end. The final situations of films are never so absolute as those in theatrical pieces because there always remains a network of physical and social contingencies, rather than the victory of one disengaged voice.

Whether or not any of these theorists has correctly characterized theater, it is certainly true that the cinema, because of its attention to the accidents and contingencies which define our life, has at last broken with the theatrical notion of autonomous scenes linked one to the other. In Mitry's language cinema has come to see its domain as "process and change itself" rather than as the linking together of set scenes. The breakdown of space within scenes, the dynamic interweaving of time through editing, and the use of the mobile camera have all helped cinema free itself from the tyranny of the all-powerful scene.

Structurally the cinema is much closer in nature to the novel. Many of the statements we make today about movies were made about the novel when it developed in the eighteenth century. It was from the outset considered a "profane" form which tantalized people's natural curiosity about how things work. It treated ordinary people, characterizing them by ordinary speech. It showed the vast networks of interdependencies (social and physical) lying beneath all situations and it pointed these up artistically by a careful use of the accidents of life. Furthermore its structure has always been a mixture of scenes, commentaries, and descriptions. It is a pluralistic form capable of incorporating all kinds of writing. While Mitry never writes very specifically about the question of cinematic organization, he does imply that it is, like the novel, free. Its only constraints are those which protect it from the absolutism of the "totally meaningful" world of theater. Film and novel must create human worlds but we must always be made to feel the chore of this creation, the emergence of meaning from the mud of inchoate experience.

And here cinema has the final word, for it is the art in which our mute perceptions take on meaning and value. If the novel makes us feel the interdependence of man and man or of men and the world, it does so abstractly, through words and figures of speech; film, on the other hand, does so through the normal process of brute perception. Hence the impossibility of true adaptation. One may try to retain in a film the structure of a novel but one must do this by means quite foreign to the novel and to the reading experience. In the epigrammatical conclusion to his study of this problem Mitry asserts that "the novel is a narrative that organizes itself in the world, while the cinema is a world that organizes itself into a narrative."[7] Once again we find Mitry synthesizing opposing traditions. Just as the "frame" acts to reveal to us the chaotic world of perception, while forcing that world into patterns of aesthetic meaning, so the open narrative of film organizes the world on the screen into an aesthetic form, but enables us at the same time to see through its organization to the unorganized world beyond.

Mitry's careful and lengthy untangling of the problem of adaptation, too elaborate to summarize here, leads him to the coda of his theory by isolating the special method and function of cinema among the arts. Cinema, he concludes, is perception which *becomes* a language. In Kracauer's terminology, it works from the bottom up. Mitry argues vigorously that the basic material of cinema has nothing to do with language. If cinema becomes a language, it is not the language we speak but the language of art or poetry. By this he means that the filmmaker can lift his images into meaningful and directed expression through the carefully controlled system of implications he develops via his camera, his sound, and above all his editing.

To take one example, the words we speak or write to represent the ocean are mediated. They are first arbitrary sounds whose abstract functioning allows us to conceive of the ocean. The poet takes these abstract words and, by attending to the physicality of their sounds and the images they evoke, he creates a second language atop ordinary language, one made up of codes of rhythm, rhyme, figures, and structure which give body and *solidity* to his thoughts. The filmmaker works the other way around. Moving pictures of the ocean have nothing to do with language. They show us immediately some aspects of the ocean. The filmmaker takes these images which, unlike words, are already solid and, through a quasi-poetic process, he makes them express themselves at a higher level. Mitry wants to call this procedure of intensifying nature a "language" because it seems to operate under rules and because it results in meaning. Nevertheless he insists that this cinematic language is utterly different from our ordinary conception of language. To analyze filmic signification, it is far better to begin at the level of poetics than at that of linguistics.

Let's recapitulate. The filmmaker chooses certain brute perceptions from reality with which to form a complete film world of his own. He can make this world radiate meanings far beyond itself if he takes advantage of all the implications of his material, transforming them by means of his "poetic codes." In the greatest film-poems we as "spectators-participants" join a complex world which speaks to us a broad human meaning yet through which we can always recognize the haphazard reality we experience every day. The filmmaker gives reality a tongue, but a tongue which speaks the words of that filmmaker. Reality thus participates in its own apotheosis, being transcended by the artistry of the filmmaker yet never being utterly consumed in the process. Without this tension between a brute reality we always recognize and the human meaning it is made to speak anew in each film, the cinema loses its power.

The expressionists and rhythmic avant-gardists wanted to leave reality behind in search of a more refined and direct style. But in truth they left cinema itself behind. Similarly those films which have adopted theatrical dramaturgy construct worlds which keep us from reality, which use the perceptions of reality as so many signs in a drama which has nothing to do with perception. But true films, even bad ones, make us aware of a contingent meaning by allowing us to look through the poetry, through the filmmaker's world, and through the images he has taken, to the bare perceptions which are at the basis of our lives. In this way every film lets us attribute a new world and a new set of meanings to the reality we daily live with. This reality is thereby greatly enriched. At the same time we can understand, can experience directly, the world view of our neighbor.

The *aesthetic* process of film joins a deep *psychological* reality and satisfies our desire to understand the world and each other in a powerful yet necessarily partial way. The aesthetics of film is based on this psychological truth and need. And so cinema is the greatest of the arts because it meets this need by showing us the *process* of the transformation of the world. The other arts can show us merely the end result of such transformation, the human-ized art world. In cinema human beings tell each other what real-ity means to them, yet they do so through reality itself, which surrounds their work like an ocean.

Mitry's deepest beliefs in cinema stem, like Bazin's and Kra-cauer's, from a passion for a reality which cinema alone can bring to light. Unlike them, however, he has a constructivist view of real-ity. Cinema doesn't allow the world's meaning to shine through. It shapes that reality and shakes it until it bears a human meaning, the only kind of meaning it can bear. Experience for both Mitry and Arnheim is this process of the perpetual transformation of partial and brute perception into rounded human forms. For Arn-heim this meant that cinema should deal only in abstractions giving us pictures of those human forms. Mitry comes to a different conclusion; he demands a cinema which, while unabashedly human, will leave itself open to brute perception.

Mitry's is a genuinely synthetic theory. He has managed to maintain a view which accommodates Bazin's "openness to Being" while insisting that Being is meaningful only insofar as man transforms it through all the devices, powers, and limitations at his command. In this venture cinema is his greatest tool, for while proceeding like natural perception it builds another, more intense world alongside that natural perception. It thereby allows us to compare our ways of seeing and valuing reality with those of other people. It allows us to project new meanings back on reality, meanings which necessarily enrich us and pay tribute to the inexhaustible world in which we live.

Christian Metz
and the Semiology of the Cinema

In his lengthy and adulatory review of Jean Mitry's *Esthétique et psychologie du cinéma*,[1] Christian Metz proclaimed a new era of film theory. Mitry, he wrote, was served well by all the theorists before him, as well as by his knowledge of philosophy and psychology. With vigor and tenacity he did what no other theorist to his day has done: he has systematically worked through the major problems of the cinema. Certainly other theorists have been systematic, but they developed their ideas, Metz feels, in a haphazard way, treating only those problems which most intrigued them. Bazin wrote incessantly about the relation of film to reality, while Eisenstein devoted himself to the topic of montage.

Mitry's achievement was not only to persevere in the tradition of these early theorists, but also to extend its methods comprehensively in a point-by-point elucidation of the basic structures and forms of the medium. His 900 pages comprise a vast logically organized resume of most of the arguments about most of the issues of film theory. This is why Metz can call Mitry's work a powerful and at times glorious finale to the first epoch of film theory.

Despite Mitry's thoroughness, indeed all the more because of it, Metz is convinced that film theory must achieve a reorientation. For him the first fifty years produced at best a diverse, intelligent, and sometimes astounding view of the medium, but in every case a view which must be termed "general." Every theorist was compelled to work out what he believed to be cinematic art or cinematic experience and to subtend this with a comprehensive philosophy. In arguing about cinema, then, theorists have in fact been arguing for and against differing world views, using cinema as a field of battle. Mitry's two volumes make up a grand-scale relief map of that field and those battles.

From Metz's point of view it is time to stop thinking generally about film, or at least time to stop publishing our general thoughts. As he put it, this often brilliant age of theory will grow old badly and become decrepit if it goes on much longer. Let us use Mitry's gigantic work to ease ourselves into a second phase of theory, he suggests, an era of specific rather than general study, an era ostensibly more limited but infinitely more precise than what has gone before. Let us begin the scientific study of the cinema.

Mitry would be incensed to be considered unscientific. He has an undying respect for science and its methods, dating from his training in physics. When Mitry speaks of a poetry of the cinema, he certainly does not do so poetically. His rigor is most apparent in the organization of his project and in the thoroughness of his research. Indeed Metz claims that any new study of film could profitably base itself on Mitry's outline, each chapter serving as a portal to an exhaustive and precise formulation.

Mitry's shortcomings in Metz's view are a product of his desire to encompass all areas of film with his theory. Because he proposed to study no less than the whole domain of cinema, Mitry was often obliged to think generally and impressionistically rather than precisely and scientifically. Metz's reproach is far from haughty. He knows that in the first years of any new field of study this kind of broad belles lettres approach is both natural and healthy. Once the problems in the field have been brought out, however, the general should begin to make way for the precise. Mitry has done film theory an incomparable service by touching virtually every problem film theorists need encounter. But let us not close his books with the feeling that all has been done because all has been touched upon. Let us, Metz proclaims, painstakingly retrace Mitry's outline, testing, proving, and discarding where he had only the time and in-clination to offer but another philosophy of film.

Now Mitry's philosophy is hardly separable from his film theory. It subtends all his thought and surfaces in the second volume of his theory for 120 pages of direct statement. This vision of man's state in the universe and the function of art gives Mitry the norms with which he has to judge what is cinematic from what is not. It is this vision which unites in a remarkably successful way the vastly diverse problems he treats. But it is this vision also which neces-sarily undercuts the objectivity of his research, at least according to his critics. His is one more "idealist" view of cinema, one more scheme which demands that the facts of cinema submit to a logic beyond them. The material reality of cinema is therefore at the mercy of the ideal reality of philosophic thought, whether that logic comes from Kant (as it does for Munsterberg), from Ge-stalt psychology (Arnheim), from Bergson and Sartre (Bazin), or, as in Mitry's case from Bertrand Russell, Edmund Husserl, and a host of others.

In an age which disparages metaphysics, distrusts speculative thinking, and relies more and more on the scientific ideal of the neutral observer, it is easy to see why Mitry is under siege. As leader of the new, Metz would launch a precise and rigorous study of the material conditions which allow cinema to function. His goal is nothing more nor less than the exact description of the processes of signification in the cinema. Following Charles Peirce and Ferdi-nand de Saussure he calls this enterprise a "semiotics" of the cinema.

The modern theorist will have a conception of himself and his work radically different from that of the theorists we have already examined. He sees his investigations as specific inquiries into spe-cific problems; Metz, for instance, has not hesitated to devote lengthy essays to such small and relatively isolated problems as "Images and Pedagogy," and "Trickery and Cinema." He feels himself to be a scientist prepared to try to solve whatever questions are pressed upon him rather than a philosopher, charged with the comprehensive understanding of the film phenomenon. Of course

Metz does hope that his work will eventually result in a comprehensive understanding, but this hope is merely the horizon of his labor. He is more eager to do field and laboratory work rather than to sit back, pipe in mouth, to ruminate about the origin, purpose, and general laws of film.

This workaday approach toward his subject forces two other new attitudes about film theorizing. First, Metz treats each of his essays as a work-in-progress which he hopes to surpass in later writing. His published essays are full of footnotes indicating the evolution or outright revision of his thought since such and such a point was first formulated. Theorists of "the first epoch" were less inclined to such visible repair work on their thought, for they saw their writing as the fluid development of a total view of the art. Once an essay conformed to the logic and general philosophy of this total view, it could be left alone. Metz, however, has reversed the order of labor, beginning with particular problems and searching only later for the potentially unifying relations between the problems. A problem, then, might readily be rewritten in the light of answers given to subsequent problems. For example, Metz has changed many of his earliest ideas concerning the impression of reality, because of his more recent studies of the concept of analogy in the film image.

A second fruit of Metz's scientific attitude toward film theory is his reliance on the work of others. He has, in effect, doled out promising research topics to his students and kept abreast of the incoming results. In addition, the larger international community of cinema semioticians has had a visible impact on Metz's writing, giving it a tone of give-and-take, and making possible revisions and sudden leaps. By attending conferences on semiotics, exchanging manuscripts and bibliographies with scholars from virtually every country, and by arguing with colleagues in other branches of semiotics, Metz's theory consciously builds on gains made by others. In this way he has indeed given to film theory at least the outward appearances of a progressive human science. No longer must one total view of cinema be opposed dramatically to another (as Bazin is seen against Eisenstein or Kracauer against Anrheim).

Now theorists can partake in the piece-by-piece elucidation of a phenomenon which exists *materially* beyond all individual world views. This at least is the ideal.

THE RAW MATERIAL

Of Semiology

The actual work of the school of cinema semiotics is comparatively slight. Like most contemporary, self-conscious movements much of its early energy has been expended in self-definition, self-justification, and preparatory mapping. Christian Metz's writings, for example, fall into two parts: (1) the establishment of the foundations of a science of the cinema and (2) the analysis of particular film problems by means of this science. Metz sees the first project as the necessary context within which he can carry out the particular studies which intrigue him. While semiology is by definition a method of uncovering the workings of cinema rather than a belief about the nature of cinema, this context amounts to a set of assumptions on which the scientist relies.

Semiology's extreme self-consciousness is immediately apparent, for it begins by examining its own raw material before tackling the raw material of cinema. It demands a precise understanding of its own subject and goals. It begins at the beginning. Of all possible questions which the enormous field of film raises, which ought the scientific film scholar study? How can such a growing and ever-shifting subject be broken down, staked out, and readied for the work of the researcher?

Starting with calling on a position developed years ago by the French theorist Gilbert Cohen-Séat, Metz cleaves the field in two parts, the filmic and the cinematic. The filmic is that illimitable area of questions dealing with film's relations to other activities. This includes all those aspects which go into the making of a film (technology, industrial organization, directors' biographies, and so on) as well as those aspects which can be thought of as the result of the existence of films (censorship laws, audience response, the cult of stars). The cinematographic is the narrower subject of the films themselves cut off both from the complexities which brought them into being as well as the complexities which result from them.

Semiology leaves the study of the filmic, the externals of film, to other related disciplines, to sociology, economics, social psychology, psychoanalysis, physics, and chemistry. It is the internal study of the mechanics of films themselves which Metz and his followers elect to investigate. Semiology in general is the science of meaning and film semiotics proposes to construct a comprehensive model capable of explaining how a film embodies meaning or signifies it to an audience. It hopes to determine the laws which make the viewing of film possible and to uncover the particular patterns of signification which give individual films or genres their special character. For example, the semiotician would like to discover the general possibilities for meaning within the zoom shot; at the same time he would also like to know the particular function the zoom plays alongside other techniques in, say, the films of Robert Altman. At the heart of the field of film is the cinematographic fact and at the core of the cinematographic fact is the process of signification. The semiotician delves directly into this core.

Of Film

What exactly is this core? Where does the semiotician begin to look for signification in film? What is the raw material out of which meaning somehow arises? Every artform, indeed every communicational system, has, Metz says, a specific material of expression which marks it off from other systems. We distinguish between cinema and painting or between painting and speech, not on the basis of the kinds of signification each customarily transmits but on the basis of the material through which any signification is possible in each. In speech we attend to a flow of discrete sounds; in painting to a two-dimensional framed organization of lines and colors. For Metz the raw material of cinema is by no means reality itself or a particular means of signification like montage attractions. For him, quite simply, the raw material are the channels of information to which we pay attention when we watch a film. These include:

1. images which are photographic, moving, and multiple
2. graphic traces which include all written material which we read off the screen
3. recorded speech
4. recorded music
5. recorded noise or sound effects.

The film semiotician is the analyst interested in signification coming from this and only this mélange of material. Of course one can add minor material variations without seeming to undertake the study of a new medium, as we might study films in color or 3-D and still feel comfortable in our domain. But if one of these 5 primary materials is significantly altered or deleted, every viewer would have to rethink his experience. A film with no dialogue, for instance, would make us take note, but we would still watch it as a film. But an artwork made up of a series of still photographs, while it has some of the traits of the material of film, is a different sort of artwork and we give it a different name, the photo-roman.

Curiously, Metz likes to link cinema and television at the level of material of expression. The differences between them, he feels, are cultural rather than semiotic since both employ the same five channels of material. Yet Marshall McLuhan would argue that Metz's description of the image is too general and does not take into account the fact that in one case the image is reflected (film) toward the spectator and in the other case (television) the image is projected directly at him. McLuhan sees this as a material difference; Metz does not. For Metz the student who studies a film on a movieola (which uses rear projection instead of reflection) or even on a TV-playback system is nevertheless studying the full semiotic system of that film. What he lacks is merely the customary cultural context in which we watch films, and this the semiologist, concerned only with the inner workings of film, may feel free to ignore.

Something of the caution and neutrality of Metz's whole approach is visible in this discussion of material, especially in his refusal to accord privileged status to the image channel. Most theorists claim, suggest, or clearly believe that the cinema is primarily an art of images which the soundtrack supports. Metz forces himself to think only of the bare theoretic possibilities of his problem before checking them against the weight of film history. Most films have been made as though the image were predominant; nevertheless it is possible to conceive of films whose balance of materials would favor the dialogue or even the music. The semiotician must take film history into account without becoming blind or seduced by it. He must be prepared to study anything coming to him through those five material channels of expression.

Itemizing film's materials of expression and differentiating these from the materials of other forms of communications is obviously a first though minor task. It merely tells us how to recognize the "cinematographic fact" and where to begin looking for signification. It is the signification itself which is of foremost concern. And signification is a different thing altogether from the material through which it appears.

THE MEANS OF SIGNIFICATION IN CINEMA

Film Is Not a True Language

How can material of expression be made to signify? How can raw images and the various aspects of the soundtrack be made to bear meaning? From the earliest days of film theory this question has been asked always in relation to verbal language which is by far our most developed and well-understood signification system. The semiotics of the cinema, like the study of all systems of signification, takes its point of departure directly from linguistics. We have already seen how quickly Arnheim and his disciples tried to apply certain linguistic concepts and formulae to the cinema. At the very beginning of his career, Christian Metz likewise posed the question: "In what ways and to what extent is cinema like verbal language?"

Metz's first responses to the film/language analogy were characteristically critical and thorough. He suggested that the analogy is strained at the level of appearance, for filmic signification doesn't at all look like verbal language. At the level of function, or the use of these systems, the analogy becomes stretched even further.

It is the arbitrariness of verbal language which has stunned the consciousness of our age and made possible the vast progress of the science of linguistics. The rapport between any signifier and its signified (between, say, the sounds *laf-ter* and the image of a person emitting certain raucous sounds while in a happy frame of mind) is terribly distant. This distance allows the speaker of the language to play around with the sound level of his utterance while hovering about the same signified. For instance the suffix endings which can change "laugh" into "laughter" or "laughing" or "laughed" or "laughable" have no substantial referent of their own but make possible the subtle modulation of the signified. Such sound particles permit verbal language to become a fine network for the production of countless gradations of sense. The user of the language must be able to operate at two levels, comprehending the function of sounds (phonemes, the units of the signifier) and meaning (monemes, the units of the signified). In our example he must understand the word "laugh" and the effect on that word of certain formal deflections such as "d" or "ing." This ability of language to function at two levels is known as its power of double articulation; and while this power belongs to certain other languages it in no way belongs to cinema. Cinema's signifiers are just too closely tied to their signifieds: images are realistic representations and sounds are exact reproductions of what they refer to. One cannot break up the signifiers of film without dismembering their signifieds at the same time. A picture of a man laughing cannot be modulated internally to allow it to play differently with other pictures in the way that the word "laugh" can. There is not even any internally natural way to give filmic signifiers tense. While some filmmakers have resorted to using color for present tense scenes and black and white for past or conditional (dream) tenses, this is clearly a sophisticated convention added to cinema rather than an indigenous aspect of the language itself.

At the most basic level we find that cinema does not have smallest units. The fact that verbal language is comprised of a finite group of interrelatable sound makes it a perfect kind of digital computer. Film would have to be compared to an analogue computer and one which functions through five, not one, materials of expression. Metz has been highly critical of all the failed attempts to find equivalents of phonemes in cinema.

The same is true for monemes, though here Metz's attack has been quite original. Film, he says, has nothing even comparable to the simple noun. A picture of a revolver, far from being a subject or object of some film sentence, is like a sentence itself. It is an assertion! Here is a revolver. At best Metz feels that cinema is like a series of sentences. Thus it can have no dictionary, no list of words and synonyms. How could there be synonyms when the signifier is so closely tied to its signified? Another picture would call up another referent altogether; or if we take several pictures of the same referent (several different angles of a house) the signifiers themselves would be so similar as to preclude comparison with verbal synonyms (like the words house, domicile, living quarters, pad, etc.). There can never be a dictionary of cinematic expressions.

Turning to the other visible characteristic of language, Metz finds that the cinema can hardly even lay claim to a grammar. While there certainly are rules of usage, these are neither so strict nor so intricate as those of verbal language. We are even unable, Metz says to clinch his point, to tell an ungrammatical film construction from a grammatical one. We would never think of correcting a filmmaker for incorrect syntax or for the wrong choice of images. Our tastes may be different from his; we may have wished another image or another order, but we are unable, strictly speaking, to call his utterance ungrammatical. Everything in cinema seems to make sense. Clearly film language *looks* utterly unlike verbal language.

But what about its method of employment? Perhaps these systems *function* in ways which permit comparison. Metz quickly qualifies this hope by pointing first to the obvious fact that language is exchanged between people whereas film utterances are given by a source to an audience. Film, therefore, seems to function far more like novels or symphonies than like verbal language. It is a smooth and continuous message unrolling before a silent spectator.

More telling, though less easy to see, is cinema's lack of any kind of "basic usage." In verbal language we can point to ordinary speech which simply employs the existing system correctly in order to perform its duties. When I write a letter to a publisher asking him to send me copies of certain books, I'm using a system which long preceded me and which I adopt to accomplish my purpose. Beyond such basic uses the speaker or writer may bring into play his poetic or artistic sensibilities. He does this by bending, stretching, and in every way deforming basic speech so that his discourse "speaks a new meaning."

In cinema there is no basic usage, primarily because we don't converse with images. Film is a weak system of communication in which every use must be poetic or inventive, even the most crassly prosaic. Put somewhat more technically, in verbal language the connotative level of signification exists quite separately from the denotative level. A computer can punch out a clear utterance which will be perfectly and correctly informational, while a poet, struggling at the level of the signifiers, will torture the sounds and images of his language until that denotation carries a second level, the connotative. In film the connotation comes in the same door as the denotation. Because signifier and signified are so tightly bound we see the denotation of an image at the same time as we sense the filmmaker's attitude toward it. Indeed we are hardpressed to distinguish a separation between these levels or even to state what in an image is denotative and what connotative. This is as true of newsfootage as it is of *Citizen Kane*.

In attacking the analogies which have been made between both the appearance and function of film and language, Metz aligns himself quite closely with Mitry and even Bazin. It is the notion of "expression" which brings these theorists together and which lets us hear echoes of the "metaphysical" even within Metz, the semiotician. For all of them the film image has a natural level of expressivity. The world speaks through the images in a normal or somewhat deflected way. It is up to the filmmaker to amplify, direct, and in every way work on these primary expressions if he wants to signify his own meaning. Film, then, remains a medium of expression more than a system of communication and its rules are *ad hoc* rather than rigid. The filmmaker doesn't construct a signification piece by piece as does the user of verbal language. He organizes, points, and releases a flow of expression that comes as much from the natural world as it does from himself.

Nevertheless Film Is Like a Language

Within Metz's lengthy and devastating attack on the film/language analogy runs a counter-current, a scarcely submerged tone which struggles to be heard. This tone reveals his fascination with the rules and regulations of the admittedly loose system of cinema. Through the years Metz has slowly purged himself of the influences of Mitry and Bazin and has concentrated precisely on the conventional and conventionalizing properties of the medium. This interest has culminated in his *Language and Cinema,* a fullblown systematic treatment of the problem. Metz seemingly spent his first years deconstructing the prevailing notions of film and language so that he could reconstruct them again in his own way, that is, systematically.

The failure of early film/language analogies came not from too much use of linguistics applied to cinema, but from too little use of it. The relationships between these media are not simple and, once initiated, the linguistic study of film must be pursued to the end if one wants to see exactly the kind of signifying system cinema is. True, cinema is not a complexly interwoven calculus like verbal language; it seems more like a *place* of signification rather than a *means* of it. Nevertheless, to understand how this medium works for and toward signification we must investigate its methods of formalizing what appears through it. This too calls for a return to linguistics.

Metz feels quite comfortable applying the whole panoply of linguistic concepts to film insofar as these concepts refer to aspects of general communication theory. As we have seen, it is clearly imprecise to apply to cinema such notions as phonemes or words since they refer to the particular material of expression of language. On the other hand, terms like *code, message, system, text, structure, paradigm,* and so on are available to the film theorist (are necessary, Metz would say) since they pertain to all systems of communications, even though it is linguistics which has best elaborated them to date.

Metz begins his semiologic project by quietly, even surreptitiously formulating a definition of "signification." Signification is the process by which messages are conveyed to a spectator. Semiotics refuses to consider any kind of signification other than messages systematically conveyed by a code in a text. It thus denies the notion of *immediate* significance. Every meaning possible in film is *mediated* by a code which enables us to make sense of it. Bazin's cosmophany, his belief that the world could speak directly to us through its appearance in cinema, is openly denied by the semiologist. For signification is defined precisely as the human process of asserting messages by means of systems of signs. Signification does not exist in perception itself but in the sign values which perception delivers to us. In cinema such sign values come to us as messages coded in texts. They are the semiotician's primary categories.

1. Code/Message

Semioticians talk endlessly of codes. A code is nothing other than the logical relationship which allows a message to be understood. Codes do not exist in films; rather they are the rules which allow the messages of a film. They are in fact constructs of semioticians, who, after studying groups of films, formulate the rules at work (the codes) in those films. Thus codes have a real existence but it is not a physical one. Codes are the opposite of the materials of expression. They are the logical forms pressed onto this material to generate messages or meaning.

The filmmaker uses codes to make his material speak to the spectator. The semiotician works in the opposite direction, using the messages of a film to help him construct the codes which transcend those messages. Most film discussions and film criticism concentrate on what a film says (on its messages); semiotics aims at the laws governing those messages, at the possibility of filmic speech itself. It does not want to repeat what the text (the film) says; rather it hopes to isolate all the logical mechanisms which permit the raw material to speak such messages.

Codes have at least three basic characteristics which enable us to understand and analyze them: 1. degrees of specificity, 2. levels of generality, and 3. reducibility to subcodes. By the concept of specificity Metz is able to factor out those codes which are indigenous to the medium of film and found nowhere else. Metz's favorite example of a specific code is "accelerated montage." Here a certain form is imprinted on the images and sounds (image A and image B alternate in progressively shorter and quicker fragments). This code delivers a distinct message that no normal viewer will miss (the signified of image A and that of image B, while existing in separate spaces, are interlocked in time and are converging on each other spatially or dramatically). Nor could this message exist except for its being delivered via cinema. If Faulkner and certain other modern authors mimic this technique in their narratives, it is only in vague imitation and never with the same result, for accelerated montage is a cinema-specific code.

On the other end of the spectrum lie the countless non-specific cultural codes which do not depend on cinema for their existence but which are transferred live into the movies. These include our basic habits of perception which, according to many semiologists, transform even our vision of nature. Most obviously they include the products of the culture itself which clearly have an ability to speak to us. In Jacques Demy's *Lola,* for example, the long-lost sailor returns to his home town in a white Cadillac convertible. Every viewer with any experience of contemporary western culture will read obvious messages from this use of the "car code." And if the viewer has been to France the message will be still more clear, for he will realize how ostentatious such an immense white vehicle would seem in that country of tiny cars, whose luxury brands are customarily black Citroens or imperially grey Mercedes Benzes.

In between specific and non-specific codes are a number of codes which cinema shares with other media. Metz likes to point here to chiaroscuro lighting, a code specific to painting but one which was employed endlessly in German expressionist films. Similarly most narrative techniques, such as flashbacks or stories told within other stories, can be found in literature as well as in cinema. One of the primary tasks of the film semiologist is the enumeration of the kinds of codes appearing in film or in certain groups of films, and the determination of the various levels of specificity of these codes.

Next, codes can be distinguished according to their degree of generality. Some codes pertain to all films while others belong only to smaller groups of films. The panorama shot, says Metz, is a general code because it can logically play a part in any film, even though some films prefer to abstain from its use. Such general codes can be made to bear numerous kinds of signification. A pan shot can in one scene signify a description of a landscape while in another scene it can follow the direction of a moving car or even imitate the ho-hum flow of a boring dialogue between two actors. In every case the panoramic movement conveys a meaning by differentiating itself at the outset from static modes of photography.

Far more interesting is the category of particular codes for it is by identifying particular codes that we identify genres, periods, and *auteurs* in film. The particular code is one which appears only in a certain number of films. Its meanings are consequently far more limited and direct than those of general codes. Cowboy films are rife with particular codes of dress, landscape, and behavior which appear in no other kinds of films, at least not all at once. Genres are popularly defined by the codes that distinguish them. The same holds true for periods, as we have seen with the example of chiaroscuro lighting in German expressionist films or the public narrator called the benshi in silent Japanese cinema. Most interesting perhaps is the realization that *auteur* studies can be reduced to attempts to enumerate the particular codes a given director is prone to use throughout his career. Max Ophuls was drawn to specific codes like the freely tracking camera shot and to such non-specific ones as the love triangle. In nearly all his films these two codes among many others reappear obsessively. The critic tries to extract from a director's films those codes which were imposed upon him by the exigencies of the script, the production situation, or other competing personalities such as producers and stars, in order to construct "the transcendental Ophuls." For the dedicated *auteur* critic, Max Ophuls is a name designating an eternal source of particular codes available for countless messages and countless films.

This is why such a critic can even feel free to speak seriously of films Ophuls never actually made but only contemplated.

Codes, then, are transcendent in relation to films. They always refer to a possibility lying beyond any given use of them in an individual film. But the semiotician is able to break down this apparent limitlessness of codes by establishing a series of subcodes within every code. The subcode is one type of use of the code, one kind of selection or answer to a coding problem. For instance, all normal fiction films employ the code of acting to help create their significations; but different eras of film achieve different kinds of acting, each of which functions with the energy and authority of a true code. We must learn the specific characteristics of expressionist or neorealist acting styles in order for the full significance of these films to be manifest.

What we usually think of as a stylistic history of film is in reality a study of selected codes and their subcodes. The history of film, as far as the semiotician is concerned, is nothing other than a succession of different solutions (subcodes) to coding situations (acting, lighting, blocking, camera movement and so on). At the level of the code, then, the semiologist has two basic areas of study. As we have seen he may examine and describe as many codes as interest him in the whole history of film; but he may also attend to the fate of one code across the years, marking and describing the various subcodes which have given body to its existence.

2. System/Text

Inseparable from the notions of code and message are those of system and text. Codes and messages in cinema are never experienced purely or in isolation; they are always found interwoven with others in a text. The text is the place, when the countless messages come together. It is a delimitation of a certain amount of material which has been formed or coded.

The privileged text is, of course, the single film. To the creators of film, the single film marks the boundaries of their work. It is the product which they are paid to complete. To distributors and theater managers, the single film is the unit of commerce par excellence of the industry. To the spectator the single film is the text he pays to encounter. It has for him a beginning and an ending which he respects as much as he respects the money he puts down at the box office.

The semiologist, unconcerned with these external filmic facts of production, distribution, and psychological impact, may take for his text something larger or smaller than the individual film. While he usually considers the single film as the locus of message organization, an individual sequence like the Odessa Steps from *Potemkin* or the color finale of *Ivan the Terrible II* may take on a life of its own, if not for the average spectator at least for the analyst. Similarly, a group of films may become the true text, especially in the cases of serials and genres. Viewers go to the movies often to see not a film (a single system) but a Tom Mix western (part of a larger text which comprises many single systems). Film critics have always felt free to choose for discussion such extended texts as a whole genre or the *oeuvre* of an *auteur*. In sum, the text is the ensemble of messages which we feel must be read as a whole.

Filmmakers, spectators, and analysts all think in terms of texts, because the text adds something to the individual messages it contains by creating a context for meaning. The text is structured in such a way that the individual messages play proper roles in the creation of a total experience or signification. Looked at from another angle, the various codes of a film do not simply exist side by side in the mind of the viewer as he passively looks on; they are systematized. The text becomes a vibrating system for both spectator and analyst, and a system which bends the codes into a particular configuration, forcing them to release their messages in a prepatterned context. The text is much more than a collection or ensemble; it is for the analyst and for the successful viewer a particular logical system of a given number of codes, capable of conferring value on messages.

The text organizes the messages of a film along two axes, the syntagmatic and the paradigmatic. The syntagmatic axis is the horizontal flow of messages linked one after the other in the chain of the text. All studies of the narrative schema of a text attempt to follow certain lines of syntagmatic signification within the complex fabric of messages. They seek the "what follows what" level of signification. In John Ford's *My Darling Clementine,* for instance, a syntagmatic study might trace the progressive domestication of Wyatt Earp or the special function played by the character Chihuahua, in bringing together, albeit inadvertently, the antagonists of the drama.

At the same time there is operating in this and every text a vertical dimension of selectivity. Films make meaning by drawing on and creating paradigms. When we associate the construction of the new church in *My Darling Clementine* with the coming of the schoolteacher, we are experiencing a paradigmatic (or "what goes with what") signification. The paradigm in the example has to do with the institutions of civilization and would contain countless other items from throughout the film: gestures, speeches (the travelling actor's soliloquy from Shakespeare, for example), music, and so on. The paradigmatic dimension of meaning appears during the narration of the film, but is not dependent on that narration. A product of sheer selection of details, this kind of meaning is created no matter when or in what order its signifiers appear. The full meaning of the text is the complex interweaving of the two axes of selection and organization.

We must not forget that all the sets of terms mentioned in this summary are best seen as complementary. They are artificial constructs of the analyst. Syntagmatic and paradigmatic codes (together with their possible messages) transcend individual films and can be studied only across a body of texts or systems. The semiologist interested in a given code (e.g., acting) must investigate numerous systems where that code plays a role. On the other hand, the semiologist may prefer to study a given text, constructing its system by discovering and relating all the codes within it. Here acting style is merely one code related to and qualified by camerawork, editing, lighting, and the innumerable non-specific codes within the subject filmed.

The new scientific investigation of the internal workings of cinema can now be outlined. The semiotician as *theorist* will carefully disengage each code he finds operating in cinema. He will explicate it, paying attention to its level of specificity, to its degree of generality, and to its interaction with other codes. As *critic,* the semiotician will attend to individual film texts (single systems, genres, *auteur* studies, etc.) showing how the nearly countless codes within them are systematized or knotted. He will explicate not the possibility of filmic messages as does the theorist but their actual structure in a particular case. Finally, as *historian* he will examine the development and evolution of various subcodes, both specific and non-specific. He might trace the kinds of lighting used in different epochs or the treatment of women on the screen from era to era. In this way, we are told, we will slowly begin to understand signification in cinema.

THE FORMS AND POSSIBILITIES OF FILM

The concepts of code, message, system, text, paradigm, and syntagm are common to all forms of communication and may be applied freely to all types of material of expression. By themselves these concepts do not in the least define cinema. They say nothing about the way it can look, the way it has looked, the way it should look. In short, they touch neither the form nor the purpose of cinema. Only the practical work of the semiotician can begin to give the abstract semiologic project substance and value. Let us survey, then, the actual *travaux pratiques* of Christian Metz and of those he has influenced in order to see how semiologists deal with questions of cinematic shape and purpose.

Metz's definition of cinema flows logically out of the body of his theory: it is for him the sum of all codes, together with their subcodes, which can possibly produce signification in the materials of expression of the medium. Both the history of film and all "programs for film" ("theories" in the old sense of normative definition) cut subsets out of this parent definition. As we have seen, film history is comprised of a set of subcodes which have been employed in the past. Similarly, programs for cinema are nothing other than a kind of censorship which upholds some codes at the expense of others and which seeks to create the film history of the future. The historian customarily makes statements like, "After 1914 cinema progressively rid itself of the false reliance on theatrical acting which it naturally had in its infancy," while the theoretician might well advance a proposition like this: "Cinema must find its way to its proper domain by eliminating all unmotivated, super-added musical accompaniment." Both types of remark seek to establish the category of "the cinematic" which has obsessed every thinker we have studied. For the historian the "cinematic" exists in certain privileged epochs or has been gradually coming into existence through an evolution which progressively filters out false or impure codes. For the theorist, the "cinematic" will exist only when certain codes, perhaps glimpsed in the past, begin to dominate the production of signification in film.

Film history, then, is a subset of actual film practices within the larger set of possible film practices and the semiologist has an obligation to trace the size and shape of this subset. He may do this in one of two ways; either by pointing to a future cinema full of possibilities which the past and present have ignored, making us realize that the cinema can be, perhaps should be, something else; or by analyzing the texts of the cinema to date, marking out the pattern of the subset we call film history and determining why these possibilities rather than others have been actualized.

Every theorist must choose his approach and Metz has opted for the second. He has further narrowed his project by concentrating on the conventional narrative film, on what for most of us is "cinema" par excellence. While we would claim that there is nothing intrinsically privileged about his project and that all semiologic projects are equal in value, one cannot help but feel that Metz knows he has grasped the heart of the problem of cinematic form and function. His curiosity, coupled with a political instinct, has driven him to hunt out the key critical issues of the past in order to open our understanding of the present and our action in the future.

Strangely enough, these critical issues seem to have been passed down to him directly from Jean Mitry. The cinema as it has existed can best be understood and criticized by an analysis of three levels of signification which should be familiar to us: the realism of the image, the shaping role of narrative, and the higher connotations of a film. Now these are precisely the levels of signification disengaged for study by Mitry. While taking over Mitry's *area* of study, Metz has gradually shifted away from his *method* and toward the precise but dry formulations of semiotics. Most of his practical analyses have dealt with the first two levels of signification, realism and narrative, as they manifest themselves in classic and modern films. He has to date largely avoided the difficult study of connotation.

In the very first article of his first book, Metz inquired into the relation of film to reality. While not a semiotic investigation of the problem, this essay does try to formulate some "scientific" rules about the creation of the impression of reality. Metz found that the interaction of mental activity together with the brute physical properties of the film image is responsible for this impression.

From the physical point of view, we can count the number and kinds of indices of reality every film image contains. For instance, while the image of an object on the screen is seldom the same size as the object in reality, the relation of that object's size to the objects around it is maintained on the screen, at least for objects photographed in the same plane. If a distorting lens is used in the photography, this index is lost. Similarly, while the sounds of the words a character speaks on the screen do not emanate precisely from his lips but from speakers behind or beside the screen, these sounds are synchronized with the movements of his lips so that our senses of sight and hearing confirm the existence of the person before us as they do in real life. If asynchronous sound is used this index too is lost. In Metz's view there is surely a minimum number of indices of reality needed before an image will be able to impress us as real.

But indices of reality are not enough. On the other side the impression of reality refers more immediately to that capacity and need of the mind to "realize" a full and consistent world in perception. This Gestaltist notion would seem to have come directly from Mitry. Lastly, Metz argues that the impression of reality is sealed by movement on the screen which is always *actual* movement, and which we readily accept as the movement of things in reality rather than as the movement of light and shadow.

In his more recent writings Metz has tried to break the power of this impression in two ways. First he has aimed directly at the spectator to discover what allows him to perceive things as real. He is currently studying the properties of "normal" vision, especially those of focus and binocularity, as well as the psychological states associated with representation and identification.

Second, he has supported a critique of the realistic representational image itself (usually termed an "analogue" or "icon"). Here he has essentially refuted his first essay by urging that we go beyond the image instead of being caught up in its fascinating likeness to reality. We must begin to examine, he says, two sorts of codes: those which are added to the image and those which allow us to see the image in the first place. Metz claims that no image is pure, that each has added to it or interwoven within it socio-cultural codes of all sorts. A Hollywood scene depicting, say, the carnival in Rio de Janiero will add to the basic representation of the carnival a kind of coloring and composition which will convey a familiar, poster look. The possibilities for study here are endless, for the culture we live in constantly codes and frames our visible world. For instance, our sense of landscape is likely based on the frame of the automobile windshield through which most of us have come to see and recognize landscapes in our daily lives. Metz demands a rigorous look at film images to spot these layers of cultural meaning pressed onto the representations.

And what of those representations themselves? Can they ever be pure? Responding to the work of the Italian semiologists, Metz is currently calling for an analysis of the codes which permit the basic message of representation to be delivered. In his most pronounced, though least developed, attack on the heritage of Bazin and Mitry, Metz now proclaims the film image itself to be a culturally determined product. What are the codes, he asks, which enable one kind of entity (a film image is only light and shadow) to become a message for another kind of entity (something in the real world it resembles)? What is this code of resemblance? While Metz has yet to try to answer this question thoroughly, the very fact that he has posed it gives us an indication of his beliefs. All signification is the product of culture, convention, and work. The filmmaker must work (usually unconsciously) just to make the film appear to represent the world. With customary frankness, Metz is not embarrassed by how far this view is from his early work in which he saw the world's significance flowing naturally to the spectator across the image.

Metz has had a similar change of viewpoint in his approach to narrative. From the first, and under the heavy influence of Mitry, Metz has been virtually unable to study cinema except as a narrative form. His initial essay on the subject was an attempt to define exactly the relation of narrative to film. In it he built up a definition of narrative as "A closed discourse that proceeds by unrealizing a temporal sequence of events"[2] and then went on to show how such a discourse is ideally suited to the medium of film. The basic unit of narrative, he argued, is the assertion, the predicate, and film is a chain of events or predicates. For Metz, film functions by a kind of innate logic of assertions, more basic than the "learned" logic of verbal language. Shots and assertions are to him more natural primary units than phonemes and monemes. Thus the basic units of narrative and cinema are congruent and film has every reason, can hardly fail, to adopt this complete way of perceiving and thinking the world.

Metz almost immediately saw the same danger here as he had seen in his early writings on "realistic perception" in cinema. There was in both cases a pulling up short, a nearly mystical refusal to go beyond a stunning phenomenon. First, the representational image seemed sacrosanct; now it was narrative which seemed to be a self-sufficient and valuable mode of human life. But as in the case of the realistic image, Metz wanted to go beyond, to get outside the mystifying phenomenon of narrative in order to construct its rules or codes.

The result of his lengthy study was his famous catalogue of "La Grande Syntagmatique du cinéma."[3] Here the narrative capacity of cinema is seen as the product of the application of a code of interrelationships between shots. Metz has extracted eight major possible kinds of links between events in the normal fictional film such as the shot-sequence, the alternating syntagm, the scene, and so on. He has gone on to suggest that by examining the particular use of links within individual genres, *auteurs,* or periods, we can learn exactly how the narrative capacity of cinema was actually employed in given circumstances. He has added to this study an essay on punctuation in the fiction film, the specific code of visual signals between large units in a film (fades, dissolves, wipes, cuts, etc.).

There is hardly room here to develop or criticize Metz's arguments, but the general pattern of his work should now be fairly clear. After focusing in a generally reflective way on a major property of cinema (realism, narration, connotation), Metz pushes through this property by breaking it down into the codes which permit it to function. Then, having grasped something of the workings of the phenomenon, he proceeds to apply his findings to specific and critical examples of cinema.

The best illustration of this is his excellent essay "The Modern Cinema and Narrativity."[4] The rigor of this study shames most reflective criticisms on the subject. Metz's scientific semiology has gained him the right to be precise about narration in film and that right lets him expose the weaknesses of the flabby truisms which have posed as theories of the modern cinema. If modern cinema is somehow new, as every critic has suggested, its newness lies not in some mystical absence of a storyteller, or reduction of spectacle, or ascendancy of "film-writing," or any other formula of new freedom which has been advanced. Its newness must lie in the development of new subcodes, especially of the *grande syntagmatique* and of punctuation. Intelligibility and signification are always the result of codes, and if cinema since 1955 has entered a new era of narrative signification, it is up to the semiologist to specify the precise recasting of the narrative codes which have led it there.

For his part, Metz has focused consciously on the great age of narrative cinema, which he defines as the fiction film from 1933 to 1955. He sees his work as incomplete and the project of semiotics as scarcely begun. We are at the same state in cinema, he says, as were the linguists of the late nineteenth century. Still overwhelmed by the beauties and varieties of film, we are only just beginning to see the system underlying this seemingly chaotic domain. It was the work of de Saussure, published in 1916, which transformed the impressionistic art of philology into the exact human science of linguistics. Similarly it will be some years yet before we can see any real scientific gains in the semiotics of the cinema.

But one thing can be said with certainty: that cinema, despite its freedom from exact parallels with language, does seem to move ever closer to degrees of formalization. Our stories get told in comprehensible ways, our acting has a rule behind it, the sets we use have a purposeful look, and the camerawork which delivers all this to us moves meaningfully within the world it photographs. Semiotics has begun to specify the rules it can see at work here. While results are meager thus far, it has done us the service of keeping our minds and senses tuned to this urge to schematization which, for the semiologist, underpins every aspect of this cultural product which can never again be naïvely construed as realistic.

SEMIOLOGY AND THE PURPOSES OF FILM

In the minds of most people, cinema consists of the narrative films which play and have played at their local theaters. Christian Metz plunged directly into this popular cinema to discover that its laws and logic comprise a small and definable set of subcodes within the true domain of cinema, the domain of the possible. What has caused society to demand this one set of subcodes and repress all others?

Noel Burch in his *Theory of Film Practice* (1969) concerned himself directly with the realm of the possible. While he employs none of the concepts Metz borrowed from linguistics, the spirit of his work is at one with semiotics. His book has the appearance of a conventional "formative" primer because it breaks cinema down into a group of major elements, but it goes well beyond such primers in its exactness and in its polemical attitude. For instance, Burch doesn't simply mention cinema's startling ability to vary time and space relations; he actually computes and spells out the fifteen possible relationships between succeeding shots. With a swift glance at the past Burch can point out which possibilities have served the film history we know. He can show that conventional cinema, in its search to tell "representational" stories, has relied on only 3 or 4 of the fifteen kinds of continuity. Burch then praises those revolutionary directors like Antonioni and Alain Resnais who have intentionally broken with classical continuity and have given to the cinema of the future a chance to use every kind of spacio-temporal relationship just as the modern painter may use every color on his palette and every kind of composition, not just those which give us the sense of the natural.

Burch is looking for a "structural" use of cinema because he has ceased to believe in a natural or realistic use of it. Art for him is the discovery of new physical properties through a conscious restructuring of the elements of a medium. Like Bazin, Burch believes in an evolution of the cinema; but unlike him Burch feels this should be guided only by the formative will of artists rather than by some basic realism of the medium. In this way, cinema will ultimately be able to leave its childhood and take its place alongside contemporary music, painting, dance, the experimental "new" novel, and all the other arts which work not to gratify our impulses but to extend our senses and our consciousness of them.

Theory of Film Practice reads like a complete semiotic system for film. In reality, as its author so often candidly admits, it is hardly a beginning, merely a signpost for the semiology of the future and perhaps for a "new" cinema. Such revolutionary fervor frequently underlies this so-called science of signs. While Christian Metz has kept himself remarkably free of predictions or programs for the future of the art, even his day-to-day practical work contains a larger function, for it puts film in an implicitly political context. Not only has film history held down the true potentialities of the art, as Burch decries, it has also helped hold down the honest, vital urges of man for personal and political freedom. Metz's most recent work has delved into the psychological and political repression which is the story of film history. While straying outside semiotics proper and into Freudian psychology, Metz's current study aims to discover the real causes of our preferences. In what way does the conventional cinema appeal to us?

The militant critics at *Cahiers du cinéma* and *Cinéthique* go a step further and accuse the conventional narrative cinema of supporting the dominant ideology of a modern repressive culture.

While everyone realizes that ideology plays its part in the financing, production, distribution, censorship, and criticism of films, these critics are the first to claim that the very basis of cinematic signification is corrupted by a lie which destroys every possibility of meaning except for the neurotic repetition of the dominant ideology.

This lie is the product of our culture's insistence on the representation of the real. It insists first that reality is visible; second that the scientific instrument of the camera can capture it. The Marxist-Leninist critics launch their attack even here, claiming that the supposedly scientific instrument of the camera is far from neutral, that, like all science, it serves the ruling class. It does this by propagating the visual codes of Renaissance humanism (perspective) which put the individual at the center of a kind of theater spectacle unrolling before him. In addition, the camera has been raised far above other instruments of film production such as film material, optical processing, sound mixing, and so forth, thereby perpetuating the ideology that the real is the visible (after all we say "I see" when we mean "I understand") and that the real exists beyond our ability to change it. For them, the real is the "work" by which we transform matter into significance. Far from hiding this work, cinema should expose it at every level. We should see the struggle to attain an image, to fabricate a story, and to create a theme, instead of falling under the hypnosis of the image, the narrative, and the ideological message.

To them the conventional cinema must be seen as a mindless repetition used by the culture to insist on the reality of the world we live in and the way we live in it. We must, they plead, create a new culture, a new reality, one which will stop repressing all but bourgeois desires and all but certain social classes. A whole new vision of the world is needed and cinema can *work* to help create it.

The Marxists call for a critical cinema which will "deconstruct" itself at every moment. Instead of fabricating an illusion, this cinema will let the viewer see beneath the images and the story to the process of creation itself. Godard's most recent films are considered models of this kind of film. To the anger of the spectator, who hopes only to be carried away into a ready-made fictional world,

Godard makes him instead struggle with the building of new significations, makes him unable to use his normal (and ideology-infested) codes of vision. Every subject should be exposed for its socio-economic underpinnings; every signification (every image and narrative relation) should expose its own work. This way we can strive toward the conscious reshaping of the world.

Semiotics serves a major function in this plan because it allows us to see beyond the petty cinema of the past and toward the vast domain of untried and repressed significations. With this freedom comes a vast responsibility. Signification doesn't simply exist; it must be created. We can't let the world give us its meaning, for it will give us only the meaning of the dominant ideology. The camera captures nothing. In the fullest sense it is a process of creation, and with it we must create a new physical vision which will be the basis of a new organization of the world. This world will at last respond to the underlying psychological and economic facts of life, no longer repressing our desires but releasing them to take their proper freedom in a true society. Such is the project and such is the place of film theory within it. Scientific semiotics serves to criticize and expose the cinema we know (this is Metz's work) and to give us a desire for that cinema, as yet unknown, which we must struggle to bring into being, so that it, in its turn, can struggle for our liberation.

The extreme difficulty one has in understanding the positions of *Cahiers du cinéma* and *Cinéthique* stems largely from the fact that their view of cinema is part of a general critique of culture which employs a vocabulary and a system of concepts quite foreign to the normal film student. Their work is part of a large and growing movement centered on the review *Tel Quel* in Paris, a journal intent on restructuring culture by taking in hand its various means of social interaction. For them the very processes of human understanding are culturally determined and determining rather than natural and common to all men. We must wrench ourselves out of the patterns by which we think and by which we communicate our thoughts.

In every field of study adherents to the *Tel Quel* philosophy rely heavily on Marx, Freud, and de Saussure. Marx developed a science capable of determining the laws of social organization and of criticizing the repression of actual systems; Freud similarly founded a science of the laws of personal psychological organization, capable of criticizing cases of individual aberration or repression; finally, de Saussure began the modern scientific study of signifying systems, uncovering the laws of human understanding and informational transaction. These laws are seen as the basis of all human life, both personal and social. Marx, Freud, and de Saussure, then, form an interlocking system capable of elaborating the reasons behind all human problems and of revolutionizing personal and social behavior by re-forming the human being at his deepest level, his level of signification and communication.

The work of such re-formation takes place in the particular domains of signification of which the cinema is only one. It is not surprising, then, to discover within an article on film technique in *Cinéthique* or a review of a recent film in *Cahiers du cinéma* references to Marx, Freud, de Saussure and their modern elaborators such as Julia Kristeva, Jacques Lacan, and Louis Althusser. The revolutionary film theorist must utilize this complex system adding to it the particular findings of cinema semiotics. In this way the laws of cinema will be understood not as they exist in themselves but as they participate in the larger context of human activity and human nature.

And so semiotics, which began as an attempt to deal with cinema scientifically, has quickly adopted a total world view and an ethics. Metz may have at one time been attracted to the ideal of a neutral science of communication, but he has become increasingly aware of the counter-charges that there is no neutral science and that every analysis of signifying systems must implicitly invoke the social and psychological systems within which signs function. Metz has more and more frequently invoked Marx and Freud.

Whether or not semiotics is bound to function only within this one dogmatic world view is hard to say, for to date the semiotics which has reached us has come from Paris where this world view gives the appearance of being universally accepted. Perhaps with the transplanting of this methodology to America, a country which has traditionally shied away from the overt acceptance of total pictures, the values of a semiotics of the cinema will receive the debate it both deserves and demands.

Whether semiotics remains an instrument of a certain group of radical culture critics, or whether it falls into the hands of critics of all persuasions, its most bitter enemies will always come not from those who are opposed to it on political grounds, but from those who feel it is too abstract, too removed from the living texture of the films it purports to treat. We must, however, recall that film theory can never be "like" its subject. Just as flowers appear simple and natural to us, botany is a complex, technical, and altogether artificial activity which we nonetheless deem valuable. Can we expect less of film theory?

9

The Challenge of Phenomenology: Amédée Ayfre and Henri Agel

Let there be no question about it; the scientific endeavor epitomized by Metz's semiotics has a firm grasp on current film theory. It is stabilized by the ascension of film theory to university status and by general atmosphere applauding "the sciences of man." The semioticians hope to replace all other film theory either because they find it impressionistic, flimsy, and sentimental, or because, as in the cases of Mitry and Bazin, it is "tainted" with philosophy.

But like every theory, semiotics stands upon some first principles which it cannot prove by its own methods, and which its opponents can reject. The semioticians suppress the philosophical approach to cinema because they are dogmatically materialistic. For them the material conditions of language, of social ideology, and of personal psychology dictate the actual institutions of culture and their development. As we saw in the last chapter, the most radical theorists of this sort hope to bring human beings to an awareness of these material conditions and force them to alter the basic structures of their life by achieving new material conditions in violently rejecting the old. Others, like Michel Foucault, are simply deterministic and feel that man has never been, nor can he ever be, in control of these conditions. He is a mere insect following out a pattern which exists beyond his ability to change it and nearly beyond his ability to understand it.

Both this optimistic (revolutionary) and this pessimistic (determinist) materialism are modern manifestations of a position which dates back to the Greeks and which has existed in every epoch of Western civilization. However, there has always been an opposing view which credits man and his imagination with a freedom to explore the world which, far from being a closed and fatal system, is a mystery to be discovered. This view sees art not as another product of given conditions of the human situation, but as a means to look beyond that situation to a world of possibilities otherwise unknown and unknowable.

In this century it has been the phenomenology of Heidegger, Sartre, Merleau-Ponty, and Dufrenne which has best given expression to this view of "art as freedom," and it is against their philosophy that the materialism and anti-humanism of structuralism and semiotics has revolted. Phenomenology proved to be a rich philosophical basis on which theories of psychology, art, music, and literature were developed up through the 1950s. But during this period film study was hardly a peer of these more traditional disciplines and the possibilities of a phenomenological film theory were never systematically explored.

While still exerting enormous influence in most fields, phenomenology is hardly visible in film theory today because of the early deaths of its two most brilliant practitioners, André Bazin in 1958 and Amédée Ayfre in 1963. Recently Henri Agel has tried to rejuvenate the thought of his close friend Ayfre in order to oppose semiotics and structualism. In his *Poétique du cinéma,* Agel admits that materialist inquiries into the sign-system of cinema or into the ideology and psychology which determines works of cinema are of obvious importance, but he complains that they have tried to erase all studies which begin from the supposition that works of art, not their material pre-conditions, are absolute. The semiotician, as semiotician, is unwilling and unable to learn anything truly new from the films he studies. He may increase his knowledge of the system which he analyses but he cannot look beyond it. From Agel's "essentialist" position, the artwork is always in control. The theorist pursues a vision opened to him in his experience, trying to account for it, describe it, or prolong it.

Agel, following Ayfre, complains that most studies of art seek to get at it from the outside. They impose on it laws taken from psychology, linguistics, general semiotics, sociology, etc., and hem in the work of art by discovering its conditions for life. But they never study the life itself. They never submit themselves to the work or approach it on its own grounds which, after all, are the grounds not of knowledge and science but of experience. An artwork is not an object like any other. Despite the metaphors we so often employ, it is neither like a flower nor a computer whose inner workings can be exposed and studied. An artwork is ethereal, because it exists only for experience and only as experienced. A different kind of science is needed to comprehend or appreciate it.

There are many kinds of truths, says Ayfre, and the phenomenological theorist wants to unveil the kind of truth which can't be reduced to logic. In Merleau-Ponty's vocabulary, art is a *primary* activity, a natural, immediate, and intuitive way of understanding life. All theory is *secondary,* placing the primary activities within a schema constructed to make their interrelationships clear. Psychology, for example, doesn't clarify dreams so much as it lets us see the connection between our dreams and our other behavior.

Phenomenology warns us against the engulfing power we accord reason in our society, reason which so often overwhelms and disfigures the primary processes it claims to understand. In the Introduction to this book I suggested that in modern culture there is a tendency to let the knowledge of an activity replace that activity, and I pointed to the flourish of books on religion, sexuality, small group dynamics, as well as art. For Merleau-Ponty, Ayfre, and Agel this is the direct result of an unbridled rationality which would devour all experience or, better, which would lay it out, dissected and organized, under glass. But rationality is only one mode of behavior, one manner of approaching reality, of understanding and responding to it. If it castrates sexuality or if it philosophizes religion, our lives are impoverished as is the world we inhabit and express. We become the automotons of Foucault, determined not by our instinct and ideology so much as by our reason.

When Agel demands that we put ourselves at the disposition of cinema he means at the disposition of nature. The phenomenologist, especially one like Merleau-Ponty, believes that primary activities and especially art are gateways leading out of the useless labyrinth of logic and to the riches of experience. These activities let nature be realized in man's imagination; they let man take his proper stances in nature. Art is a formal gesture organizing our bodies and our imaginations in response to basic experience. Reason can never replace this gesture though it can describe it and talk around it. Agel consolidates his position by quoting Bazin:

> We can coldly isolate patterns in music or logic in dreams as does the psychoanalyst, but, more warmly, we can begin to live the rhythm of the music as an invitation to dance and to vibrate; and we can feel in it a sense, as an unveiling of the world expressed in the epiphany of the sensible.[1]

Bazin here has opened up a magical panoply, the vocabulary of the philosophy of his age. Listen to the words he uses. Man is "invited" to the world by art; he doesn't simply reproduce his own patterns on the world, as the semiologists insinuate. Similarly where the semiotician would say that in art we understand a certain signification, Bazin claims that "we feel in it a sense." *Signification* is that which is imposed on an object by man; *sense* is something an object naturally possesses and radiates. Art, he says, "unveils a world" which was hidden and which will always be hidden to the cold logic of analysis. This world is "expressed" (not "communicated," as semioticians would prefer) by the "epiphany of the sensible." In other words, the hidden depth of the world is suggested by the vision art gives us of its true sensual surface. Mikel Dufrenne has called the whole enterprise of art "the progressive thickening of a surface" through which we experience the expression of a full and vibrant world or of a way of being in the world.

Agel moves quickly to the most mystical implications of this train of thought. He quotes Gaston Bachelard, for whom nature (not man) is the mother of images. Man merely leaves himself open, in his best moments, to receive such primordial clusters as fire and water. Art is for Agel what it was for the romantic poets, a place where we go from the visible to the invisible by means of a "forest of correspondences" which we traverse not so much by "the paths of logic as by those of analogy."[2] For his part, the spectator submits himself to art in order to listen to the analogies and correspondences of the world which the artist, thanks to his labor and genius, managed to enclose within the structure of his work.

Agel turns his argument away from art in general and toward the cinema by suggesting that semioticians tend to value only one strain of film, a cinema of "signification" whose greatest exponent is Eisenstein. His films are films based on a syntax of significant shocks and jolts which develop into a powerful human statement. But there is another kind of cinema generally neglected by semioticians: the cinema of contemplation. Flaherty, Dreyer, Kenji Mizoguchi, Rossellini and Renoir all let the variety of meaning in reality live within their film. They refuse to overwhelm the spectator with their meaning, preferring to let the sense of the world slowly appear. In their great works a multitude of meaning congeals into powerful images which have the strength of transcendence about them because nature, not man, is speaking from the screen.

Agel here has tried to revivify the debate begun years earlier by Bazin between cinema of the image and that of reality, only he has greatly increased the moral stakes. For him Eisenstein's montage represents an analytic, violent approach to life which has invaded even the content of films until today spectators demand violent scenes cut with violent technique. This is the cinema of man, showing above all his maladjustment to the world he lives in. Mizoguchi and Dreyer, on the other hand, represent the synthetic, sacred approach to life, as they patiently grope through the analogies provided in concrete experience to reach a transcendent reality. For Agel, semiotics, as an analytical theory and method, supports a cinema which analyzes the world; whereas phenomenology offers us a "poetics" which values the great films of life, unity, accord, and synthesis. Only these latter can open for us a glimpse of the transcendent laws which silently organize our everyday vision, our everyday experience. He summarizes his position by redefining the structuralist term *écriture* for the cinema. Whereas semioticians feel that filmmakers spell out a meaning on the world with a mechanism of signs and syntax, Agel claims that the great filmmakers read the meaning of the world, not mechanically, but as one reads the palms of the hand. This cinema is the *écriture* of nature isolated by the filmmaker for examination and contemplation.

Agel's theory involves at least two major beliefs which are not crucial to phenomenological theory as a whole. First of all, he believes that certain films are qualitatively different from the common commerce of films which are shown each night on our televisions and in our theaters. His theory is thus a kind of ethics of filmmaking and film viewing based on the "morally correct" aesthetic vision of certain directors. Second, there is the problem of transcendence. Agel not only has confidence that cinema, in certain privileged moments, can lead us to the realm of the absolute, he also has confidence, as a Christian, in the value of that absolute, of its goodness and importance to us.

In a little known but beautifully written book entitled *Contre l'image* Roger Munier has avoided both of Agel's conclusions while remaining very much within the framework of phenomenology. The first portion of his work is a fertile meditation on Bazin's image of the genetic link between the image and its referent. Unlike all other arts, cinema is a discourse of the world, not of men. Along with television it dominates us, demanding that we notice what before we had been able to disregard. Exploring the sinister implications of this conception, Munier discovers that all films, be they masterpieces or not, are composed of images which go far beyond the story they help narrate. All announce a pre-logical world which dominates and controls our imagination. Before the invention of mechanically generated images man's imagination was free to conjure and play with boundless possibilities. But since that invention, he can only tell stories and conjure images within the domain of the real world reproduced by the camera. To be sure, this domain fascinates us and we peer into it hoping for some message from beyond. But what message can we find, he asks, except an inhuman one? Munier agrees with Agel that cinema peers beyond human speech and human intrigue; but the transcendence which it opens is, for him, the cold transcendence of an inhuman physical world.

Like the discovery of atomic energy, cinema is an invention which has released a power in nature capable of destroying man. Nature has been given speech and her speech necessarily hypnotizes us, reducing our human hopes and imagination to insignificance. Cinema, he says, is like an immense imaginary man, generating images autonomously and pathologically.

We try with our pathetic film syntax, with our editing and camera placement, to organize a discourse or at least a view of the world; but it is always the world which has the last word. Forever opaque, it outlives the transparence of human speech. We have created machines and tools which no longer serve us but which serve a world that now commands us.

The positions of both Munier and Agel leave film scholars little room to maneuver. Agel's positive transcendent demands that we meditate only on certain moments in certain privileged films; Munier's negative, "earthly" transcendent is too vast to be grasped or studied. Both are reductive theories. Agel reduces filmmaking and viewing to a gateway to the beyond, erasing from focus all the ordinary conditions and work involved in the process of cinema; Munier reduces man's part in cinema until nature overwhelms him. No matter what film one makes or what statements one makes about a film, nature has the last word, a word we can never fully understand and which always dominates us.

While phenomenological film theory may tempt one to skip to such reductionism, it doesn't do so necessarily. Amédée Ayfre was able to maintain a precise and well-informed phenomenological approach (as friend of Gabriel Marcel and student of Merleau-Ponty), while opening up a program of film theory that only his early death prevented him from developing. Ayfre took a long time finding this compatibility between phenomenology and the study of film. His first essays, brilliant though many of them were, depended crucially on his belief in the aesthetic superiority of neorealism and therefore suffer the same limitation found in Agel's book. These essays form an ethic of neorealism but hardly a fulcrum for a full theory of film. In this early work Ayfre showed, more clearly than Bazin, that neorealism was the only movement in film to that date which utilized the full capacity of the medium to account for the accidents of life. He opposed it to "verism" and "socialist realism" in which man controls what reality signifies. He opposed it likewise to all direct cinema or *cinéma-vérité* in which man's desires and values are ignored in favor of a brute reality. Neorealism was for him and for Bazin a human realism which illustrated in its very technique man's incessant dialogue with physical reality.

Starting from this notion of dialogue, Ayfre went on to explore many aspects of the film experience. One can examine cinema, he claimed, from the position of its creator (auteur, studio, etc.) and seek the world view of the author, whose intentions become our goal and whose sincerity is our criterion. One can focus instead on the audience and determine this time the effect of the film, the practical change cinema makes in man and his culture. One can, finally, aim at reality itself in its most normal sense, seeking some kind of scientific truth or knowledge in the images. But it is only when we consider film in its totality that we encounter its *human* truth. The author's intentions are valuable only when they are modified and formed in symbiosis with the world. The film, far from being a cold record of the world, is a record of that symbiotic rapport between intention and resistance, between author and material, mind and matter. The audience alone (including the author when he reviews his film) transforms this dull physical record into a vibrant human reality by experiencing that drama of mind and matter. When the semiotician spreads a film out for analysis, he stops the flow of time, the flow of the experience, and he risks treating the film like an object in nature. But the film is a hyper-natural object where truth exists only in the experiencing of it.

How does one get at this experience? In the mid-1950s Ayfre wrote several articles trying to open up this closed world of experience. He wrote about the function of time in the cinema and about the physical presence of the human body in relation to other objects on the screen. In an essay entitled "Cinema and our Solitude"[3] he focused on the viewing situation of the audience. In each of these essays his descriptive phenomenology quickly gives way to his ethical concern, as he pleads for a quiet cinema of dialogue with the world in which the audience can actively play a role as it seeks out the depth of the spirit behind the shadows on the screen.

The semioticians object on the grounds that throughout all of his investigations into the experience of cinema, Ayfre neglects the most essential component, the system by which an *auteur* and an audience mediate the world. Recall that he spoke of author, reality, and audience, but never of the system of signs which allows these three to be brought together. In one essay devoted to film language, Ayfre defined the film situation as "someone speaking to me about something in a certain manner."[4] He treats every aspect of language except its possibility: *how* in fact can someone speak at all?

Ayfre's neglect of film language is typical of phenomenology, for even Merleau-Ponty, despite his vast knowledge of linguistics, emphasized the language event or "gesture of the mind" that transcends the language *system* which conveys it. For Merleau-Ponty and Ayfre, the rules of the system (verbal language or film syntax) are basic conditions which every user of the language surpasses in expressing himself. The rules of film language are not the rules of art, and what interested Ayfre was the manner in which a given series of images could transcend its author, its audience, and the normal rules of cinema, becoming adequate to itself, fulfilling rules of its own creation. Like the human beings who act in films, the syntax of cinema and all the laws of semiotics, while still existing in the real world, dissolve magically into the characters and life of the artwork whose criterion is no longer scientific truth but aesthetic authenticity.

Ayfre felt obliged to deal directly with this notion of authenticity. All films give us images connected by a syntax, but only some of these are authentic expressions of a personal vision. Most films must finally be termed either propagandistic in that they put the filmmaker in a role of power and urge the spectator to submit to him or pornographic in that the spectator's needs (erotic, psychological) become the goal of the experience and the filmmaker cravenly submits himself to satisfying those needs. In neither case can cinema enrich our lives in the world; in neither case can the film break loose from its status as tool or toy in the service of pre-formed ideas (propaganda) or pathological needs (pornography).

The authentic film ties the filmmaker and spectator together in a dialogue with the earth, and the resultant work of art frees itself from "service" status, becoming a self-sufficient life-force. We will always have both kinds of cinema, but we must obviously strive for authenticity which makes us free of our needs and free from the domination of others, giving us a chance to see and express life. In effect, Ayfre can ask in all innocence: "wouldn't you rather live in the Greece of Sophocles than in the Rome of the Circus Maximus?"

Ayfre's final task was to try to describe the process by which a work disengages itself from everything else, becoming an authentic image through which we can reorganize our perception and behavior. The imagination, he claims, has an essential role to play in our life in the world. As the most formal product of the imagination, as a structured and finished image itself, the authentic work of art is not merely a refuge from reality. Nor is it, as the surrealists believed, the deliverer of a truth which reason can never comprehend. Insisting once more on the values of dialogue, Ayfre conceives of a reciprocity between the imagination and reason which allows us to extend our knowledge of life and our ability to express the world. Phenomenologists in general tend to minimize the separation of human capabilities, as does Ayfre when he suggests that the real is a relation between the true and the dream, between science and the imagination, between the discursive, verifiable idea and the primitive ambiguous image.

The filmmaker must generate images which move toward the abstraction of ideas without being allegorical substitutes for ideas. If the image is blocked at the outset and is unable to rise to clarity, then it will remain on the level of mere toy, madly proliferating itself without the capability of direction. If the image, on the other hand, is overwhelmed by the idea, it becomes nothing but a tool, losing its ability to direct thought because it is itself already directed by thought.

Proper images, especially as refined in works of art, stun us by their immediacy and intensity. They seem the opposite of reasoned ideas, yet they possess the power to clarify and simplify thought, driving the reason to find and explain the correspondences which they spontaneously create. The psychoanalyst is an emblem for discursive reason as he tries to trace a latent logic in the dreams of his patient. The patient supplies the imagination, the analyst brings a measure of logic, and the dialogue between the two (between image and truth) is able to heal the patient, granting him a glimpse of the reality underlying both.

This same dialectic applies in art as well. The artist provides an image or series of images, beautiful in themselves, yet capable as well of consolidating and initiating new ideas. The critic (and every spectator is in part a critic) elaborates the ideas latent in the work and connects them to the great network of ideas we call knowledge. The image comes out of pre-logical experience and rises toward idea. The critic grabs the image in its ascent and draws out its rational truths. But Ayfre says the process here is not yet complete, for the critic, enriched with his ideas, must then resubmit himself to the image and descend to the level of experience, letting the image sink back into the flux of inner life. The critic must follow the image by responding anew to reality.

The salutory power of the image can function only if this process is allowed to flow to completion. There is the danger in the first place that our public censors or our private ideology will fail to let us experience the brute image at all. When we leave a film and call its subject matter ridiculous, immoral, or irrational, we are refusing to submit to the imagination of another. The second danger lurks at the level of idea, where the critic is tempted to use the image as a mere tool or primer for cognitive thought. This critic submits himself to the work only long enough to transfer the level of discourse to that of ideas where he feels both comfortable and competent. It is only in plunging back into the life of the work as that life joins a larger reality that the spectator gives to the image a value beyond that of toy or tool. Ayfre says that in watching de Sica's *Umberto D* (1951) we must not be stopped by the banality or pathos of the images. Nor must we turn the film into a thesis about old age, acceptance, rejuvenation, or the like. Having watched the film closely and developed its implicit ideas, we must return to the world with its experience in our bodies. We must begin seeing old men outside the theater in a new light and allow the image to continue to work within us. The image is a seed producing a tree of ideas and a fruit which eventually fertilizes the soil from which it came.

Such is Ayfre's "organic" theory of art, a general framework for a phenomenological view of film which no one has satisfactorily pursued. Perhaps this is the kind of theory which can't be systematically developed or applied. I think, however, that had Ayfre lived, he would have linked himself to that branch of phenomenology known as hermeneutics and sought a way to talk about the experience of images through this science of interpretation. For the phenomenologist, watching a film is a process by which we interpret the signs of nature and the signs of man from our own personal perspectives.

Seen this way, the separation between the semiotician and the phenomenologist is narrowed. Semiotics must pursue its task of developing a science of the cinema so that we can understand the conditions and processes by which all films function. But phenomenology would want to go beyond this and investigate those moments when the sign language of cinema becomes another kind of sign, one with which the atomism of semiotics cannot deal. In this way semiotics may someday teach us how cinema is possible and why it generally looks the way it does. Phenomenology will continue the more uncertain venture of trying to describe for us the value and importance which all of us have sensed within certain moments of cinema. It is this sense of value which has driven us to reflect about the cinema in the first place and to engage in the dialogue we call film theory.

Notes

I. The Formative Tradition
1

1. Hugo Munsterberg, *The Film: A Psychological Study* (New York: Dover, 1970), p. 48.
2. For an in-depth investigation of Munsterberg's philosophical heritage, see Donald Frederickson, "The Aesthetic of Isolation in Film Theory: Hugo Munsterberg," unpublished doctoral dissertation, University of Iowa, 1973.
3. Munsterberg, *op. cit.*, pp. 74, 82.
4. Jean Mitry, in a private conversation with the author.

2

1. E. H. Gombrich develops this point at length in his monumental *Art and Illusion* (New York: Pantheon Books, 1960), where he shares many ideas with Arnheim.
2. Even after decades of sound films, Arnheim still refuses to budge from his rigid preference for the silent era. See, for example, Rudolf Arnheim, *Film as Art* (Berkeley: Univ. of Calif. Press, 1967), p. 5.
3. Arnheim, *Art and Visual Perception* (Berkeley: Univ. of Calif. Press, 1969), p. viii. All citations are from this paperback edition, not from the revised and updated 1974 edition.
4. Wolfgang Köhler, *The Task of Gestalt Psychology* (Princeton: Princeton Univ. Press, 1969). It is important to note that Arnheim specifically refers to himself as a student of Köhler's (*Film as Art,* p. 3).
5. Arnheim, "On the Nature of Photography," *Critical Inquiry,* I, 1 (Fall 1974), 148-61.

255

6. Christian Metz's current seminars at the Ecole Pratique des Hautes Etudes have focused on the psychology of the viewing experience. His lectures on the psycho-physiology of filmic perception as opposed to ordinary perception have their direct source in Arnheim's *Film as Art*.

3

1. Eisenstein, Pudovkin, Alexandrov, "Statement on Sound," in S. M. Eisenstein, *Film Form* (New York: Harcourt Brace, 1949), pp. 257-59. All citations are from the paperback edition, translation by Jay Leyda.

2. I am indebted here to Jeffrey Bacal who wrote an unpublished paper on Eisenstein's debts to psychology in 1969 at the Univ. of Iowa. Very recently, indeed since this essay was written, two articles have appeared in *Screen* XIV, no i (Spring 1975), by David Bordwell and Ronald Levaco, touching on this relationship with some precision.

3. Roman Jakobson, "The Dominant," in *Readings in Russian Poetics,* edited by L. Matejka and K. Pomorska (Cambridge: M.I.T. Press, 1971), pp. 82-87.

4. Eisenstein, *The Film Sense* (New York: Harcourt, Brace, 1942), p. 11. All citations are from the paperback edition, translation by Jay Leyda.

5. Eisenstein writes in *Film Form,* p. 161: "The work has a completely individual effect on its perceivers, not only because it is raised to the level of natural phenomena, but also because the laws of its construction are simultaneously the laws governing those who perceive the work, inasmuch as the audience is also a part of organic nature. Each spectator feels himself organically related, fused, united with a work of such a type, just as he senses himself united and fused with organic nature around him."

4

1. In the first era of formative film theory this tendency led to the consistent praise of expressionist and montage films and to the comparative neglect of the more naturalistic masterpieces of Murnau, Flaherty, and von Stroheim. Bazin would make much of this in his famous essay "The Evolution of the Language of Cinema" (*What Is Cinema?,* I, pp. 26, 27).

2. Victor Shklovsky, "Art as Technique," in *Russian Formalist Criticism: Four Essays,* translated by Lee Lemon and Marin Reis (Lincoln: Univ. of Nebraska Press, 1965).

3. Fernand Léger, "A New Realism: The Object," in Lewis Jacobs, *An Introduction to the Art of the Movies* (New York: Noonday, 1960), p. 98.

4. Harry Alan Potamkin, "Phases of Cinema Unity," *Close Up,* VI, p. 470.

5. Hans Richter, "The Film as an Original Artform," in Jacobs, *op. cit.,* p. 282.

6. Rudolf Arnheim, *Art and Visual Perception,* p. 92.

7. Shklovsky, "Sterne's *Tristram Shandy*," in Lemon and Reis, *Russian Formalist Criticism*, pp. 25-60.

8. Boris Tomashevsky, "Thematics," in Lemon and Reis, *Russian Formalist Criticism*, pp. 61-98.

9. Béla Balázs, *Theory of the Film* (New York: Dover Books, 1970), p. 84. All citations are from this edition.

10. Allardyce Nicoll, *Film and Theater* (New York: Thomas Crowell, 1937), p. 53.

11. Shklovsky, "Art as Technique," p. 23.

12. Dallas Bower, *Plan for the Cinema* (London: Dent, 1936), p. 109.

13. Potamkin, "Phases of Cinema Unity," *Close Up*, V, p. 175.

14. Jean Cocteau, *Cocteau on the Film*, translated by Vera Traill (New York: Dover, 1972), p. 218.

15. Jan Mukarovsky, "Standard Language and Poetic Language," in *A Prague School Reader in Esthetics, Literary Structure, and Style*, translated and edited by Paul L. Garvin (Washington, D.C.: Georgetown Univ. Press, 1964), p. 19.

16. But surely identification has occurred before in Western art. What of the tales told of medieval crowds weeping before a new stained-glass window or being literally entranced within the space of a new cathedral. If cinema has taken over this powerful function of art, we have come a great distance from "Art as Technique." If anything is distanced, cold, and objective, it is Formalism itself.

II. Realist Film Theory

5

1. Peter Harcourt, "What, Indeed, Is Cinema?" *Cinema Journal*, Vol. VIII No. 1. Fall 1968, p. 25.

2. Siegfried Kracauer, *Theory of Film* (New York: Oxford Univ. Press, 1960), p. 15.

3. Kracauer quotes (p. 304) Gabriel Marcel with evident homage. If Kracauer and Bazin are ever to be linked it most probably would be through their mutual respect for this great existentialist philosopher whose views evidently influenced both their theories.

4. François Truffaut, "A Certain Tendency in French Cinema," *Cahiers du Cinéma in English*, I (1966), pp. 30-40.

6

1. Twenty-six of these essays have been translated by Hugh Gray in Bazin, *What Is Cinema?* and *What Is Cinema?*, II (Berkeley: Univ. of Calif. Press, 1967 and 1971 respectively). *What Is Cinema?* collects essays taken from the first two volumes of *Qu'est-ce que le cinéma?* dealing with questions of the ontology of cinema and with cinema's relations to the other arts. *What Is Cinema?*, II reproduces in translation essays from

Qu'est-ce que le cinéma? volumes 3 and 4, dealing with cinema and sociology and the aesthetics of neorealism. Wherever possible citations will be made from the paperback editions of these translations.

2. Bazin, "La Strada," *Crosscurrents,* Vol. VI, no. 3 (1956), p. 20, translated by J. E. Cunneed from *Esprit* XXIII, no. 226 (1955), pp. 847-51.

3. Bazin, "La Mort à l'écran," *Esprit,* Oct. 1949, p. 442 (my translation).

4. Eric Rohmer, "La Somme d'André Bazin," *Cahiers du cinéma,* no. 91 (Dec. 1958), p. 36.

5. Bazin and Jean Cocteau, *Orson Welles* (Paris: Editions du Chavanne, 1950), p. 57. This book-length study of Welles has been recently reprinted in French (Paris: Editions du Cerf, 1972). The introduction by Cocteau as well as many passages from Bazin have been excised, while later essays by Bazin and two interviews of Welles by Bazin have been added. All quotations from the Welles book in this essay are my translations from the original out-of-print edition. This is because several of the key quotations have been eliminated from the modern version.

6. Bazin, *Qu'est-ce que le cinéma,* I (Paris: editions du Cerf, 1959), p. 37. My translation.

7. Bazin, "Un Peu Tard," *Cahiers du cinéma,* no. 48 (June 1955), p. 47. My translation.

8. Lotte Eisner, *The Haunted Screen* (Berkeley: Univ. of Calif. Press, 1969). Translated from the French by Roger Greaves. Originally published in France in 1952.

9. Bazin, *Jean Renoir,* trans. by W. W. Halsey and William H. Simon (New York: Simon and Schuster, 1973), p. 86. While this is generally quite a good translation, the passage quoted here has unaccountably lost a key metaphor. The last phrase literally translated should read, "Renoir's films are made with the skin of things." Bazin develops this metaphor further on by describing Renoir's camera style as a "caress."

10. Bazin, *Qu'est-ce que le cinéma?,* IV, p. 102. My translation.

11. Bazin, "Le Ghetto concentrationnaire," *Cahiers du cinéma,* no. 9 (Feb. 1952), p. 60.

12. Bazin, *Qu'est-ce que le cinéma?,* I, p. 74.

13. *Ibid.,* p. 160.

14. Alexandre Astruc, "Le Camera-stylo," in Peter Graham, *The New Wave* (Garden City, N.Y.: Doubleday, 1968), pp. 17-24.

III. Contemporary French Film Theory

1. Christian Metz, *Language and Cinema,* tr. by D. J. Umiker-Sebeok (The Hague: Mouton Press, 1974).

2. Charles Barr, "Cinemascope: Before and After," in Gerald Mast and Marshall Cohen (eds.), *Film Theory: Introductory Readings* (New York: Oxford Univ. Press, 1974). First published in *Film Quarterly* XVI, no. 4 (1963).

3. Stanley Cavell, *The World Viewed* (New York: Viking Press, 1971).
4. George Linden, *Reflections on the Screen* (Belmont, Calif.: Wadsworth Press, 1970).

7

1. Christian Metz, *Essais sur la signification au cinéma,* II (Paris: Editions Klincksieck, 1972), p. 34.
2. David Bordwell, "Mitry on Montage," an unpublished seminar paper (Univ. of Iowa, May 1972).
3. Jean Mitry, *Esthétique et psychologie du cinéma,* volume 1 (Paris: Editions Univérsitaires, 1963), p. 119.
4. *Ibid.,* pp. 283-285.
5. Close examination of versions of *October* available in the United States fails to support Mitry's example. He was perhaps familar with earlier and more complete copies of this much tampered with film. In any case his example does certainly characterize certain tendencies in montage, tendencies which do exist throughout the film *October.*
6. Metz, "Current Problems in Film Theory," *Screen* XIV, nos. 1, 2 (Spring, Summer 1973), p. 61.
7. Jean Mitry, "Remarks on the Problem of Cinematic Adaptation," *The Bulletin of the Midwest Modern Language Association,* Spring 1971, p. 8.

8

1. Christian Metz, *Essais sur la signification au çinéma,* II, Chapters 1 and 2. 1974), p. 28.
2. Christian Metz, *Film Language* (New York, Oxford University Press, 1974).
3. *Ibid.,* p. 119.
4. *Ibid.,* pp. 175-227.

9

1. André Bazin, cited in Henri Agel, *Poétique du cinéma* (Editions du Signe, 1973), p. 9.
2. Here Agel is citing both Baudelaire and Gaston Bachelard. *Ibid.,* p. 15.
3. Amédée Ayfre, "Le Cinéma et notre solitude," in *Le Cinéma et sa vérité* (Paris: Editions du Cerf, 1969), pp. 41-58.
4. Ayfre, "La Language cinématographique et sa morale," *ibid.,* p. 92.

Bibliography

GENERAL WORKS ON FILM THEORY

Books

MacCann, Richard Dyer, ed. *Film: A Montage of Theories*. New York: E. P. Dutton & Co., 1966.

Mast, Gerald, and Marshall Cohen, eds. *Film Theory and Criticism: Introductory Readings*. New York: Oxford University Press, 1974.

Perkins, V. F. *Film as Film*. Baltimore: Penguin Books, 1972.

Talbot, Daniel. *Film: An Anthology*. Berkeley: University of California Press, 1970.

Tudor, Andrew. *Theories of Film*. London: Secker and Warburg, 1974.

Wollen, Peter. *Signs and Meanings in the Cinema*. London: Secker and Warburg, 1974.

Articles

Harrah, David. "Aesthetics of the Film: The Pudovkin-Arnheim-Eisenstein Aesthetic." *Journal of Aesthetics and Art Criticism,* Dec. 1954, pp. 163-74.

Henderson, Brian. "Two Types of Film Theory." *Film Quarterly,* XXIV, No. 3, 33-41 (Spring 1971).

Katchadourian, Haig. "Film as Art." *Journal of Aesthetics and Art Criticism* XXXIII, No. 3 (Spring 1975), 271-284.

Mast, Gerald. "What Isn't Cinema?" *Critical Inquiry* I, No. 2 (Dec. 1974), 373-393.

Sesonske, Alexander. "Aesthetics of Film." *Journal of Aesthetics and Art Criticism* XXXIII, No. 1 (Fall 1974), 51-59.

MUNSTERBERG BIBLIOGRAPHY

Works by Munsterberg

Munsterberg, Hugo. *The Eternal Values.* Boston: Houghton, Mifflin, 1909.

————. *The Film: A Psychological Study* (The unaltered and unabridged republication of *The Photoplay: A Psychological Study,* originally published by D. Appleton, New York, in 1916.) Foreword by Richard Griffith. New York: Dover, 1970.

————. "The Opponents of Eternal Values." *The Psychological Bulletin,* VI (Oct. 15, 1909), 329-338.

————. *The Principles of Art Education.* New York: Prang Educational, 1905.

————. "The Problem of Beauty." *Philosophical Review,* XVIII (March 1909), 121-146.

————. "Psychology and Art." *Atlantic Monthly,* Nov. 1898, pp. 22-32.

————. *Psychology and Life.* Boston: Houghton Mifflin, 1899.

————. *Psychology and the Teacher.* New York: D. Appleton, 1909.

————. *Psychology: General and Applied.* New York: D. Appleton, 1914.

————. *Psychotherapy.* New York: Moffat, Yard, 1909.

————. *Science and Idealism.* Boston: Houghton Mifflin, 1906.

————. "Why We Go to the Movies." *Cosmopolitan,* Dec. 15, 1915, pp. 22-32.

Works on Munsterberg

Frederickson, Donald. "The Aesthetic of Isolation in Film Theory: Hugo Munsterberg." Ph.D dissertation, University of Iowa, 1973.

Lindsay, Vachel. "Photoplay Progress." Review of *The Photoplay, A Psychological Study,* by Hugo Munsterberg. *New Republic,* Feb. 17, 1917, pp. 76-77.

Munsterberg, Margaret. *Hugo Munsterberg: His Life and Work.* New York: D. Appleton, 1922.

Strong, Charles A. "Dr. Munsterberg's Theory of Mind and its Consequences." *Philosophical Review,* I (March 1892), 179-195.

Other Works of Interest
Casebier, Allan. "The Concept of Aesthetic Distance." *Personalist,* LII (Winter 1971), 70-91.
Cassirer, H. W. *A Commentary on Kant's Critique of Judgement.* London: Methuen, 1938.
Cormier, Romona. "The Concept of 'Isolation' in Contemporary Aesthetic Theory." *Tulane Studies in Philosophy,* XLX, No. 1, pp. 1-19.
Kant, Immanuel. *Critique of Judgement.* Translated by J. H. Bernard. New York: Hafner, 1951.
Lindsay, Vachel. *The Art of the Moving Picture.* First published New York: Macmillan, 1916. New York: Liveright, 1970.
Stolnitz, Jerome. "On the Origins of 'Aesthetic Disinterestedness.' " *Journal of Aesthetics. and Art Criticism,* XX (Winter 1961), 131-143.
Wolfe, G. Joseph. "Vachel Lindsay: The Poet as Film Theorist." Ph.D. dissertation, University of Iowa, 1964.
Wolman, Benjamin. "Immanuel Kant and His Impact on Psychology." *Historical Roots of Contemporary Psychology.* Edited by Benjamin Wolman. New York: Harper & Row, 1968.

ARNHEIM BIBLIOGRAPHY

Works by Arnheim
Arnheim, Rudolf. "Abstraction and empathy in retrospect." *Confinia Psychiatrica,* 1967, Vol. 10, pp. 1-15.
———. *Art and Visual Perception.* Berkeley and Los Angeles: University of California Press, 1967.
———. "The Critic and the Visual Arts." Fifty-second Biennial Convention of the American Federation of Arts in Boston. New York: American Federation of Arts, 1965.
———. *Entropy and Art: an Essay on Disorder and Order.* Berkeley: University of California Press, 1971.
———. "Fiction and Fact" *Sight and Sound,* Vol. 8, No. 32 (Winter 1939-40), 136, 137.
———. *Film.* Translated from the German by L. M. Sieveking and

Ian F. D. Morrow, with a preface by Paul Rotha. London: Faber and Faber, 1933.

———. *Film as Art*. (An adaptation of *Film*) Berkeley: University of California Press, 1957.

———. *Film Culture*. A series of six short articles, including three originally destined for the *Enciclopedia del cinema,* appeared in the issues of *Film Culture* numbered 11, 16, 17, 18, 24, and 42, running from 1957 to 1966.

———. "Gestalt and Art." *Journal of Aesthetics and Art Criticism,* No. 2, 1943, pp. 71-75.

———. "Gestalt Psychology and Artistic Form." From *Aspects of Form*. Edited by L. L. Whyte. Bloomington: Indiana University Press, 1951.

———. "On the Nature of Photography." *Critical Inquiry,* I (Sept. 1974), 148-161.

———. *Picasso's Guernica: The Genesis of a Painting*. Berkeley and Los Angeles: University of California Press, 1962.

———. "Psychological Notes on the Poetical Practice." From *Poets at Work*. Arnheim, et al. New York: Harcourt Brace, 1948.

———. "Psychology of the Dance." *Dance Magazine,* Aug. 1946, pp. 20 and 38.

———. *Radio*. Translated by Margret Ludwif and Herbert Read. London: Faber and Faber, 1936.

———. "Second Thoughts of a Psychologist." From *Essays in Teaching*. Edited by Harold Taylor. New York: Harper, 1950.

———. *Toward a Psychology of Art*. Berkeley and Los Angeles: University of California Press, 1966.

———. *Visual Thinking*. Berkeley and Los Angeles: University of California Press, 1969.

———. "Visual Thinking." In *Education of Vision*. Edited by Gyorgy Kepes. 1-15. New York: Braziller, 1965.

Works on Gestalt Psychology

Gombrich, E. H. *Art and Illusion: A Study in the Psychology of Pictorial Representation*. New York: Pantheon Books, 1960.

Köhler, Wolfgang. *The Task of Gestalt Psychology*. With an introduction by Carroll C. Pratt. Princeton: Princeton University Press, 1969.

Rhyne, Janie. *The Gestalt Art Experience*. Monterey, Calif.: Brooks/Cole Publishing Company, 1973.

EISENSTEIN BIBLIOGRAPHY

Works by Eisenstein

Eisenstein, Sergei M. *Film Essays and a Lecture.* Edited and translated by Jay Leyda. Foreword by Grigori Kozintsev. New York: Praeger, 1970.

————. *Film Form: Essays in Film Theory.* Edited and translated by Jay Leyda. New York: Harcourt Brace & Co., 1949.

————. *The Film Sense.* Edited and translated by Jay Leyda. New York: Harcourt Brace & Co., 1942.

————. *Ivan the Terrible, a Screenplay.* Translated by Ivor Montagu and Herbert Marshall. Edited by Ivor Montagu. New York: Simon and Schuster, 1962.

————. *Notes of a Film Director.* Originally published as "Zametki kinoryezhissyora," Foreign Languages Publishing House, Moscow, after 1948. Translated into English by X. Danko. With a note by Richard Griffith. New York: Dover Publications, 1970.

————. *Potemkin, a Film.* Translated by Gillon R. Actken. New York: Simon and Schuster, 1968.

Works on Eisenstein

Barna, Yon. *Eisenstein.* Bloomington: Indiana University Press, 1973.

Kuiper, John Bennett. "An Analysis of Four Silent Films of Sergei M. Eisenstein." Ph.D. dissertation, University of Iowa, 1960.

————. "Cinematic Expression: A Look at Eisenstein's Silent Montage." *The Art Journal,* Fall 1962, pp. 34-39.

Montagu, Ivor. *With Eisenstein in Hollywood, a Chapter of Autobiography.* New York: International Publications, 1967.

Newcomb, James. "Eisenstein's Aesthetics." *Journal of Aesthetics and Art Criticism* XXXII, No. 4 (Summer 1974), 471-477.

Nizhnii, Vladimir. *Lessons with Eisenstein.* Edited and translated by Ivor Montagu and Jay Leyda. New York: Hill and Wang, 1962.

Pleynet, M. "The 'Left' Front of Art: Eisenstein and the Old 'Young' Hegelians." *Screen,* Spring 1972, pp. 101-119. Translated from *Cinéthique* 1969, No. 5.

Potamkin, Harry Alan. "Eisenstein and the Theory of the Cinema." *Hound and Horn,* July 1933, pp. 678-89.

Seton, Marie. *Sergei M. Eisenstein, a Biography.* New York: Grove Press, 1960.

Seydor, Paul. "Eisenstein, a Dissenting View." *Sight and Sound,* Winter 1973/74, pp. 38-43.

Other Works of Interest

Kuleshov, Lev. *The Principles of Film Direction*. Moscow, 1941.

Levaco, Ronald, ed. and trans. *Kuleshov on Film*. Berkeley: University of California Press, 1975.

Pudovkin, V. I. *Film Technique and Film Acting*. Translated by Ivor Montagu. London: Vision Press, 1954.

BALÁZS BIBLIOGRAPHY

Works by Balázs

Balázs, Béla. *Theory of the Film: Character and Growth of a New Art*. Translated by Edith Bone. London: Dobson, 1952.

Works on Formalist Aesthetics

Erlich, Victor. *Russian Formalism*. The Hague: Mouton, 1955.

Garvin, Paul, ed. and trans. *A Prague School Reader on Esthetics, Literary Structure, and Style*. Washington, D.C.: Georgetown University Press, 1964.

Jameson, Fredric. *The Prison-house of Language*. Princeton University Press, 1972.

Lemon, Lee, and Martin Reis, eds. *Russian Formalist Criticism: Four Essays*. Lincoln: University of Nebraska Press, 1965.

Matejka, Ladislav, and Krystyna Pomorska, eds. *Readings in Russian Poetics: Formalist and Structuralist Views*. Cambridge, Mass.: M.I.T. Press, 1971.

KRACAUER BIBLIOGRAPHY

Works by Kracauer

Kracauer, Siegfried. "Challenge of Qualitative Content Analysis." *Public Opinion Quarterly*, 1952, pp. 631-642.

————. "Conquest of Europe on the Screen." *Social Research*, Sept. 1943, pp. 337-357.

————. "Decent German: Film Portrait." *Commentary*, Jan. 1949, pp. 74-77.

————. *From Caligari to Hitler: A Psychological History of the German Film*. Princeton: Princeton University Press, 1947.

————. *History, The Last Things Before the Last*. New York: Oxford University Press, 1969.

————. "Hollywood's Terror Films." *Commentary,* Aug. 1946, pp. 132-136.

————. "Jean Vigo." From *Introduction to the Art of Movies.* Edited by Lewis Jacobs. New York: Noonday Press, 1960, pp. 223-227.

————. "National Types as Hollywood Presents Them." *Public Opinion Quarterly,* 1949, pp. 53-72.

————. *Orpheus in Paris: Offenbach and the Paris of his Time.* New York: A. A. Knopf, 1938.

————. "Psychiatry for Everything and Everybody." *Commentary,* March 1948, pp. 222-228.

————. "Revolt Against Rationality." *Commentary,* June 1947, pp. 586-587.

————. *Theory of Film: The Redemption of Physical Reality.* New York: Oxford University Press, 1960.

Kracauer, Siegfried, and Paul L. Berkman. *Satellite Mentality: Political Attitudes and Propaganda Susceptibilities of Non-Communists in Hungary, Poland, and Czechoslovakia.* New York: F. A. Praeger, 1956.

Works on Kracauer and General Interest

Arnheim, Rudolf. "Melancholy Unshaped." In *Towards a Psychology of Art.* Berkeley and Los Angeles: University of California Press, 1966, pp. 181-191.

Auerbach, Erich. *Mimesis: The Representation of Reality in Western Literature.* Translated by Willard R. Trask. Princeton: Princeton University Press, 1953.

Corliss, Richard. "The Limitations of Kracauer's Reality." *Cinema Journal,* Vol. 10, No. 1 (Fall 1970), 15-20.

Harcourt, Peter. "What Indeed, Is Cinema?" *Cinema Journal,* VI, No. 1 (Fall 1968), 22-28.

Kael, Pauline. "Is there a Cure for Film Theory?" *Sight and Sound,* Spring 1962, pp. 56-64.

BAZIN BIBLIOGRAPHY

Books by Bazin in English

Bazin, André. *Jean Renoir.* Translated by W. W. Halsey and William H. Simon. New York: Simon and Schuster, 1973.

————. *What Is Cinema?* Selected and translated by Hugh Gray from the first two volumes of *Qu'est-ce que le cinéma?* Berkeley: University of California Press, 1967.

————. *What Is Cinema?* Volume II. Selected and translated by Hugh

Gray from the last two volumes of *Qu'est-ce que le cinéma?*
Berkeley: University of California Press, 1971.

Books by Bazin in French

Bazin, André, *Cinema de la cruauté*, ed, by F. Truffaut. Paris: Flammarion, 1975.

————. *Jean Renoir*. Paris: Editions Champs Libre, 1971.

————. *Le Cinéma de l'occupation et de la résistance*. Paris, 1975.

————. *Orson Welles*. Paris: Les Editions du Cerf, 1972.

————. *Qu'est-ce que le cinéma?* In 4 volumes. Paris: Les Editions du Cerf, 1959, 1960, 1962.

Bazin, André, and Eric Rohmer. *Charlie Chaplin*. Paris: Les Editions du Cerf, 1972.

Works on Bazin in English

Andrew, J. Dudley. "André Bazin." *Film Comment* IX, No. 2 (March-April 1973), 64-67.

————. "Realism and Reality in Cinema: The Film Theory of André Bazin and Its Source in Recent French Thought." Ph.D. dissertation, University of Iowa, 1972.

Cadbury, William. "The Cleavage Plane of André Bazin." *Journal of Modern Literature* III, No. 2 (Spring 1973), 253-267.

Graham, Peter. *The New Wave*. Garden City: Doubleday, 1968.

Harcourt, Peter. "What, Indeed, Is Cinema?" *Cinema Journal* VI, No. 1 (Fall 1968), 22-28.

Henderson, Brian. "The Structure of André Bazin's Thought." *Film Quarterly* XXV, No. 4, Summer, 1972 pp. 15-27.

Kael, Pauline. "Behind the New Wave." *The New York Times,* Sept. 10, 1967, Sec. 7, p. 1.

Michelson, Annette. Introduction to *Theory of Film Practice* by Noel Burch. New York: Praeger, 1973.

————. Review of "What Is Cinema?" *Artforum* VI, No. 10 (1968), 66-71.

Roud, Richard. "Face to Face: André Bazin." *Sight and Sound* XXVIII, Nos. 3-4 (1959), 176-179.

————. "André Bazin: His Rise and Fall." *Sight and Sound* XXXVII, No. 2 (1968), 94-96.

Trope, Zippora. "A Critical Application of André Bazin's *Mise en Scène Theory.*" Ph.D. dissertation, University of Michigan, 1974.

Williams, Christopher. "Bazin on Neorealism." *Screen* XIV, No. 4 (Winter 1973-74), 61-68.

MITRY BIBLIOGRAPHY

Works by Mitry in English
Mitry, Jean. "Remarks on the Problem of Cinematic Adaptation." Translated by Richard Dyer. *The Bulletin of the Midwest Modern Language Association,* Spring 1971, pp. 1-9.

Works by Mitry in French
Mitry, Jean. *John Ford.* Paris: Editions Universitaires, 1954.
―――. *S. M. Eisenstein.* Paris: Editions Universitaires, 1955.
―――. *Charlot et sa "fabulation" Chaplinesque.* Paris: Editions Universitaires, 1957.
―――. *Dictionnaire du cinéma.* Paris: Larouse, 1963.
―――. *Esthétique et psychologie du cinéma.* 2 volumes. Paris Editions Universitaires, 1963, 1965.
―――. *Histoire du cinéma.* 3 volumes to date. Paris: Universitaires, 1967, 1969, 1971.
―――. *Le Mot et l'image. n.p. Edition du Signe,* 1972.

Works on Mitry in English
Atwell, Lee. "Notes on a Film History in Progress." *Film Quarterly* XXV, No. 1 (Fall 1971), pp. 58-63.
Dreyfus, Dina. "Cinema and Language." *Diogenes* No. 35 (Fall 1961), 23-33.
Lewis, Brian. "Jean Mitry on Film Language." *SubStance,* No. 9 (1974), 5-14.
Metz, Christian. "Current Problems of Film Theory: Christian Metz on Jean Mitry's *L'Esthétique et psychologie du cinéma,* Volume II." Translated by Diana Matias. *Screen,* Spring/Summer 1973, pp. 40-87.

BIBLIOGRAPHY OF CINEMA SEMIOTICS IN ENGLISH

Works by Metz in English
Metz, Christian. *Film Language: A Semiotics of the Cinema.* Translated by Michael Taylor. New York: Oxford University Press, 1974.
―――. *Language and Cinema.* Translated by Donna Jean Umiker-Sebeok. The Hague: Mouton, 1974.
―――. "The Imaginary Signifier." Translated by Ben Brewster. *Screen* XVI, No. 2 (Summer 1975), 14-76.

Works on Metz

Carroll, Noel. "Review of Film Language." *Film Comment* X, No. 6 (Nov./Dec. 1974), 62.

Finn, John. "Metz' New Directions." *Jumpcut,* No. 6 (March 1975), 14-16.

Guzzetti, Alfred. "Christian Metz and the Semiology of the Cinema." *Journal of Modern Literature* III, No. 2 (April 1973), 292-308.

Henderson, Brian. "Metz *Essais I* and Film Theory." *Film Quarterly* XXVIII, No. 3 (1975), 18-32.

Nichols, Bill. "Style, Grammar, and the Movies." *Film Quarterly,* XXVIII, No. 3 (1975), 33-48.

Rohdie, Sam. "Metz and Film Semiotics." *Jumpcut* No. 7 (May-July 1975), 22-24.

Sandro, Paul. "Signification in the Cinema." *Diacritics* IV, No. 3 (Fall 1974), 42-50.

Screen XIV, Nos. 1 & 2 (Spring/Summer 1973). "Semiotics and the Work of Christian Metz." Entire Issue.

Thompson, Richard. "A Guide to Christian Metz." *Cinema,* Spring 1972, pp. 37-45.

General Works on Cinema Semiotics and Structuralism

Barthes, Roland. *Elements of Semiology.* Translated by Annette Lavers and Colin Smith. New York: Hill and Wang, 1967; available in paperback from Beacon Press, Boston, 1970.

Baudry, Jean-Louis. "Ideological Effects of the Basic Cinematographic Apparatus." Translated by Alan Williams. *Film Quarterly* XXVIII, No. 2 (Winter 1974, 75), 39-47.

Bettettini, Gianfranco. *The Language and Technique of Film.* Translated by David Osmond-Smith. The Hague: Mouton, 1974.

Burch, Noel. *Theory of Film Practice.* Translated by Helen R. Lane. New York: Praeger, 1973.

Dayan, Daniel. "The Tutor-Code in Classic Cinema." *Film Quarterly* XXVIII, No. 1 (Fall 1974), 22-31.

Eckert, Charles. "The English Cine-Structuralists." *Film Comment* IX, No. 3 (May/June 1973), 46-51.

Harpole, C., and Hanhardt, J. "Linguistics, Structuralism, Semiology: A Bibliography with an Introduction." *Film Comment* IX, No. 3 (May/June 1973), 52-59.

Henderson, Brian. "Critique of Cine-Structuralism." (essay in two parts) *Film Quarterly.* Fall 1973, pp. 25-34, and Winter 1973-74, pp. 37-46.

du Pasquier, Sylvain. "Buster Keaton's Gags." *Journal of Modern Literature,* III, No. 2 (April 1973), 269-291. One of Metz's students here performs a close analysis of the signifying structure of a certain technique in comedy.

Screen. Virtually every issue since 1973 has touched upon or actually focussed on semiology, structuralism and post-structuralism in relation to the cinema.

SubStance, No. 9 (1974). Entire Issue.

CINEMA AND PHENOMENOLOGY

Film Works in English with a Phenomenological Viewpoint

Cavell, Stanley. *The World Viewed.* New York: Viking Press, 1971.

Earle, William. "Revolt Against Realism in the Film." *Journal of Aesthetics and Art Criticism* XXVII, No. 2 (Winter 1968).

Linden, George W. *Reflections on the Screen.* Belmont, Calif.: Wadsworth, 1970.

Munier, Roger. "The Fascinating Image," *Diogenes,* No. 38 (1962), 85-94.

Thompson, David. *Movie Man.* New York: Stein and Day, 1967.

French Phenomenology of the Cinema

Agel, Henri. *Le Cinéma et le sacré.* Paris: Editions du Cerf, 1961 (written in collaboration with Amédée Ayfre).

———. *Poetique du cinéma.* n.p. Edition du Signe, 1973.

Ayfre, Amédée. *Cinéma et mystère.* Paris: Editions du Cerf, 1969.

———. *Le Cinéma et sa vérité.* Paris: Editions du Cerf, 1969.

———. *Conversion aux images?* Paris: Editions du Cerf, 1964.

Morin, Edgar. *Le Cinéma ou l'homme imaginaire.* Paris: Editions Minuit, 1958.

Munier, Roger. *Contre l'image.* Paris: Gallimard, 1963.

General Works on the Aesthetics of Phenomenology

Dufrenne, Mikel. *Phenomenology of the Aesthetic Experience.* Translated by Edward S. Casey *et al.* Evanston: Northwestern University Press, 1973.

Kaelin, Eugene. *Existentialist Aesthetics.* Madison: University of Wisconsin Press, 1965. This book deals with the aesthetic theories of Sartre, Merleau-Ponty, and Dufrenne. It also has a large bibliography of important sources for the further study of this area.

Merleau-Ponty, Maurice. *Sense and Non-sense.* Translated by Hubert and Patricia Dreyfus. Evanston: Northwestern University Press, 1964.

Index

NOTE: For a breakdown of the key concepts used in this book (e.g. raw material) or for major terms specific to a single theory (e.g. the art machine, system/text), consult the Table of Contents.